The
Princeton
Review®

SAT Subject Test™

FRENCH

PREP

17th Edition

The Staff of The Princeton Review

PrincetonReview.com

| Penguin
| Random
| House

The Princeton Review
110 East 42nd St, 7th Floor
New York, NY 10017
Email: editorialsupport@review.com

Published in the United States by Penguin Random House LLC, New York, and in Canada by Random House of Canada, a division of Penguin Random House Ltd., Toronto.

Terms of Service: The Princeton Review Online Companion Tools ("Student Tools") for retail books are available for only the two most recent editions of that book. Student Tools may be activated only once per eligible book purchased for a total of 24 months of access. Activation of Student Tools more than once per book is in direct violation of these Terms of Service and may result in discontinuation of access to Student Tools Services.

SAT Subject Tests is a trademark owned by the College Board, which is not affiliated with, and does not endorse, this product.

The Princeton Review is not affiliated with Princeton University.

ISBN 978-0-525-56896-4
ISSN: 2687-8429

Editor: Eleanor Green
Production Editor: Emily Epstein White and Emma Parker
Production Artist: John Stecyk
Content Contributors: Terry Serres and Sophie Rose

Printed in the United States of America.

10 9 8 7 6 5 4 3 2 1

17th Edition

Editorial
Rob Franek, Editor-in-Chief
David Soto, Director of Content Development
Stephen Koch, Student Survey Manager
Deborah Weber, Director of Production
Gabriel Berlin, Production Design Manager
Selena Coppock, Managing Editor
Aaron Riccio, Senior Editor
Meave Shelton, Senior Editor
Chris Chimera, Editor
Eleanor Green, Editor
Orion McBean, Editor
Brian Saladino, Editor
Patricia Murphy, Editorial Assitant

Penguin Random House Publishing Team
Tom Russell, VP, Publisher
Rebecca Holland, Publishing Director
Amanda Yee, Associate Managing Editor
Ellen Reed, Production Manager
Suzanne Lee, Designer

Acknowledgments

Special thanks to Terry Serres and Sophie Rose for their contributions to this title. As always, we appreciate the time and attention given to each page by Emily Epstein White, Emma Parker, and John Stecyk.

Special thanks to Adam Robinson, who conceived of and perfected the Joe Bloggs approach to standardized tests and many of the other successful techniques used by The Princeton Review.

Contents

Get More (**Free**) Content

at **PrincetonReview.com/prep**

As easy as **1·2·3**

1 Go to PrincetonReview.com/prep and enter the following ISBN for your book:
9780525568964

2 Answer a few simple questions to set up an exclusive Princeton Review account. *(If you already have one, you can just log in.)*

3 Enjoy access to your **FREE** content!

Once you've registered, you can...

- Get our take on any recent or pending updates to the SAT Subject Test in French

- Take a full-length practice PSAT, SAT, and ACT

- Get valuable advice about the college application process, including tips for writing a great essay and where to apply for financial aid

- If you're still choosing between colleges, use our searchable rankings of *The Best 385 Colleges* to find out more information about your dream school.

- Access comprehensive study guides and a variety of printable resources, including vocabulary lists

- Check to see if there have been any corrections or updates to this edition

Need to report a potential **content** issue?

Contact **EditorialSupport@review.com** and include:

- full title of the book
- ISBN
- page number

Need to report a **technical** issue?

Contact **TPRStudentTech@review.com** and provide:

- your full name
- email address used to register the book
- full book title and ISBN
- Operating system (Mac/PC) and browser (Firefox, Safari, etc.)

Look For These Icons Throughout The Book

 PROVEN TECHNIQUES

 APPLIED STRATEGIES

Part I
Orientation

Chapter 1
Introduction

You have chosen to take the SAT Subject Test in French, and now it is time to demonstrate all you have learned during the course of your advanced study. This book will help you understand the format of the Subject Test and will give you all the tools you need to do your best.

This book is divided into five parts. Part One gives you an orientation of the SAT Subject Test in French and reveals some basic strategies. Part Two contains a practice test along with answers and explanations for the test. Part Three gives you the format for each section of the test and reviews key grammar and vocabulary words. Part Four contains answers and explanations for the drills found in Part Three. Part Five contains another practice test along with answers and explanations for the test.

WHAT ARE THE SAT SUBJECT TESTS?

They are a series of one-hour exams developed and administered by the Educational Testing Service (ETS) and the College Board. The SAT Subject Tests are designed to measure specific knowledge in specific areas. There are many different tests in many different subject areas, such as biology, history, French, and math. They are scored separately on a 200–800 scale.

How Are SAT Subject Tests Used by College Admissions?

Because the tests are given in specific areas, colleges use them as another piece of admissions information and, often, to decide whether an applicant can be exempted from college requirements. A good SAT French score might place you in second-year French instead of first-year French or exempt you from a foreign language requirement altogether.

Should I Take the SAT Subject Tests? How Many? When?

About one-third of the colleges that require SAT scores also require that you take two or three Subject Tests. Your first order of business is to start reading those college catalogs. College guidebooks, admissions offices, and guidance counselors should have this information as well.

As to which tests you should take, the answer is simple:

1. those Subject Tests that you will do well on
2. the tests that the colleges you are applying to may require you to take

The best possible situation, of course, is when the two overlap.

Some colleges have specific requirements; others do not. Again, start asking questions before you start taking tests. Once you find out which tests are required, if any, part of your decision-making is done. The next step is to find out which of the tests will highlight your particular strengths.

Possibilities range from math, English literature, U.S. or world history, biology, chemistry, and physics to a variety of foreign languages.

As to when you should take the tests, schedule them as close as possible to your school's corresponding academic calendar. If you plan to take the SAT Subject Test in Chemistry, for example, and you are currently taking chemistry in high school, don't postpone the test until next year.

When Are the SAT Subject Tests Offered?

In general, you can take from one to three Subject Tests per test date in October, November, December, January, May, and June at test sites across the country. Not all subjects are offered at each administration, so check the dates carefully. The College Board's website has tons of helpful information about all of the SAT Subject Tests: sat.collegeboard.org/about-tests/sat-subject-tests.

How Do I Register for the Tests?

To register by mail, pick up *The Paper Registration Guide for the SAT and SAT Subject Tests* at your guidance counselor's office. You can also register at the College Board website at www.collegeboard.org. This site contains other useful information such as the test dates and fees. If you have questions, you can talk to a representative at the College Board by calling 1-866-756-7346.

You may have your scores sent to you, to your school, and to four colleges of your choice. Additional reports will be sent to additional colleges for—you guessed it—additional money. Scores are made available to students via the College Board's website. To find out about the timeline of when scores are made available, please visit sat.collegeboard.org/scores.

Have You Heard About Fee-Waiver?

Are you a lower-income student whose family is unable to afford these test fees? Fear not. You may qualify for a fee waiver. Your high school counselor or an authorized community-based organization can give you a waiver if you qualify. Fee waivers can be used for the SAT and SAT Subject Tests. More information and the requirements for qualification can be found at sat.collegeboard.org/register/sat-fee-waivers.

A Couple of Words About Score Choice™

The good news about the SAT Subject Test is that you can choose which test scores you want colleges to see. Why is this such good news? Well, if you take more than one SAT Subject Test on a given test date, you'll be able to choose which tests from that date you'd like to submit to colleges. So if, for example, you take the French test followed by the chemistry test, but don't think the chemistry test went very well, you can simply opt out of having that chemistry score sent to your schools.

Score Choice is optional for students. This means that you aren't required to opt in and actively choose which specific scores you would like sent to colleges. If you decide not to use the score reporting, then all of the scores on file will automatically be sent when you request score reports. You should feel fine about sending along all of your scores, since most colleges consider a student's best score.

For more information about score reporting options, go to the College Board website at www.collegeboard.org.

What's a Good Score?

That's hard to say, exactly. A good score is one that fits in the range of scores the college of your choice usually looks for or accepts. However, if your score falls below the normal score range for Podunk University, that doesn't mean you won't get into Podunk University. Schools are usually fairly flexible in what they are willing to look at as a "good" score for a particular student.

Along with your score, you will also receive a percentile rank. That number tells you how you fit in with the other test takers. In other words, a percentile rank of 60 means that 40 percent of the test takers scored above you and 60 percent scored below you.

What Is The Princeton Review?

The Princeton Review is a test-preparation company founded in New York City. We have branches across the country and abroad. We've developed the techniques you'll find in our books, courses, and online resources by analyzing actual exams and testing the effectiveness of those techniques with our students. What makes our techniques unique is that we base our principles on the same ones used by the people who write the tests. We don't want you to waste your time with superfluous information; we'll give you just the information you'll need to get great score improvements. You'll learn to recognize and comprehend the relatively small amount of information that's actually tested. You'll also learn to avoid common traps, to think like the test writers, to find answers to questions you're unsure of, and to budget your time effectively.

You need to do only two things: trust the techniques, and practice, practice, practice.

The College Board publishes a book called *The Official Study Guide for all SAT Subject Tests* with practice exams for all 20 SAT subjects offered. You can also go to the College Board website for more information and practice questions. After you have worked through the review chapters and completed the practice tests in this book, try out your new skills on real SAT Subject Test questions.

What Makes This Book Different?

Most prep books for foreign language tests are written by academics who ramble on about the subtleties of the syntax of their chosen language. Their cups runneth over with more rules about grammar than you could ever absorb in a limited period of time. Most of all, they take more interest in teaching you French with a capital F than in preparing you for the particular challenges of this test. Rather than waste your time rehashing every tedious rule of grammar, we'll cover only those points needed to improve your score on the test. We want you to study effectively.

Some prep books can harm you more than help you by misleading you about the types of questions or by giving you so much to review that you don't know where to begin or what's most important. In more than twenty years of test-prep experience, we've learned what you truly need to know to score your best.

What Is the SAT Subject Test in French?

You can choose to take one of the two French Subject Tests: French or French with Listening. While the SAT Subject Test in French is generally offered on every SAT Subject Test date (except November), French with Listening is given only in November. It has an additional audio portion, which evaluates your ability to comprehend spoken French. You listen to a recording and answer multiple-choice questions. If you intend to continue your French language study, this is useful for placement purposes. You are not tested on your speaking or writing ability on either of these tests.

> **Test Changes!**
> Be advised: after November 2020, the French with Listening Subject Test will only be offered in May (starting with May 2021).

Will Slang or Casual Expressions Be Included on the Test?

Only authentic and widely accepted French language is used on the test. The French Subject Test is testing what should have been taught in a minimum of two years of regular French study in high school. Of course, the more you study, the better your scores will be.

What Does It Test?

The SAT Subject Test in French tests vocabulary, structure (grammar), and reading comprehension. Reading comprehension and structure each comprise between 30% and 40% of the test. Vocabulary in Context comprises 30% of the test. A strong vocabulary will help you score well on the Vocabulary and Reading Comprehension sections. Our review groups words by category for easier recall and gives you tips for learning vocabulary.

> Please note that the SAT French with Listening requires you to bring a portable CD player or Discman with you to the testing center. You will not be permitted to sit the exam if you do not have this device.

As you probably know, French grammar is complex, but your Subject Test requires you to know only a small portion of all grammar. You do not need to know spelling, where the accents go, or correct word order in a sentence. You don't need to know how to conjugate the *passé simple* or the imperfect of the subjunctive. We'll review only those points of grammar that serve you best on the test.

Now for the Good News

In the scheme of standardized tests, the French Subject Test isn't all that bad. Any standardized test provides you with a wealth of opportunity. Wouldn't you rather take a test in which you can use the Process of Elimination and guessing techniques than walk into a room and speak to a French person? By using an approach that has been developed over the years at The Princeton Review, you'll have the confidence and the ability to ace the SAT Subject Test in French.

> You can't master all of the French language in a few weeks or even a month. Focus on the vocabulary and grammar that helps you on the test.

How Is the SAT Subject Test in French Scored?

The scoring system for the SAT Subject Test in French is similar to that for the SAT. You are given a raw score based on the number of questions you got right minus one-third of a point for every wrong answer. The raw score is then converted to a scaled score ranging from 200 to 800.

How Will I Improve My Score?

Unfortunately, reading through this book may not be enough. It is important that you apply our techniques during the practice sections so that our approach will be second nature when you take the actual test.

> Although this book can be used alone, you may find it handy to have a French/English dictionary and a grammar book available as references while you read through the text. Don't use them on the practice tests, though!

Read one section of the book at a time and immediately apply what you have learned to the practice section that follows it. Then, carefully read through the explanations, looking for patterns in the mistakes that you made. If you notice that one type of question or topic is giving you trouble, go back and review the relevant section. Finally, before taking the diagnostic tests at the back of the book, review both the general test-taking strategies and the specific question strategies. Again, after taking the test, notice where your mistakes were, and use that information to adjust your pacing and intensify your review.

This book is designed to help you focus on those points that will help you score higher. It assumes that you have a basic French vocabulary and a rough grasp of grammar. The grammar section highlights the rules that are actually tested, giving you a concise explanation of each rule and examples of test questions. If you are someone who likes detailed explanations, you may want to have your school grammar book handy to use alongside this review book.

For more information visit www.PrincetonReview.com.

OVERALL STRUCTURE OF THE TEST

The French Subject Test consists of four types of multiple-choice questions. You are free to work on the sections or questions in any order that you choose. You will have 60 minutes to answer 85 questions.

The layout of each test will look something like this:

- Part A—Vocabulary Completions
  (approximately 20–26 questions)
- Part B—Grammar Blanks
  (approximately 15–20 questions)
- Part C—Paragraph Blanks
  (approximately 12–20 questions)
- Part D—Reading Comprehension
  (approximately 27 questions)

The exact breakdown of questions varies from test to test. The list above gives you the approximate number of each type of question.

If Reading Comprehension contains "schedules and tickets" questions as well as traditional passages, then Reading Comprehension will have more questions and Grammar will have slightly fewer.

> Schedules and tickets questions show time-tables, advertisements, or flyers.

Summary

Did you get all that?

o   There are two different French Subject Tests: the traditional French Subject Test and the French with Listening Subject Test. Most of you will take the traditional test, but if you have a lot of experience speaking French, consider taking the French with Listening Subject Test. Keep in mind that the listening test is only administered once a year!

o   The good news is that you can use the same strategies to prepare for both exams!

  • Read articles from French magazines, newspapers, and journals. Find academic articles, short stories, and pop culture articles to challenge and broaden your vocabulary.

  • Practice speaking French with your friends or family.

  • Listen to French radio stations or watch French TV shows and films.

o   Don't stress! By preparing the right way and taking time to relax, you'll be able to take the test with confidence.

Chapter 2
General Strategy

In this chapter, we'll discuss the best way for you to approach the SAT Subject Test in French. Pacing, Process of Elimination, and knowing when or whether to guess are all important factors that can determine how many points you accumulate as you work. You will also get a first look at the structure of the exam so you can plan your study time accordingly. Good luck!

HOW TO IMPROVE

As on any multiple-choice standardized test, you can learn to leverage your knowledge into the best possible score by following a few simple principles.

Attitude

Do not be intimidated by the test! This is only a test that stamps you with a number so that you can be easily classified by the colleges to which you apply. It measures some vocabulary, some minor rules such as which phrases take the subjunctive, but above all, it measures how well you do on standardized tests.

We can't make up for what you did or didn't learn in school, but we can teach you to make the most of what you do know and boost your test-taking savvy. We'll teach you new ways of approaching the test: pacing yourself, spotting wrong answers, and using guessing skills that put you in control.

Pacing

In school, most of us were trained to answer every question on a test. That made sense because those tests were usually written so that there was time to answer every question. On standardized tests, such thinking can lower your score. These tests are designed so that 99 percent of the population cannot finish the test without rushing and making careless mistakes. Slowing down—finding a pace at which you can work carefully and confidently—is the first step to improving your score. Remember: You are not given a negative score on a question you leave unanswered.

> Standardized tests aren't like school tests. They are actually designed so that hardly anyone can finish all of the questions. Don't stress about answering every question or getting through the entire test.

There is no advantage to answering all the questions on a test if you answer so hurriedly that you get most of them wrong. Think of each question as an investment in your score. Take enough time to make the work you put in pay off in terms of points. Most people don't realize that they can get a terrific score by doing fewer questions. While this philosophy holds true for all standardized tests, it is especially important for the SAT Subject Tests, in which one-third of a point is deducted for each wrong answer.

One caution: Working slowly and carefully is great. Spending five minutes to get an answer on a single question is not. Don't let your pride keep you struggling with a question that's giving you a hard time; each question has the same value. Do what you can, eliminate wrong answer choices, and guess. Then move on to a new question.

You'll have one hour to work on the entire test. You are not timed on each section. That means you can spend less time on sections that you are stronger in, or just move at a steady, careful pace through the whole test.

Work for Accuracy, Not for Speed

The scoring system used by the College Board rewards you for slowing down. It is better to do fewer questions well than to do many questions badly.

The following guide tells you approximately how many questions you have to answer to get a particular score. (This is the approximate number you should answer—not counting guesses—making no more than five errors.) Keep in mind that the scale changes each year, depending on the difficulty of the exam.

To get this score:	Answer this many questions (out of 85):
500	25
550	35
600	45
650	55
700	65
750	75
800	85

So, to get a 600 you have to answer barely half of the test. You can skip the questions that give you the most trouble.

As you do each practice section, you can check your pacing by comparing the number you got right with the number you got wrong. If you made more than two careless errors in that section (not counting guesses), you may want to slow down and attempt fewer questions on the practice test.

> You could skip as many as 20 questions and still score a 700.

Which Ones Should You Skip?

On Parts A and B, the questions are arranged roughly in order of increasing difficulty, so unless you are aiming for more than a 600, you may skip the last third of each part. On Parts C and D, there is no clear order of difficulty. Skip questions or passages that are difficult for you and spend time on those that you can comprehend.

You don't have to answer the same proportion of questions on each part. For most people, reading comprehension is the most difficult and vocabulary is the easiest. If that's true for you, do extra vocabulary and fewer Reading Comprehension questions.

Tailor your pacing strategy to your strengths and weaknesses. If your reading ability is strong and your grammar is weak, pace yourself accordingly.

Process of Elimination

No matter how good you are at French, you may still come across a question or two that will stump you. What can you do? Look for obviously incorrect answers, and get rid of them. It is often easier to find three wrong answers than it is to find one right one. If the sentence completion has something to do with going to the beach, an answer choice that means "pincushion" is probably not what you're looking for. The College Board also has some favorite ways to trap test takers who aren't completely sure of themselves. Once you know how they trick you, you're protected from falling into that trap and you're one answer choice closer to the correct one. On some occasions, you may even be able to eliminate all but the correct choice.

Make Only Smart Guesses

Eliminate as many of the wrong answer choices as possible, then guess. The way the test is scored, you get one point for each right answer, but you lose one third of a point for each wrong answer. You lose nothing if you leave the question blank. Therefore, you should skip the question if you really have no clue. However, if you can eliminate even one or two answer choices, it's to your advantage to guess. If you're down to two choices and can't decide, guess and move on to the next question.

Random vs. Educated Guessing
Make a distinction between random guessing and educated guessing. Random guessing (when you have no clue at all) won't help your score. Educated guessing (when you know enough to eliminate at least one answer choice) boosts your score.

Part II
Practice Test 1

Practice Test 1

FRENCH SUBJECT TEST 1

SECTION 1

Your responses to the SAT French questions must be filled in on Section 1 of your answer sheet (at the back of the book). Marks on any other section will not be counted toward your score.

When your supervisor gives the signal, turn the page and begin the SAT Subject Test in French.

FRENCH SUBJECT TEST 1

Part A

Directions: This part consists of a number of incomplete statements, each having four suggested completions. Select the most appropriate completion and fill in the corresponding circle on the answer sheet.

1. Les documents dont j'ai besoin pour mon travail sont toujours dans ma . . . au bureau.

   (A) douche
   (B) mallette
   (C) fourneau
   (D) pot à fleur

2. Il fait beau dehors; veux-tu te . . . après le dîner?

   (A) laver
   (B) demander
   (C) lever
   (D) promener

3. Le soldat attendait avec impatience la fin de . . .

   (A) la route
   (B) la gare
   (C) la guerre
   (D) l'immeuble

4. Il n'est pas permis d'amener votre chien . . . le café; veuillez le laisser à l'extérieur.

   (A) dans
   (B) avec
   (C) en dehors de
   (D) après

5. Paul a besoin d' . . . pour soutenir son pantalon.

   (A) un bras
   (B) une poche
   (C) une jambe
   (D) une ceinture

6. Pour son anniversaire, le garçon a reçu plusieurs . . .

   (A) jours
   (B) talents
   (C) jardins
   (D) cadeaux

7. Le tailleur nous a fait de nouveaux . . .

   (A) pneus
   (B) pains
   (C) vêtements
   (D) ameublements

8. Le . . . de mon immeuble est 564.

   (A) nombre
   (B) guide
   (C) numéro
   (D) nom

9. Il y a douze . . . dans un an.

   (A) mois
   (B) jours
   (C) heures
   (D) saisons

10. La route est fermée; nous ne pouvons pas . . . n'importe où.

    (A) conduire
    (B) acheter
    (C) jouer
    (D) sauter

GO ON TO THE NEXT PAGE

11. Quand je me suis marié, j'ai placé la bague sur . . . de ma femme.

    (A) le nez
    (B) le doigt
    (C) les lèvres
    (D) la tête

12. Je suis d'accord avec lui; je pense qu'il a . . .

    (A) tort
    (B) raison
    (C) mal
    (D) nécessité

13. Le magasin n'est pas . . . de mon bureau, alors je peux y aller à pied en cinq minutes.

    (A) en haut
    (B) tout près
    (C) sur
    (D) loin

14. Le héros a . . . une fille qui était en train de se noyer.

    (A) sauvé
    (B) nagé
    (C) remercié
    (D) traîné

15. L'été, il faut porter des . . . de soleil pour se protéger les yeux.

    (A) spectacles
    (B) cheveux
    (C) lunettes
    (D) rayons

16. Il est important de . . . des questions à votre enseignant si vous ne comprenez pas votre manuel.

    (A) enseigner
    (B) poser
    (C) être ennuyé avec
    (D) exiger

17. Ce n'est pas gentil de . . . tes amis.

    (A) lire
    (B) remplir
    (C) taquiner
    (D) tolérer

18. Le bruit constant m'. . .

    (A) énerve
    (B) enseigne
    (C) enlève
    (D) enferme

19. Le boulanger avait . . . mon pain et a dû en faire un autre.

    (A) brûlé
    (B) destiné à
    (C) établi
    (D) couvert

20. La dame a . . . le bras pour attraper le ballon.

    (A) tendu
    (B) renversé
    (C) retiré
    (D) perdu

GO ON TO THE NEXT PAGE

21. L'étudiant a écrit . . . sur les œuvres de Maupassant.

    (A) une boulette
    (B) une recette
    (C) une dissertation
    (D) un témoin

22. Si nous ne rentrons pas vite chez nous, nous serons rattrapés par . . .

    (A) les pleurs
    (B) la pousse
    (C) la pluie
    (D) la peur

GO ON TO THE NEXT PAGE

Part B

Directions: Each of the following sentences contains a blank. From the four choices given, select the one that can be inserted in the blank to form a grammatically correct sentence and fill in the corresponding circle on the answer sheet. Choice (A) may consist of dashes that indicate that no insertion is required to form a grammatically correct sentence.

23. Le monsieur ------- à vous suggérer.

    (A) n'a quelque chose
    (B) n'a pas
    (C) n'a rien
    (D) a rien

24. À ------- est ce manteau vert?

    (A) que
    (B) qui
    (C) lequel
    (D) quoi

25. Je n'aime pas cette nouvelle ------- qui habite dans mon immeuble.

    (A) garçon
    (B) serveur
    (C) homme
    (D) dame

26. Aimez-vous la plage? Nous ------- allons après la classe.

    (A) en
    (B) où
    (C) y
    (D) là

27. La semaine prochaine je rends visite à ma cousine à -------.

    (A) Mexique
    (B) France
    (C) Paris
    (D) Chine

28. Il faut toujours savoir ------- tu veux.

    (A) ce que
    (B) ce dont
    (C) a quoi
    (D) de quoi

29. Jean-Claude est venu avec -------.

    (A) ils
    (B) leur
    (C) eux
    (D) soi

30. C'est une décision ------- laquelle je vais beaucoup réfléchir.

    (A) à
    (B) sans
    (C) avec
    (D) dont

31. Elle est la personne la plus gentille que ------- jamais connue.

    (A) a
    (B) j'ai
    (C) j'aie
    (D) sois

32. Je vais nager à la plage ------- il ne fasse nuit.

    (A) après qu'
    (B) puisqu'
    (C) avant qu'
    (D) dès qu'

GO ON TO THE NEXT PAGE

33. Pierre ------- dehors quand le téléphone a sonné.

    (A) est
    (B) était
    (C) soit
    (D) serait

34. Nous ------- bientôt si elle a réussi son examen.

    (A) saura
    (B) saurons
    (C) saurait
    (D) savait

35. ------- les mains avant de manger!

    (A) Lavez
    (B) Brossez-vous
    (C) Serrez
    (D) Lavez-vous

36. Il n'a pas ------- signer les papiers.

    (A) décidé
    (B) le droit
    (C) envie
    (D) voulu

37. Je me ------- du souci pour votre santé.

    (A) feras
    (B) fasses
    (C) fait
    (D) faisais

38. C'est à cause de ------- que nous avons raté le train.

    (A) il
    (B) moi
    (C) se
    (D) leur

39. Est-ce que ------- cette dame qui va nous montrer la chambre?

    (A) c'est
    (B) ce soit
    (C) c'était
    (D) sera

40. Mon travail est ------- que le vôtre.

    (A) si difficile
    (B) le meilleur
    (C) pire
    (D) trop

41. N'appuyez pas trop fort sur le crayon, ------- il peut déchirer le papier.

    (A) avant que
    (B) sinon
    (C) durant
    (D) afin de

42. ------- m'a écrit.

    (A) Celui qui
    (B) Tu
    (C) C'est lui qui
    (D) Personne

GO ON TO THE NEXT PAGE

Part C

Directions: The paragraphs below contain blank spaces indicating omissions in the text. For some blanks, it is necessary to choose the completion that is most appropriate to the meaning of the passage; for other blanks, to choose the one completion that forms a grammatically correct sentence. In some instances, choice (A) may consist of dashes that indicate that no insertion is required to form a grammatically correct sentence. In each case, indicate your answer by filling in the corresponding circle on the answer sheet. Be sure to read the paragraph completely before answering the questions related to it.

Il est trois heures et demie du matin quand j' __(43)__ avec ma femme, sur le terrain de l'aérodrome pour le grand départ. Après avoir __(44)__ pendant plusieurs jours un temps __(45)__ , nous sommes __(46)__ prêts à partir __(47)__ Tokyo. Ma femme, qui __(48)__ née __(49)__ Japon, n'a __(50)__ visité la capitale, Tokyo. Elle voulait __(51)__ y aller.

43. (A) arrivais
    (B) arriverais
    (C) arrive
    (D) étais arrivé

44. (A) attendu
    (B) attendue
    (C) attendus
    (D) attendues

45. (A) passé
    (B) mauvais
    (C) triste
    (D) favorable

46. (A) loin d'être
    (B) jamais
    (C) enfin
    (D) simplement

47. (A) dans
    (B) sans
    (C) en
    (D) pour

48. (A) était
    (B) soit
    (C) est
    (D) es

49. (A) en
    (B) au
    (C) à
    (D) dans

50. (A) toujours
    (B) pas toujours
    (C) jamais
    (D) guère

51. (A) souvent
    (B) parfois
    (C) simplement
    (D) tellement

GO ON TO THE NEXT PAGE

Trois ou quatre cents personnes sont là pour __(52)__ à notre envol. Je ne sais pas comment cela se fait, __(53)__ que nous n'avions dit à personne que nous partions. Je suis très __(54)__ , mais notre avion est très chargé et la piste est couverte de neige. Je connais bien les dangers qu'il y a à __(55)__ dans ces conditions. Tout a été longuement __(56)__ , discuté entre nous depuis des __(57)__ , avec une très grande attention. Maintenant, j' __(58)__ l'esprit tranquille.

52. (A) assister
    (B) assommer
    (C) asseoir
    (D) aspirer

53. (A) malgré
    (B) parce
    (C) sans
    (D) dès

54. (A) fière
    (B) énervé
    (C) calme
    (D) lourd

55. (A) débarrasser
    (B) déborder
    (C) développer
    (D) décoller

56. (A) étudié
    (B) étudier
    (C) étude
    (D) étudiant

57. (A) minutes
    (B) secondes
    (C) moments
    (D) semaines

58. (A) ai
    (B) avais
    (C) aurais
    (D) ai été

GO ON TO THE NEXT PAGE

Part D

Directions: Read the following texts carefully for comprehension. Each is followed by a number of questions or incomplete statements. Select the completion or answer that is best according to the text and fill in the corresponding circle on the answer sheet.

Je croyais connaître admirablement tous les entours de la commune ; mais passé la ferme de la Saudraie, l'enfant me fit prendre une route où jusqu'alors je ne m'étais
Ligne jamais aventuré. Je reconnus pourtant, à deux kilomètres
5 de là, sur la gauche, un petit lac mystérieux où jeune homme j'avais été quelquefois patiner. Depuis quinze ans je ne l'avais plus revu, car aucun devoir pastoral ne m'appelle de ce côté ; je n'aurais plus su dire où il était et j'avais à ce point cessé d'y penser qu'il me sembla,
10 lorsque tout à coup, dans l'enchantement rose et doré du soir, je le reconnus, ne l'avoir d'abord vu qu'en rêve.

(*La Symphonie Pastorale,* André Gide, Folio, 1925, pages 12–13)

59. Qu'est-ce que le narrateur a cru avant d'aller avec l'enfant ?

(A) L'enfant vivait dans une ferme.
(B) Le narrateur a visité tous les endroits de sa paroisse.
(C) L'enfant était perdu.
(D) Le narrateur fera un tour de la commune.

60. Où se trouve le narrateur ?

(A) à Saudraie
(B) dans un village
(C) dans un parc
(D) à la campagne

61. Depuis combien de temps habite le narrateur à cet endroit ?

(A) Toute sa vie
(B) Moins d'une année
(C) Pour quinze ans
(D) Depuis sa jeunesse

62. Qu'est-ce que l'auteur veut dire avec l'expression « l'enchantement rose et doré » ?

(A) que le narrateur est un magicien
(B) qu'il y a beaucoup des fleurs sur la route
(C) que le narrateur voit le coucher du soleil
(D) qu'il faisait presque matin

63. On comprend que le narrateur

(A) rêve du lac
(B) se sent très fatigué
(C) est étourdi
(D) se rappelle soudainement le lac

GO ON TO THE NEXT PAGE

Il y a, au fond de beaucoup de Français, un champion de course automobile qui sommeille et que réveille le simple contact du pied sur l'accélérateur. Le citoyen
Ligne paisible, qui vous a obligeamment invité à prendre place
5 dans sa voiture, peut se métamorphoser sous vos yeux en pilote démoniaque. Jérôme Charnelet, ce bon père de famille, qui n'écraserait pas une mouche contre une vitre, est tout prêt à écraser un piéton au kilomètre, pourvu qu'il se sente "dans son droit." Au signal vert, il voit rouge.
10 Rien ne l'arrête plus, pas même le jaune. Sur la route, cet homme, qui passe pour rangé, ne se range pas du tout. Ce n'est qu'à bout de ressources, et après avoir subi une klaxonnade nourrie, qu'il consentira de mauvaise grâce à abandonner le milieu de la chaussée.
(*L'Auto,* Hachette)

64. L'auteur écrit dans un style

(A) sérieux
(B) neutre
(C) drôle
(D) scientifique

65. Qu'est-ce qui fait apparaître le "champion de course automobile"?

(A) l'action de se mettre au volant de l'automobile
(B) le lever du soleil
(C) l'action de se réveiller
(D) un klaxon

66. D'après le passage, Jérôme Charnelet est d'habitude

(A) un champion de course
(B) d'une disposition aimable
(C) impatient
(D) généreux

67. Comment Jérôme réagit-il au signal vert?

(A) Il s'arrête.
(B) Il écrase une mouche.
(C) Il ne réussit pas à voir les couleurs.
(D) Il devient un conducteur démoniaque.

68. D'après le passage, qu'est-ce qui convaincrait Jérôme de changer de position sur la chaussée?

(A) la réalisation qu'il est au milieu de la route
(B) son sens de ses obligations envers les autres conducteurs
(C) les klaxons des autres conducteurs
(D) la couleur du signal

69. On comprend que Jérôme conduit d'une manière

(A) ordonnée
(B) rangée
(C) gracieuse
(D) obsédée

GO ON TO THE NEXT PAGE

92 HAUTS DE SEINE
Le confort du neuf, le charme de l'ancien

Résidence "Le Valvert." Aux portes de Paris et près d'un accès autoroutier, dans immeuble du XIXe siècle, 10 appartements en cours de rénovation (du studio au 4 pièces). Parking privé dans cour intérieure. Proche du centre ville avec vue exceptionnelle sur parc aux arbres centenaires.

Prix à partir de 110000

Livraison 3ème trimestre 2005.

Bureau de vente et appartement-témoin:
01 587 45 35 12

Du lundi au samedi de 9 h 30 à 19 h, le dimanche uniquement sur rendez-vous.

70. Ces appartements

(A) vont être rénovés en 2005
(B) ont été rénovés au XIXe siècle
(C) sont en train d'être rénovés
(D) sont rénovés

71. Cette publicité s'adresse à

(A) des acheteurs éventuels
(B) de futurs locataires
(C) des personnes âgées
(D) des vendeurs

72. Après avoir lu cette publicité, on connaît tout SAUF

(A) la proximité de Paris de la résidence
(B) les heures d'ouverture du bureau de vente
(C) l'adresse exacte de la résidence
(D) l'existence d'un appartement modèle

GO ON TO THE NEXT PAGE

En mars 1973, un journal parisien a demandé à des jeunes de 14-15 ans quel était, pour eux, le plus mauvais moment de la journée; plus de la moitié (57%) ont *Ligne* répondu: "Quand je pars le matin pour l'école" et 23%
5 "le temps que je passe à l'école." Tout le monde aussi le sait: beaucoup de lycéens s'ennuient; ils en ont assez, ils en ont "ras le bol." Ce sont des mots qu'on entend et qu'on lit souvent. Certains disent: "Les examens, ça sert à trouver du travail, à avoir un beau métier. Sans
10 diplôme, on ne trouve rien." Mais d'autres pensent que l'école ne sert à rien, qu'ils apprennent plus de choses à la radio, au cinéma, à la télévision ou en voyageant; et aussi que l'école est souvent coupée de la vie et qu'elle est construite, comme la société, avec des chefs, une trop
15 grande hiérarchie.
(*Les Jeunes Aujourd'hui,* Hachette)

73. Ce passage concerne

(A) le nombre d'étudiants dans le système éducatif
(B) les attitudes des adolescents français
(C) le moyen de changer l'attitude des lycéens
(D) des changements récents dans le système éducatif

74. Que veut dire l'expression "ils en ont ras le bol"?

(A) qu'ils n'ont pas assez à manger
(B) qu'ils se plaignent des études
(C) qu'ils doivent se raser
(D) qu'ils ne veulent plus de quelque chose

75. D'après l'avis de certains étudiants, où est-ce qu'on apprend le plus?

(A) en famille
(B) à l'école
(C) dans une hiérarchie
(D) dans la vie

76. Selon les étudiants qui n'aiment pas l'école, quelle est la critique la plus forte contre le système d'éducation courant?

(A) Il y a trop de travail.
(B) Les étudiants s'ennuient.
(C) Les études n'ont rien à voir avec la vie.
(D) Il n'y a pas assez de chefs.

GO ON TO THE NEXT PAGE

Peu après, le patron m'a fait appeler et, sur le moment, j'ai été ennuyé parce que j'ai pensé qu'il allait me dire
Ligne de moins téléphoner et de mieux travailler. Ce n'était pas cela du tout. Il m'a déclaré qu'il allait me parler
5 d'un projet encore très vague. Il voulait seulement avoir mon avis sur la question. Il avait l'intention d'installer un bureau à Paris qui traiterait ses affaires sur la place, et directement, avec les grandes compagnies et il voulait savoir si j'étais disposé à y aller. Cela me permettrait de
10 vivre à Paris et aussi de voyager une partie de l'année. "Vous êtes jeune, et il me semble que c'est une vie qui doit vous plaire." J'ai dit que oui mais que dans le fond cela m'était égal.
(Camus, *L'Étranger,* Folio)

77. Le narrateur s'attend à

  (A) être grondé par son patron
  (B) recevoir une augmentation de salaire
  (C) discuter un projet avec le patron
  (D) ennuyer le patron

78. Que fait le patron?

  (A) Il ennuie le narrateur.
  (B) Il lui commande d'aller à Paris.
  (C) Il demande ce que pense le narrateur d'une
      suggestion.
  (D) Il refuse de laisser aller le narrateur à Paris.

79. Que veut faire le patron à Paris?

  (A) Il veut y habiter.
  (B) Il veut travailler pour une grande compagnie.
  (C) Il veut ouvrir un bureau.
  (D) Il veut trahir sa compagnie.

80. Selon le passage, pour quelle raison le patron a-t-il suggéré le projet au narrateur?

  (A) parce que le narrateur ne travaille pas bien
  (B) parce que le patron pense que le narrateur
      serait content de cette vie
  (C) parce que le patron est trop jeune pour le faire
      lui-même
  (D) parce que tout est égal au narrateur

81. Quelle est la réaction du narrateur à l'idée d'aller à Paris?

  (A) Il est énervé.
  (B) Il est content.
  (C) Il se sent rajeuni.
  (D) Il ne s'y intéresse pas beaucoup.

GO ON TO THE NEXT PAGE

Quand une rivière est bouchée par une grosse pierre, elle attend, grossit, grossit encore. Et tout à coup la pierre saute, et l'eau, enfin libre, peut continuer son chemin. Il se passe souvent la même chose dans l'histoire des arts.

Ligne

5 Charles Trenet a fait sauter ce qui bouchait la chanson française, il a fait d'elle un art mais lui a donné, en même temps, une très grande liberté, liberté dans la musique, dans les paroles, et aussi dans les gestes du chanteur sur la scène. Après Trenet, il n'y a plus une chanson, il y a
10 dix, vingt, cent chansons: après lui les artistes se sentent plus libres de faire, d'écrire, de chanter, ce qu'ils veulent.
(*La Chanson Française Aujourd'hui,* Hachette)

82. Selon le passage, qu'est-ce qui rend une rivière plus grosse?

   (A) l'augmentation de l'eau qui sort de la bouche de la rivière
   (B) la présence de quelque chose qui bloque le chemin
   (C) la présence de pierres
   (D) la liberté de l'eau

83. Pourquoi l'auteur décrit-il une rivière?

   (A) pour caractériser la musique de Trenet
   (B) pour expliquer la nature
   (C) pour montrer l'importance de Trenet
   (D) pour faire une analogie avec le développement de la chanson

84. D'après ce passage, on comprend qu'avant Trenet la chanson

   (A) était plus comme une rivière
   (B) était plus compliquée
   (C) avait moins de possibilités
   (D) était plus artistique

85. On comprend que Trenet

   (A) a introduit une nouvelle façon de présenter une chanson
   (B) aimait beaucoup la nature
   (C) a écrit cent chansons
   (D) n'était pas aimé par les autres chanteurs

STOP
If you finish before time is called, you may check your work on this test only.
Do not work on any other test in this book.

Practice Test 1:
Answers and
Explanations

PRACTICE TEST 1 ANSWER KEY

Question number	Correct answer	Right	Wrong
1.	B	_____	_____
2.	D	_____	_____
3.	C	_____	_____
4.	A	_____	_____
5.	D	_____	_____
6.	D	_____	_____
7.	C	_____	_____
8.	C	_____	_____
9.	A	_____	_____
10.	A	_____	_____
11.	B	_____	_____
12.	B	_____	_____
13.	D	_____	_____
14.	A	_____	_____
15.	C	_____	_____
16.	B	_____	_____
17.	C	_____	_____
18.	A	_____	_____
19.	A	_____	_____
20.	A	_____	_____
21.	C	_____	_____
22.	C	_____	_____
23.	C	_____	_____
24.	B	_____	_____
25.	D	_____	_____
26.	C	_____	_____
27.	C	_____	_____
28.	A	_____	_____
29.	C	_____	_____
30.	A	_____	_____
31.	C	_____	_____
32.	C	_____	_____
33.	B	_____	_____
34.	B	_____	_____
35.	D	_____	_____

Question number	Correct answer	Right	Wrong
36.	D	_____	_____
37.	D	_____	_____
38.	B	_____	_____
39.	A	_____	_____
40.	C	_____	_____
41.	B	_____	_____
42.	C	_____	_____
43.	C	_____	_____
44.	A	_____	_____
45.	D	_____	_____
46.	C	_____	_____
47.	D	_____	_____
48.	C	_____	_____
49.	B	_____	_____
50.	C	_____	_____
51.	D	_____	_____
52.	A	_____	_____
53.	B	_____	_____
54.	C	_____	_____
55.	D	_____	_____
56.	A	_____	_____
57.	D	_____	_____
58.	A	_____	_____
59.	B	_____	_____
60.	D	_____	_____
61.	D	_____	_____
62.	C	_____	_____
63.	D	_____	_____
64.	C	_____	_____
65.	A	_____	_____
66.	B	_____	_____
67.	D	_____	_____
68.	C	_____	_____
69.	D	_____	_____
70.	C	_____	_____

Question number	Correct answer	Right	Wrong
71.	A	_____	_____
72.	C	_____	_____
73.	B	_____	_____
74.	D	_____	_____
75.	D	_____	_____
76.	C	_____	_____
77.	A	_____	_____
78.	C	_____	_____
79.	C	_____	_____
80.	B	_____	_____
81.	D	_____	_____
82.	B	_____	_____
83.	D	_____	_____
84.	C	_____	_____
85.	A	_____	_____

PRACTICE TEST 1 EXPLANATIONS

The possible choices are examined for clues that should have indicated the correct answer. To help explain why a choice is right or wrong, resemblances between English and French words are noted, grammatical explanations are given, and an analysis of the Comprehension questions is provided.

Part A

1. **B** The sentence means, "The documents that I need for work are always in my...at the office. The key word or phrase is *pour mon travail*. Choice (A) means shower, (B) means briefcase, (C) means oven, and (D) means flower pot. The only answer that works is (B).

2. **D** The sentence means, "It's nice outside; do you want to...after dinner? The key phrase is *Il fait beau*. Choice (A) means to wash, (B) means to ask, (C) means to get up, and (D) means to take a walk. Choices (A) and (B) do not logically complete the sentence, while (C) does not closely relate to the weather outside being nice. The answer is (D).

3. **C** The sentence means, "The soldier was waiting impatiently for the end of the..." The key phrase is *soldat*. Choice (A) means the road, (B) means the train station, (C) means the war, and (D) means building. Choices (A) and (D) do not logically link to something a soldier would wait for. Be very careful with confusing (B) and (C) which look similar. The answer is (C).

4. **A** The sentence means, "It is not permitted to bring your dog...the café; please leave him outside." The key phrases are *n'est pas permis* and *à l'extérieur*. Choice (A) means in or inside, (B) means with, (C) means apart from, and (D) means after. Choices (B) and (D) are not things you would do with your dog and a café. Choice (C) has the word *dehors* by itself means outside, but the sentence is negated (*n'est pas*), so the opposite answer is needed. This is a trap answer. The answer is (A).

5. **D** The sentence means, "Paul needs...to hold up his pants." The key phrase is *soutenir son pantalon*. Choice (A) means an arm, (B) means a pocket, (C) means a leg, and (D) means a belt. Choice (A) doesn't connect to pants. Choices (B) and (C) are things associated with pants, but are wrong since they do not relate to holding up (*soutenir*) the pants. The answer is (D).

6. **D** The sentence means, "For his birthday, the boy received many..." The key word is *anniversaire*. Choice (A) means days, (B) means talents, (C) means gardens, and (D) means presents. Choice (A) is tricky since the words look similar to the word for toys (*jouets*). Choices (B) and (C) do not link to the key word. The answer is (D).

7. **C** The sentence means, "The tailor made us new...." The key phrase is *Le tailleur*, which looks very similar to tailor in English. Choice (A) means lungs, (B) means bread, (C) means clothes, and (D) means home furnishings. The only answer that works is (C).

8. **C** The sentence means, "The…of my building is 564." The key phrases are *immeuble* and *564*. Choice (A) means number, (B) means guide, (C) means number, and (D) means name or noun. Choices (B) and (D) don't match, but (A) and (C) have the same English translation. The difference is in the usage. In French, *nombre* refers to a collection or group of things. For example, *un grand nombre de participants* means a large number of participants. In contrast, *numéro* refers to a list of digits. For example, *mon numéro de telephone* is my telephone number. Since 564 is a list of digits, the answer is (C).

9. **A** The sentence means, "There are twelve…in a year." The key words are *douze* and *dans un an*. Choice (A) means months, (B) means days, (C) means hours, and (D) means weeks. The answer is (A).

10. **A** The sentence means, "The road is closed; we cannot…anywhere." The key phrase is *La route*. Choice (A) means drive, (B) means buy, (C) means play, and (D) means jump. The answer is (A).

11. **B** The sentence means, "When I got married, I put a ring on the…of my wife." The key phrases are *je me suis marié* and *la bague*. Choice (A) means nose, (B) means finger, (C) means lips, and (D) means head. If the meaning of *la bague* was unknown, use the word *marié* to eliminate (A) and (D). The answer is (B).

12. **B** The sentence means, "I agree with him; I think he is…" The key phrase is *d'accord*. Choice (A) means wrong, (B) means right, (C) means suffers, and (D) means needed. The answer is (B).

13. **D** The sentence means, "The store is not…from my office, so I can walk there in five minutes." The key phrases are *n'est pas* and *à pied* en cinq minutes. Choice (A) means up high, (B) means very near, (C) means on, and (D) means far. Choices (A) and (C) do not logically match the key phrases. Choice (B) is a trap answer. Since the very is negated, the opposite word is needed. The answer is (D).

14. **A** The sentence means, "The hero…a woman who was drowning." The key phrases are *Le héros* and *en train de se noyer*. Choice (A) means saved, (B) means swam, (C) means thanked, and (D) means dragged. Even if the meaning of *se noyer* is unknown, use the key phrases of *Le héros* to eliminate (B) and (C). *Sauvé* is a cognate with the English word saved and is a best guess even if the word *traîné* is unknown. The answer is (A).

15. **C** The sentence means, "In summer, you should wear…[of sun] to protect your eyes." The key phrase is *se protéger les yeux*. Choice (A) means a show or large event, (B) means hair, (C) means sunglasses in the context of *de soleil*, and (D) means a ray of sunshine in the context of *de soleil*. Choices (B) and (D) are not items that are worn, so these can be eliminated. Choice (A) is a *faux-ami* and is a trap answer. The answer is (C).

16. **B** The sentence means, "It is important to…questions to your teacher if you do not understand your textbook." The key phrases are *à votre enseignant* and *si vous ne comprenez pas*. Choice (A) means teach, (B) means ask, (C) means be bored with, and (D) means to demand. Choices (C) and (D) do not match the key phrases. Answer (A) is a look-alike word to a word in the sentence and is a trap. The answer is (B).

17.   **C**   The sentence means, "It is not nice to…your friends." The key phrase is *n'est pas gentil*. Choice (A) means to read, (B) means to fill up, (C) means to tease, and (D) means to tolerate. Choice (A) doesn't match the negative tone of the sentence. Choice (B) is a possible trap since it looks like the word for replace. Choice (D) doesn't logically mesh with the sentence. The answer is (C).

18.   **A**   The sentence means, "The constant noise…me." The key phrase is *bruit*. Choice (A) means annoys, (B) means teaches, (C) means removes, and (D) means shuts up. The question is made challenging since all the words are similar in appearance. The answer is (A).

19.   **A**   The sentence means, "The baker had…my bread and he had to make another one." The key phrases are *Le boulanger* and *a dû en faire un autre*. Choice (A) means burned, (B) means destined to, (C) means established, and (D) means covered. Choice (D) can be confused with *cuit au four,* which means baked. The answer is (A).

20.   **A**   The sentence means, "The woman…her arm to catch the ball." The key phrases are *le bras* and *attraper*. Choice (A) means to hold out, (B) means turned around, (C) means withdrew, and (D) means lost. The answer is (A).

21.   **C**   The sentence means, "The student wrote…on the works of Maupassant." The key phrase is *L'étudiant a écrit*. Choice (A) means a small paper ball, (B) means a recipe, (C) means an essay, and (D) means a witness. Choice (C) is a cognate with the English word dissertation, which means a very long report. The answer is (C).

22.   **C**   The sentence means, "If we don't hurry home, we will get caught in…" The key phrase is *nous serons rattrapés par*. Choice (A) means the tears, (B) means the growth (of plants), (C) means the rain, and (D) means the fear. This question is made challenging since all the answers are very similar looking. The answer is (C).

Part B

23.   **C**   *Pronouns*

The sentence means, "The man-------to suggest to you." Choice (A) has no negation word to pair with *ne*. Choice (B) has no pronoun which would be required with this negation. Choice (C) means has nothing, which is the correct *ne* plus a negation, and (D) is missing the *ne* portion of the negation pair. The answer is (C).

24.   **B**   *Pronouns*

The sentence means, "To-------belongs this green coat?" Choice (A) is wrong since *à* is a preposition and the word *que* is never used with a preposition. Choice (B) is correct since *qui* is used with prepositions and can mean whom in this context. Choice (C) means which and does not match the context of the sentence. Choice (D) means what and does not match the context of the sentence. The answer is (B).

25.   **D**   *Odds and Ends: Article agreement*

The sentence means, "I don't like this new------who lives in my building." The phrase this new (*cette nouvelle*) is feminine singular. Choice (A) is masculine and would require *ce nouveau*. Choice (B) is masculine and would require *ce nouveau*. Choice (C) is masculine and is a silent h, which would require *ce nouvel*. Choice (D) is a singular feminine noun. The answer is (D).

26.   **C**   *Pronouns*

The sentence means, "Do you like the beach? We're going ------- after class." In French, the pronouns precede the verb, while in the English translation, they follow the verb. The required pronoun needs to refer to a location or place. Choice (A) could refer to a place if the verb takes *de*; however, *aller* takes the pronoun *à*. Choice (B) means where but is a pronoun that is used to connect two phrases (like *qui* or *que*). Choice (C) refers to place and is the proper pronoun to replace the preposition *à*. Choice (D) means there, but *là* is an adverb and cannot be used in this location in the sentence. The answer is (C).

27.   **C**   *Prepositions*

The sentence means, "Next week I will visit my cousin in ------- ." The preposition *à* can sometimes refer to a country, but more often refers to a city. Additionally, countries take a definite article (*la/le*) in this context. Choice (A) would need to say *au Mexique* since Mexico takes the masculine article. Choice (B) would need to say *en France* rather than *à*. Choice (C) is the correct usage for a city. Choice (D) would need to say *en Chine*. The answer is (C).

28.   **A**   *Pronouns*

The sentence means, "You always need to know ------- you want." This question is testing relative pronouns. Many times, relative pronouns connect to prepositions. It is important to note that the verb *vouloir* does not take a preposition. Choice (A) means what and does not use a pronoun. Choice (B) would require a verb with the preposition *de*. Choice (C) would require a verb with the preposition *à*. Choice (D) does not fit the context of the sentence with the word *savoir*. The answer is (A).

29.   **C**   *Pronouns*

The sentence means, "Jean-Claude came with ------- ." The question is testing for the correct form of the pronoun after the preposition *avec*. This requires the stressed pronoun. Choice (A) is a subject pronoun. Choice (B) is an indirect object pronoun. Choice (C) is a stressed pronoun. Choice (D) is a reflexive pronoun. The answer is (C).

30.   **A**   *Prepositions*

The sentence means, "It's a decision ------ which I have to reflect a lot. The question is testing what the correct form of the pronoun is that matches with the verb *réfléchir*. Choice (A) is correct since the phrase is *réfléchir à*. Choice (B) would be *réfléchir sans*. Choice (C) would be *réfléchir avec*. Choice (D) is wrong since *dont* and *laquelle* cannot be used together. The answer is (A).

31. **C**   *Verbs*

The sentence means, "She is the nicest person that -------- ever known." The question is testing which form of the verb is needed and whether that verb also needs a subject. In French, the subject must always be explicit. When a sentence uses the superlative (nicest), subjunctive tense is required. Choice (A) is indicative and lacks a subject. Choice (B) is indicative with a subject. Choice (C) is subjunctive with a subject. Choice (D) is subjunctive without a subject. The answer is (C).

32. **C**   *Prepositions/Verbs*

The sentence means, "I'm going swimming at the beach ------- it becomes night." The question is testing which preposition would logically complete the sentence. However, the second phrase is in the form of the subjunctive, so the preposition chosen must also require the use of the subjunctive. Choice (A) means after and requires indicative. Choice (B) means since and requires indicative. Choice (C) means before and requires subjunctive. Choice (D) means as soon as and requires indicative. While all of these prepositions could logically complete the sentence, only one requires the subjunctive. The answer is (C).

33. **B**   *Verbs*

The sentence means, "Peter ------- outside when the telephone rang." The sentence is testing which form of the verb best matches with the past tense verb *a sonné*. Choice (A) is present tense, but the rest of the sentence is past. Choice (B) is imperfect (*l'imparfait*), which is one of the past tense forms. Choice (C) is present subjunctive. There is no reason to use the subjunctive or present tense. Choice (D) is conditional. There is no conditional phrase with *si* so eliminate (D). The answer is (B).

34. **B**   *Verbs*

The sentence means, "We ------- soon if she passed her exam. The key phrases here are *si* and *a réussi*. Typically, sentences with an "if" clause in the *passé composé* require future tense. Choice (A) is in the future tense, but is third person singular (he/she/it) so doesn't match *nous*. Choice (B) is in the future tense and is first person plural (we). Choice (C) is the conditional tense. Choice (D) is the imperfect tense. The answer is (B).

35. **D**   *Pronouns*

The sentence means, " ------- your hands before eating!" The sentence is testing both the correct vocabulary word and whether a reflexive pronoun is needed with this command. Choice (A) means wash but does not have a reflexive pronoun indicating who should wash what. Choice (B) means to brush and refers to teeth, not hands. Choice (C) means to shake hands and does not match eating. Choice (D) means to wash and contains the reflexive pronoun. The answer is (D).

36.   **D**   *Prepositions*

The sentence means, "He does not have/He didn't ------ to sign the papers." At first glance this sentence is testing word choice, but each word logically completes the sentence, so consider other things the SAT tests, such as prepositions. Choice (A) means decided but requires the preposition *de*. Choice (B) means the right but requires the preposition *de*. Choice (C) means desire but requires the preposition *de*. Choice (D) means want and does not need a preposition. The answer is (D).

37.   **D**   *Verbs*

The sentence means, "I ------- worry about your health." Choice (A) is the future tense. Choice (B) is subjunctive. Choice (C) is present third person (he/she/it). Choice (D) is imperfect first person (I). There is no reason to use future or subjunctive in this sentence. Past or present tense would both work; however, (C) does not match the subject. The answer is (D).

38.   **B**   *Pronouns*

The sentence means, "It is ------- fault that we missed the train." A more literal translation would be, "It is the cause of -------, that we missed the train. The question is testing the correct form of the pronoun that follows the preposition *de*. Prepositions require the stressed pronoun. Choice (A) is a subject pronoun. Choice (B) is a stressed pronoun. Choice (C) is a reflexive pronoun. Choice (D) is an indirect object pronoun. The answer is (B).

39.   **A**   *Verbs*

The sentence means, "------- the woman who is going to show us the room?" The key phrase is *va nous montrer* which is immediate future. Choice (A) is present tense with a subject. Choice (B) is present subjunctive. Choice (C) is imperfect. Choice (D) is future but lacks a subject. There is no reason to use subjunctive. Past tense does not match the second half of the sentence. Both present and future tense would work, but there needs to be a subject *ce*. The answer is (A).

40.   **C**   *Odds and Ends: comparatives*

The sentence means, "My work is ------- than yours is." The key phrase is *que le vôtre* indicating the need for a comparison. Choice (A) means so difficult and is not a comparison. Choice (B) means the best and is superlative rather than a comparison. Choice (C) means worse and can be used to compare two things. Choice (D) means too much. The answer is (C).

41.   **B**   *Prepositions*

The sentence means, "Don't push too hard on the pencil, ------- it can tear the paper." This question is testing the word that most logically connects the two phrases. Choice (A) means before and would require the subjunctive. Choice (B) means otherwise. Choice (C) means during. Choice (D) means in order to. The answer is (B).

42.   **C**   *Prepositions*

The sentence means, " ------- wrote to me." The question is testing the correct pronoun to begin the sentence. Choice (A) means he that and would leave this as an incomplete sentence. Choice (B) is a subject pronoun, but doesn't match the verb (*tu m'as écrit*). Choice (C) means that is the person who and is in the correct form of the pronoun. Choice (D) matches the verb, but the negation form requires *ne*. The answer is (C).

Part C

The following translation is for questions 43–51.

It is three thirty in the morning when I   (43)   with my wife, on the field of the airport for the grand departure. After having   (44)   for many days a   (45)   time, we are   (46)   ready to leave   (47)   Tokyo. My wife, who   (48)   born   (49)   Japan, has   (50)   visited the capital, Tokyo. She has   (51)   wanted to go there.

43.   **C**   *Verbs*

Choice (A) is imperfect, which is an ongoing action in the past. Choice (B) is conditional and requires an "if" statement. Choice (C) is in the present tense. Choice (D) is the past perfect and is an action complete in the past before another action. The answer is (C).

44.   **A**   *Verbs*

The question is testing when the participle requires agreement. Since the verb is *avoir* no agreement is necessary. Choice (A) has no agreement. Choice (B) is the feminine and is not needed. Choice (C) is the plural and is not needed. Choice (D) is the feminine plural and is not needed. The answer is (A).

45.   **D**   *Vocabulary*

The question is testing for the word that most logically completes the sentence. Choice (A) means past. Choice (B) means unpleasant weather. Choice (C) means sad. Choice (D) means favorable weather. Choices (A) and (C) are illogical. Choice (B) does not match the first sentence, which shows the couple leaving. The answer is (D).

46.   **C**   *Vocabulary*

The question is testing for the word or phrase that most logically completes the sentence. Choice (A) means far from. Choice (B) means never. Choice (C) means finally. Choice (D) means simply. The answer is (C).

47. **D** *Prepositions*

The question is testing the correct preposition to match with the verb *partir*. Choice (A) means in. Choice (B) means without. Choice (C) means to but cannot be used with cities. Choice (D) means for. The correct answer is (D).

48. **C** *Verbs*

The question is testing the correct form of the verb to precede the word born (*née*). The verb *naître* is conjugated with the present tense of the verb *être* to form the *passé composé*. Choice (A) is imperfect. Choice (B) is the present subjunctive tense. Choice (C) is the present tense. Choice (D) is present tense but is in the second person (*tu es* versus *ma femme est*). There is no need for subjunctive in this sentence. The answer is (C).

49. **B** *Prepositions*

The question is testing the correct preposition to follow *née* and precede *Japon*. Choice (A) cannot be used with *Japon*. Choice (B) is the correct preposition to precede *Japon,* since *Japon* takes the masculine article. Choice (C) is missing the article (*la/le*). Choice (D) is not the correct preposition in this context. The answer is (B).

50. **C** *Vocabulary*

The question is testing the correct negation pair to logically complete the sentence. The key phrase is *n'a…visité*. Choice (A) is not a negation pair. Choice (B) means not always. Choice (C) means never. Choice (D) means rarely. Choices (B) and (D) do not make sense in the context of the story. The answer is (C).

51. **D** *Odds and Ends: adverbs*

While this question is testing adverbs, it is also helpful to think in terms of vocabulary. The question is testing which word most logically completes the sentence. Choice (A) means often. Choice (B) means sometimes. Choice (C) means simply. Choice (D) means really (so much). In the context of the passage, (B) and (C) do not make logical sense. Choice (A) does not provide enough emphasis. The answer is (D).

The following translation is for questions 52–58.

Three or four hundred people are there to __(52)__ our flight. I do not know how that happened, __(53)__ we had not told anyone we were leaving. I am very __(54)__ , but our plane is heavily loaded and the runway is covered in snow. I fully understand the dangers that exist when __(55)__ in these conditions. All had been __(56)__ at length, discussed among ourselves for many __(57)__ , with great attention to detail. Now, I __(58)__ a tranquil spirit.

52. **A** *Vocabulary*

The question is testing the correct word that logically completes the sentence. Choice (A) means to attend. Choice (B) means to knock down. Choice (C) means to sit. Choice (D) means to aspire. The answer is (A).

53. **B** *Vocabulary*

The question is testing the correct word to use to connect the two phrases. The second phrase explains the reason for the first phrase. Choice (A) means in spite of. Choice (B) means because. Choice (C) means without. Choice (D) means as soon as. The answer is (B).

54. **C** *Vocabulary*

The question is testing the correct word to logically complete the sentence. Choice (A) means proud. Choice (B) means annoyed. Choice (C) means calm. Choice (D) means heavy. The correct answer is (C).

55. **D** *Vocabulary*

The question is testing the correct word to logically complete the sentence. Choice (A) means getting rid of. Choice (B) means overflowing. Choice (C) means developing. Choice (D) means taking off. This question is made challenging since all of the answers look very similar. The answer is (D).

56. **A** *Odds and Ends: Adjectives*

This question is testing which form of the word *étudier* to use in the sentence. The key phrase is *Tout a été*, which means Everything had been. Since the verb *être* is used, the participle or adjective form of the verb is needed and must match the gender and number of the subject *Tout*. Choice (A) is the participle or adjective form of the word. Choice (B) is the infinitive verb form. Choice (C) is a noun meaning study. Choice (D) is a noun, meaning student. The answer is (A).

57. **D** *Vocabulary*

This question is testing the correct word to logically complete the sentence. The key phrase in the sentence is *longuement*. Choice (A) means minutes. Choice (B) means seconds. Choice (C) means moments. Choice (D) means weeks. Though there is no explicit support for weeks, (A), (B), and (C) all refer to a short amount of time. The answer is (D).

58. **A** *Verbs*

The question is testing the correct tense of the verb to use. The key phrase is *Maintenant*, which means now. Also note that much of the paragraph is narrated in the present tense. Choice (A) is the present tense. Choice (B) is the imperfect tense. Choice (C), conditional. Choice (D) is the *passé composé*. The answer is (A).

Part D

The following translation is for questions 59–63.

> I believed that I had thoroughly known all the different parts of my community; but past the Saudrie farm, the boy took me down a road along which I had never traveled. All the same, I recognized, about two kilometers away, on the left, a little mysterious lake where I had sometimes swum as a young man. It has been fifteen years since I had last seen it, since no pastoral duty had called me to this area; I would not have been able to explain where it was and at this point in my life, I had stopped thinking about it when it seemed to me, all of a sudden, in the rose and golden enchantment of the evening, that I recognized it, having at first only seen it in a dream.

59. **B** The question asks, "What did the narrator believe before going with the boy?"

(A) No. "The boy lived on a farm." These are familiar words—wrong context. The passage says the boy took him past a farm.

(B) Yes. "The narrator had visited all the parts of his parish." In line 1, the passage says "*Je croyais connaître admirablement tous les entours…*"

(C) No. "The boy was lost." This answer confuses *prendre*, which means to take, with *être perdue*, which means to be lost.

(D) No. "The narrator will take a tour of his community." These are familiar words—wrong context. It is also in the future tense which does not address the question of what the narrator believed *before* going with the boy.

60. **D** The question asks, "Where is the narrator?"

(A) No. "At Saudrie." These are familiar words—wrong context. This is the name of a local farm the narrator passes.

(B) No. "In a village." There is no context for this. While the narrator mentions *commune*, which is a community, there is no evidence of a town.

(C) No. "In a park." There is no context for this. While the narrator can see a lake, there is no evidence that he is in a park of any sort.

(D) Yes. "In the countryside." The narrator mentions *commune*, which is a territorial division similar to community in English. Likewise, he mentions *un lac* and *une ferme*, both of which are more likely to be found in a rural community.

61. **D** The question asks, "How long has the narrator lived in this area?"

(A) No. "All his life." There is no context for this in the passage.

(B) No. "Less than a year." The narrator mentions that he went swimming in this area as a young man and has had pastoral duties in that area for at least fifteen years.

(C) No. "For fifteen years." These are familiar words—wrong context. The narrator says that no pastoral duty has brought him to that part of his parish for fifteen years, but it does not say that he had been living there for only fifteen years.

(D) Yes. "Since he was young." This is supported by the fact that he went swimming in the lac as a young man, but hadn't visited the area for at least the last fifteen years as a pastor.

62.   **C**   The question asks, "What does the author mean when he says 'the rose and golden enchantment'?"

(A) No. "That the narrator is a magician." These are familiar words—wrong context. There is an enchantment in a figurative rather than the literal sense.

(B) No. "That there are a lot of flowers along his route." There is no context evidence for this.

(C) Yes. "That the narrator sees the sunset." The narrator says that the rose and golden enchantment were *au soir* or "of the evening."

(D) No. "That it is nearly morning." This is contradicted by the passage. While a sunrise might make rose and golden colors, the narrator specifies *au soir*.

63.   **D**   The question asks, "It is understood that the narrator:"

(A) No. "Dreamed of a lake." These are familiar words—wrong context.

(B) No. "Feels very tired." There is no context for this. Dreaming does not mean the narrator is sleepy.

(C) No. "Is forgetful." There is no context for this. Just because the narrator had not thought of the lake for many years does not mean that he is forgetful.

(D) Yes. "Suddenly remembers the lake." This is supported when the passage says *tout à coup…je le reconnus*, which means suddenly I remembered.

The following translation is for questions 64–69.

There is, deep in the heart of many Frenchmen, a champion race car driver who lies dormant and awakens at the simple contact of the foot against the accelerator. The peaceable citizen, who politely invited you to join him in his car, can change into a demon driver before your eyes. Jerome Charnelet, that kind father and family man, who would not even squash a bug on a window, is suddenly ready to run over a pedestrian a kilometer away, since he feels it is "within his rights." At a green light, he sees red. Nothing will stop him anymore, much less a yellow light. On the road, this man, who typically lives an orderly life, will never pull over to let others pass. It is only at the end of his resources, after sustained honking, that he will consent with a bad grace to abandon the middle of the road.

64. **C**   The question asks, "The author writes in a style that is:"

(A) No. "Serious" The author makes several jokes including a word play (*qui passe pour rangé, ne se range pas du tout*).

(B) No. "Neutral." The author is doing more than just describing a scene.

(C) Yes. "Humorous." This is supported by the exaggerations and word plays in the passage.

(D) No. "Scientific." There is no context for this.

65. **A**   The questions asks, "What makes the race car driver appear?"

(A) Yes. "The act of getting behind the wheel." This is supported in line 2 when the passage says *que réveille le simple contact du pied.*

(B) No. "The sunrise." These are familiar words—wrong context. *Réveiller* does not imply a sunrise.

(C) No. "The action of waking up." These are familiar words—wrong context. *Réveiller* is used in a figurative sense here rather than a literal one.

(D) No. "A horn." These are familiar words—wrong context. *Klaxonner* is mentioned later in the passage but is not used to wake up the race car driver.

66. **B**   The question asks, "According to the passage, Jerome Charnelet is usually:"

(A) No. "A race car driver." These are familiar words—wrong context. Jerome is transformed into a race car driver when he drives. This is not what he is usually like.

(B) Yes. "Of a kind disposition." This is supported by the text *ce bon père de famille.*

(C) No. "Impatient." This is how he drives, but is not what Jerome is usually like.

(D) No. "Generous." There is no support for this in the passage.

67. **D**   The question asks, "How does Jerome react to the green light?"

(A) No. "He stops." This is a trick question about him seeing red (*il voit rouge*).

(B) No. "He swats a fly." This is familiar words—wrong context.

(C) No. "He has trouble seeing colors." This is too literal of a reading of the sentence "at a green light, he sees red."

(D) Yes. "He becomes a crazy driver." This is supported by the idiomatic expression, he sees red.

68. **C**   The question asks, "According to the passage, what convinces Jerome to change lanes on the road?"

(A) No. "The realization that he is in the middle of the road." These are familiar words—wrong context.

(B) No. "His sense of obligation to the other drivers." These are familiar words—wrong context.

(C) Yes. "The horns of the other drivers." This is supported by the passage *avoir subi une klaxonnade nourrie.*

(D) No. "The color of the traffic light." These are familiar words—wrong context.

69. **D** The question asks, "It is understood that Jerome drives in a manner that is"

(A) No. "Orderly." There is no support for this in the text.

(B) No. "Steady." This is a familiar word—wrong context.

(C) No. "Gracious." This is the opposite of the text.

(D) Yes. "Obsessive." This is supported in the text by the phrase *pilote démoniaque.*

The following translation is for questions 70–72.

92 Seine Heights. Modern comfort, antique charm.

Residence "La Valvert." On the Parisian boat docks near to a highway access, 10 apartments are in the process of being renovated (from studio to 4 bedroom). Private parking in an enclosed garage. Near to downtown with an exceptional view of a park with hundred-year-old trees. Prices starting at 110,000€. Home delivery in the 3rd trimester of 2005. Sales office and model room: 01 587 45 35 12. From Mondays to Saturdays 930a to 7p, Sundays by appointment only.

70. **C** The question asks, "These apartments:"

(A) No. "Will be renovated in 2005." There is no context for this.

(B) No. "Were renovated in the 19th century." These are familiar words—wrong context.

(C) Yes. "Are being renovated." This is supported by the passage *en cours de rénovation.*

(D) No. "Are renovated." These are familiar words—wrong context.

71. **A** The question asks, "This advertisement is aimed at:"

(A) Yes. "Prospective buyers." This is supported by the passage *bureau de vente.*

(B) No. "Future tenants." This is close but these are for sale rather than for rent.

(C) No. "Elderly people." There is no context for this.

(D) No. "Sellers." This is a familiar word—wrong context.

72.   **C**   The question asks, "After reading this advertisement, one has learned everything EXCEPT:"

(A)   No. This is learned since it is *aux portes de Paris* and *proche du centre ville*.

(B)   No. This is learned in the last line of the advertisement.

(C)   Yes. The name of the building is 92 Seine Heights, but this is not the exact address. This is not something learned from the advertisement.

(D)   No. This is learned, since the passages mentions *appartement-témoin*.

The following translation is for questions 73–76.

In March of 1973, a Parisian newspaper asked youths aged 14-15 what was, for them, the worst moment of their day; more than half (57%) answered: "When I leave in the morning for school" and 23% said "the time I spend in school." Everyone also knows that: many high school students are bored; they've had enough, they are fed up with it [literally: they have filled their bowl]. These are phrases that one often hears and reads. Some say: "tests help you find work, to have a better job. Without a diploma, you cannot find any work." But others think that school is pointless, that they can learn more from radios, movies, television, and travel; and that school is often cut off from real life and that it is fabricated, like society, with many bosses, a massive hierarchy.

73.   **B**   The question asks, "This passage is concerned with:"

(A)   No. "The number of students in the educational system." The story does provide some percentages, but no exact numbers are mentioned.

(B)   Yes. "The attitude of French youth." This is supported by the passage.

(C)   No. "The way to change the attitude of French students." There is no context for this.

(D)   No. "Recent changes in the educational system." There is no context for this.

74.   **D**   The question asks, "What does the expression "*ils en ont ras le bol*" mean?

(A)   No. "That they don't have enough to eat." This is a trap that ignores the figurative meaning of *le bol*.

(B)   No. "That they complain about their studies." These are familiar words—wrong context.

(C)   No. "That they should shave." This is a confusion of *ras* and *raser*.

(D)   Yes. "They do not want any more of something." This is supported by the phrase *ils en ont assez*.

75. **D** The question asks, "According to certain students, where does one learn the most?"

(A) No. "At home." There is no context for this.

(B) No. "At school." No, certain students are complaining about school.

(C) No. "In a hierarchy." No, these are familiar words—wrong context.

(D) Yes. "In life." This is supported by students feeling they can learn *à la radio, à la télévision,* etc.

76. **C** The question asks, "According to students who do not like school, what is the strongest criticism of the educational system?"

(A) No. "There is too much work." There is no context for this.

(B) No. "The students are bored." This is a problem, but one that *tout le monde* knows. This does not come from the students.

(C) Yes. "Studies have nothing to do with real life." This is supported by the passage *l'école est souvent coupée de la vie.*

(D) No. "There aren't enough bosses." This is the opposite of the passage.

The following translation is for questions 77–81.

A little while later, my boss called me and, at that time, I was bothered since I thought he would tell me to speak less on the phone and to work more. That is not at all what happened. He told me that he would tell me about a vague project. He only wanted to get my advice on something. He was planning on opening an office in Paris that would deal with business locally, and directly, with large companies, and he wanted to know if I felt like going there. This would allow me to live in Paris and travel a bit each year. "You are young, and it would seem to me that this would give you an enjoyable life." I told him yes, but deep down, it didn't really matter to me at all.

77. **A** The question asks, "The narrator expects:"

(A) Yes. "To be scolded by his boss." This is supported by the passage *j'ai été ennuyé.*

(B) No. "To get a raise." There is no context for this in the passage.

(C) No. "To discuss a project with his boss." These are familiar words—wrong context. It is what happens to the narrator, but not what he expected to happen.

(D) No. "To annoy the boss." These are familiar words—wrong context.

78. **C** The question asks, "What does the boss do?"

(A) No. "He annoys the narrator." These are the right words—wrong context.

(B) No. "He orders him to go to Paris." This is too strong. The boss asks rather than orders.

(C) Yes. "He asks what the narrator thinks of a suggestion." This is supported by the passage *avoir mon avis sur la question*.

(D) No. "He refuses to let the narrator go to Paris." This is opposite of the passage.

79. **C** The question asks, "What does the boss want to do in Paris?"

(A) No. "He wants to live there." There is no support for this in the passage.

(B) No. "He wants to work for a large company." These are familiar words—wrong context.

(C) Yes. "He wants to open an office." This is supported by the passage *l'intention d'installer un bureau*.

(D) No. "He wants to betray his company." There is no support for this in the passage.

80. **B** The question asks, "According to the passage, why does the boss suggest the project to the narrator?"

(A) No. "Because the narrator does not work very well." No, these are familiar words—wrong context.

(B) Yes. "Because he thinks the narrator would enjoy it." This is supported by the passage *c'est une vie qui doit vous plaire*.

(C) No. "Because the boss is too young to do it himself." These are familiar words—wrong context.

(D) No. "Because it's all the same to the narrator." These are familiar words—wrong context.

81. **D** The question asks, "What reaction does the narrator have to the idea of moving to Paris?"

(A) No. "He is irritated." There is no context for this.

(B) No. "He is happy." He says yes, but there is no context for his being happy.

(C) No. "He feels rejuvenated." There is no context for this.

(D) Yes. "He's not really that interested in going." This is supported by the passage *cela m'était égal*.

The following translation is for questions 82–85.

When a river is blocked by a large rock, it waits, grows, and grows some more. Suddenly, the rock is pushed aside, and the water, finally free, can continue on its way. The same thing often occurs in the history of the arts. Charles Trenet managed to push aside that which was blocking French song. He made it into an art from, but at the same time he gave it a greater freedom: freedom in the music, in the words, and even in the gestures of the singer on stage. After Trenet, there was not one song, there were ten, twenty, a hundred songs: after him artists felt freer to make, write, and sing anything they wanted.

82.   **B**   The question asks, "What makes a river bigger?"

(A)   No. "An increase in water from the mouth of the river." These are familiar words—wrong context.

(B)   Yes. "The presence of something that blocks the way." This is supported by the passage *est bouchée par une grosse pierre.*

(C)   No. "The presence of rocks." Careful. According to the passage, the rock must block the river. These are familiar words—wrong context.

(D)   No. "The freedom of the water." These are familiar words—wrong context.

83.   **D**   The question asks, "Why does the author describe a river?"

(A)   No. "To characterize Trenet's music." This is close, but it ignores the sentence before that mentions *la même chose.*

(B)   No. "To explain nature." There is no context for this in the passage.

(C)   No. "To show Trenet's importance." Again, this is tricky since the author discusses his importance later. However, this ignores the sentence earlier that mentions *la même chose.*

(D)   Yes. "To make an analogy with the development of song." This is supported by the passage *Il se passe souvent la même chose dans l'histoire des arts.*

84.   **C**   The question asks, "According to the passage, before Trenet songs:"

(A)   No. "Were more like a river." These are familiar words—wrong context.

(B)   No. "Were more complicated." There is no context for this.

(C)   Yes. "Had fewer possibilities." This is supported by the passage *après lui les artistes se sentent plus libres.*

(D)   No. "Were more artistic." These are familiar words—wrong context.

85.   **A**   The questions asks, "It is understood that Trenet:"

(A) Yes. "Introduced a new way of presenting songs." This is supported by the passage *Trenet a fait sauter ce qui bouchait la chanson fran*çaise.

(B) No. "Loved nature." There is no support for this in the passage.

(C) No. "Wrote a hundred songs." These are familiar words—wrong context.

(D) No. "Wasn't liked by other singers." There is no context for this.

HOW TO SCORE PRACTICE TEST 1

When you take the real exam, the proctors will collect your test booklet and answer sheet and send your answer sheet to a processing center where a computer looks at the pattern of filled-in ovals on your answer sheet and gives you a score. We are providing you, however, with this more primitive way of scoring your exam.

Determining Your Score

STEP 1   Using the answer key, determine how many questions you got right and how many you got wrong on the test. Remember: Questions that you do not answer do not count as either right answers or wrong answers.

STEP 2   Write the number of correct answers on line A.

(A) _____

STEP 3   Write the number of wrong answers on line B. Divide that number by 3.

(B) _____ ÷ 3 = _____

STEP 4   Subtract the number of wrong answers divided by 3 on line B from the number of correct answers on line A, and round to the nearest whole number. (C) is your **raw score**.

(A) _____ − (B) _____ = (C) _____

STEP 5   To determine your **real score**, look up your raw score in the left column of the Score Conversion Table on the next page; the corresponding score on the right is the score you earned on the exam.

PRACTICE TEST 1
SCORE CONVERSION TABLE

Raw score	Scaled score	Raw score	Scaled score	Raw score	Scaled score
85	800	45	630	5	410
84	800	44	620	4	410
83	800	43	620	3	400
82	800	42	610	2	400
81	800	41	610	1	390
80	800	40	600	0	390
79	800	39	600	−1	380
78	800	38	590	−2	380
77	800	37	580	−3	370
76	790	36	580	−4	360
75	790	35	570	−5	360
74	780	34	570	−6	350
73	780	33	560	−7	350
72	770	32	560	−8	340
71	770	31	550	−9	340
70	760	30	550	−10	330
69	760	29	540	−11	330
68	750	28	540	−12	320
67	740	27	530	−13	320
66	740	26	530	−14	310
65	730	25	520	−15	300
64	730	24	520	−16	290
63	720	23	510	−17	290
62	720	22	500	−18	280
61	710	21	500	−19	280
60	710	20	490	−20	270
59	700	19	490	−21	270
58	700	18	480	−22	260
57	690	17	480	−23	260
56	690	16	470	−24	250
55	680	15	470	−25 through −28	240
54	680	14	460		
53	670	13	460		
52	660	12	450		
51	660	11	450		
50	650	10	440		
49	650	9	430		
48	640	8	430		
47	640	7	420		
46	630	6	420		

Part III
Content Review
and Strategies

Chapter 3
Vocabulary

This chapter gives you several techniques to boost your score on Part A of the SAT Subject Test in French. First, get acquainted with the format and structure of the vocabulary section of the test. If you understand how the test writers think, you can get a question right even if you don't know the answer. Then you'll learn additional strategies that will get you more points— tactics to use depending on how well you understand the question. What do you do if you are not sure of the answer? What if you do not know the meaning of the sentence? What if you do not know all the words in the answer choices? Just follow the simple steps we give you, and you'll be ready to handle any of these situations.

PART A: VOCABULARY COMPLETIONS

The first part of the test consists of 20 to 26 vocabulary completions. Each question is a sentence containing a blank. Each of the four answer choices provides a word that could fill in the blank. The correct answer is the one that best completes the sentence in terms of the meaning of the word. All choices will be grammatically correct.

Here are the directions for this section as they appear on the test. Become familiar with these directions now so that you don't waste valuable time when you take the test.

Part A

Directions: This part consists of a number of incomplete statements, each having four suggested completions. Select the most appropriate completion and fill in the corresponding circle on the answer sheet.

> If your vocabulary needs work, short, frequent study sessions will help you more than long, infrequent ones. Your brain will be able to absorb only a small amount of information at a time. Ten minutes a day between now and the test will make a big difference.

The questions are arranged roughly in order of difficulty. Harder, more obscure vocabulary words will appear later in the section. Additionally, questions may have false cognates that make the questions trickier to answer correctly.

What Makes the Difference in this Section?

Vocabulary, vocabulary, vocabulary. If your vocabulary is not strong, start working on it right away. In Chapter 4, Vocabulary Review, there are several techniques designed to boost your vocabulary.

DRILL 1

Test your vocabulary by writing the English translations of the following words.
Answers can be found in Part IV.

une usine _____

la honte _____

l'œuvre _____

en vouloir à _____

mou _____

taquiner _____

la foule _____

ramasser _____

soutenir _____

repasser _____

se méfier de _____

se débarrasser de _____

If you missed more than three of the words, you may need to give vocabulary work extra attention (Chapter 4).

IF YOU KNOW THE WORDS

Fill in Your Own Word

As you read through the sentence, fill in your own word in English **before you look** at the answer choices. Cover the answer choices with your hand, if need be.

> Le film était tellement amusant qu'elle . . . sans cesse.

If something is funny, what does someone do?

Now let's look at the answer choices and see which one is closest to the English answer you decided on:

(A) dansait
(B) mangeait
(C) riait
(D) lisait

If you thought of the word "laughed" or "smiled," you can eliminate *dansait*, which means "danced," *mangeait*, which means "ate," and *lisait*, which means "read." The correct answer is *riait*, "laughed."

If you understand most of the words in the question, you'll have no problem filling in the blank.

Cover the answer choices and fill in a word for the following examples.

> Jean-Pierre a mal . . . parce qu'il a trop mangé.

(A) à l'oreille
(B) au ventre
(C) aux genoux
(D) à la tête

If someone ate too much, he would probably have a pain in the "belly." You could then eliminate (A), which means "the ear," (C), which means "the knees," and (D), which means "the head." Choice (B), meaning "the abdomen," is the correct answer.

> La banque se trouve . . . le supermarché et la poste.

(A) dans
(B) sur
(C) pendant
(D) entre

The word in the blank should give the position of the bank in relationship to the supermarket and the post office: "between" or "near." You can eliminate (A), which means "inside," (B), which means "on," and (C), which means "during." Choice (D), which means "between," is the correct answer.

Watch Out for Trap Answers

Don't immediately pick the first word that seems right. Look at all the answer choices, and leave in only those that might work. Then carefully compare the remaining choices before selecting an answer.

> Si tu n'as pas assez d'argent pour acheter le livre, tu peux le trouver à . . .
>
> (A) la librairie
> (B) l'épicerie
> (C) la bibliothèque
> (D) la papeterie

If you don't have enough money to buy a book, you will probably go to a "library." If you know the vocabulary, you might immediately identify the right answer. If not, eliminate (B), which means "grocery store," and (D), which means "stationery store." Is the answer *librairie* or *bibliothèque?* Which means "library"? The answer in this case is the less obvious one: (C), *bibliothèque. Librairie* means "bookstore." See page 100 for "Common Mix-Ups."

> On average, each Part A section contains one question that tests your knowledge of words for body parts and one question that tests your knowledge of the words for different types of stores.

IF YOU DON'T KNOW ALL THE ANSWER CHOICES

Sometimes you'll be able to fill in a word, but you won't be sure which answer choice matches the word you picked. The following guessing techniques will improve your odds of picking the correct answer.

Use Process of Elimination (POE)

First, clear out the obviously wrong options. Eliminate answer choices that you are sure do not match the word you chose. With the remaining choices, try to narrow down what each means.

Use Your English

Although it is your knowledge of French that is being tested, your own native language can often help you. Many English words are derived from French, so it makes sense that some words are nearly identical in both languages (but, again, watch out for those traps). How hard is it to guess what *régulier* means? *Transporter? Bière?*

DRILL 2

Decide what English words the following French words remind you of. Answers can be found in Part IV.

évaluer   _____

sacré   _____

retarder   _____

fréquenter   _____

nombre   _____

assurer   _____

raison   _____

plante   _____

attraper   _____

servir   _____

content   _____

accord   _____

cru   _____

Using English can help you make an educated guess about the meaning of a word. Based on that guess, you can decide to keep the word or eliminate it, narrowing the field of choices and improving your odds. Don't automatically pick the first word that reminds you of the English word you are looking for.

Use this technique with caution on hard questions. On difficult questions (especially the last five questions), use this technique only to eliminate wrong choices, not to pick the right answer. On tough questions, if an answer choice reminds you strongly of the word you're looking for in English, it's practically guaranteed that it's a trap answer.

> On easy questions (the first third of the section), the right answer will not be a tough vocabulary word. On hard questions (the final third), the right answer will not be the answer that reminds you of the word in English that you are looking for.

27. _____ des étudiants sortant de l'école a rompu le silence du quartier.

    (A) Le martelage
    (B) La chatière
    (C) Le ramassage
    (D) Le bavardage

This is a tough question. If you understand the sentence ("The _____ of the students leaving school broke the silence in the neighborhood."), you know you're looking for a word that means noise, talk, or chatter. Which answer is a trap?

Choice (B) looks like the English word "chatter." Since this is a hard question (from the final third), you know it's a trap. *La chatière* actually means "the cat/pet door." The correct answer is (D), which means "the chatting." Choice (A) means "the hammering" (*un marteau* is a hammer), and (C) means "the gathering." On difficult questions, don't pick the answer that reminds you of the word you're looking for in English.

> On hard questions, be wary of trap answers, but don't psych yourself out! If you know the meaning of all the words, the right answer is still the right answer. Don't cross off the right answer because you're afraid it's too "obvious." Trap answers have a specific feel to them.

Look for Easier Versions of Words

On difficult questions (or if your vocabulary isn't very strong), you can sometimes figure out an easier version of the answer choices. For example, in the verb *feuilleter* you may see the word *feuille,* meaning "leaf" or "sheet of paper." Could there be a verb meaning "to leaf"? Yes, just as in English, you can "leaf" through a book.

What easier words do you see in the following words?

prochainement _____

emporter _____

parapluie _____

retarder _____

Find as many opportunities as possible to hear and speak French. Check your TV or radio guides for programs in French, watch French movies, and go to French-language websites, such as www.tv5.fr www.rfi.fr www.lemonde.fr

Well? In *prochainement,* you probably saw *prochain,* which means "next," so *prochainement* probably has something to do with being next. (It means "in a short while" or "coming up next.") You probably see *porter,* which means "to carry," in *emporter,* so you might be able to guess that *emporter* has a similar meaning. It means "to carry away." And what about *parapluie?* Recognize the word *pluie,* "rain"? So *parapluie* is likely to be "umbrella." *Retarder* has the word *tard,* or "late," in it, so it's a safe bet that *retarder* means "to slow or delay."

Avoid Look-Alike Answers

The College Board sometimes tries to trick you by providing answers that look like either the correct answer or a word that appeared in the sentence.

Je dois réparer ma montre; elle ne . . . plus.

(A) casse
(B) montre
(C) donne
(D) marche

If something needs to be fixed, what doesn't it do anymore? Most likely, it doesn't work. Which answer choice means "to work"? Choice (B) is a look-alike trap here. *Montre,* meaning "show," is identical to the word *montre,* meaning "wristwatch," in the sentence. It's a trap! Eliminate it. The correct answer is (D) *marche.* The verb *marcher* used with an inanimate object means "to work or function correctly."

Please see Les Faux Amis (p. 100) for more on these look-alike trap answers.

IF YOU DON'T UNDERSTAND THE SENTENCE

Word Association

Even if you're shaky on the exact meaning of the sentence, you can still make an educated guess for the answer. Go through the words in the sentence that you do know and see if any of the answer choices are in some way associated with those words.

> You often don't need the whole sentence to figure out what word you're looking for. Usually one or two key words in the sentence point to the answer.

Le chevalier chimerique . . . au moulin.

(A) joute
(B) rattrape
(C) raméne
(D) s'enfuit

The word *chimérique* is likely unfamiliar. However, *chevalier* means knight and moulin means windmill. The answer choices are all verbs followed by the preposition *à*, which means to or toward. Use these context clues to figure out which answer choice is most likely related to knights moving toward something. The word in (A) is likely unfamiliar, but looks like joust. The words in (B), (C), and (D) mean catch, bring, and flee. The word that fits best is (A). Make the educated guess.

DRILL 3

For the following incomplete questions, pick the answer choice that makes the most sense given the words that are shown.

Answers can be found in Part IV.

1. xxxxxxx xxxxxxxx *légumes* xxxx xxxxx . . .
   vegetables

   (A) cheminée
   (B) jardin
   (C) gazon
   (D) quartier

2. xxxx xxxxxxx x *tombé* xxx xxxx . . . fallen

   (A) envolée
   (B) échappée
   (C) cassée
   (D) attrapée

3. xx x xxx xxxxx *chaises* xxxx . . . xxxx xx xxxxx.
   chairs

   (A) assommer
   (B) s'asseoir
   (C) assurer
   (D) associer

4. xxxx *ne se sent pas bien* xxxxx xxx . . . doesn't feel well

   (A) une fièvre
   (B) une armoire
   (C) un verger
   (D) une annonce

5. xxxx xxxxxxxxx xxxxx *mangé* xxx xxx . . . eaten

   (A) soutenir
   (B) emporter
   (C) avaler
   (D) évaluer

Comprehensive Drill

Answers can be found in Part IV.

Part A

Directions: This part consists of a number of incomplete statements, each having four suggested completions. Select the most appropriate completion and fill in the corresponding circle on the answer sheet.

1. Il fait froid dehors. Est-ce que toutes les . . . sont fermées?

   (A) chambres
   (B) cheminées
   (C) fenêtres
   (D) notes

2. Ne fais pas de bruit; les enfants sont . . .

   (A) venus
   (B) endormis
   (C) partis
   (D) tristes

3. Est-ce que ces fleurs sont de votre . . . ?

   (A) peinture
   (B) garage
   (C) jardin
   (D) verger

4. Ce manteau n'a pas de . . . où mettre mon porte-monnaie.

   (A) manches
   (B) portes
   (C) poches
   (D) monnaie

5. Jeanne s'est réveillée . . . pour voir le lever du soleil.

   (A) bas
   (B) haut
   (C) tard
   (D) tôt

6. Le train est parti . . . à midi.

   (A) du garage
   (B) du toit
   (C) de l'histoire
   (D) de la gare

7. Au repas du dimanche, nous mangeons un . . . avec des pommes de terre.

   (A) rôti
   (B) ruban
   (C) régime
   (D) rôle

8. Les tartes qui sont vendues dans cette . . . sont délicieuses.

   (A) pâtisserie
   (B) pharmacie
   (C) épicerie
   (D) librairie

9. Tu peux te laver maintenant. La salle de bains est . . .

   (A) gratuite
   (B) libre
   (C) livrée
   (D) seule

10. Mon . . . pour la classe est de traduire un poème de Rimbaud.

    (A) destin
    (B) composition
    (C) droit
    (D) devoir

11. Le bruit dans un club peut être tellement fort qu'on a mal . . .

    (A) aux oreilles
    (B) aux orteils
    (C) à l'orgueil
    (D) à la gorge

12. La lune est si . . . que je ne peux pas imaginer que l'homme y soit allé.

    (A) longue
    (B) fade
    (C) loin
    (D) immense

13. Ce n'est pas nécessaire de sortir la poubelle; Jean l'a . . . fait.

    (A) hier
    (B) ce matin
    (C) déjà
    (D) d'un côté

14. Nous passerons Noël avec mes grands-parents . . .

    (A) cet été
    (B) cet automne
    (C) cet hiver
    (D) ce printemps

15. Vous avez déjà fait vos devoirs? Cela . . .

    (A) m'admet
    (B) me fait mal
    (C) me trompe
    (D) m'étonne

16. N'avez-vous pas . . . d'avoir fait cette bêtise?

    (A) courage
    (B) joie
    (C) hâte
    (D) honte

17. Ce tissu est . . . comme la peau d'un bébé.

    (A) mouillé
    (B) nu
    (C) doux
    (D) cru

18. Le renard a . . . aux chasseurs.

    (A) ramassé
    (B) enfui
    (C) échappé
    (D) couru

19. Le film commence à 8 heures exactement; soyez . . .

    (A) à l'heure
    (B) au courant
    (C) au loin
    (D) à présent

20. Il y a trop de monde ici; je préfère des cafés moins . . .

    (A) doués
    (B) chargés
    (C) tranquilles
    (D) fréquentés

21. Il n'y a pas assez de preuves pour . . . cet homme.

    (A) indiquer
    (B) inquiéter
    (C) insinuer
    (D) inculper

22. Mon frère est . . . ; il ne veut jamais m'aider à nettoyer la cuisine.

    (A) serviable
    (B) paresseux
    (C) redoutable
    (D) affolé

23. Le vase que j'ai laissé tomber s'est . . .

   (A) perdu
   (B) tricoté
   (C) évanoui
   (D) brisé

24. Vous pouvez trouver la robe de mariée de votre
    grand-mère si vous cherchez dans . . .

   (A) le plancher
   (B) le grenier
   (C) l'atelier
   (D) le magasin

25. Elle s'est débarrassée de ses vêtements . . .

   (A) âgés
   (B) déprimés
   (C) abîmés
   (D) achetés

26. Diane s'est coupé les . . . pour être plus à la mode.

   (A) chevaux
   (B) chiffres
   (C) cheveux
   (D) chemins

27. Pour établir la validité de sa théorie, l'homme de
    science a fait . . .

   (A) un échec
   (B) une expérience
   (C) un résumé
   (D) un résultat

Summary

To increase your score, keep the following tips in mind.

- o   All incorrect answers should be eliminated before you bubble in the correct one.

- o   If you know all the words in the sentence
    - • eliminate obviously wrong answer choices
    - • examine remaining choices (to avoid obvious traps)
    - • pick your answer

- o   If you are not sure of the meaning of the sentence
    - • use word association
    - • read the question again, and see if there are any obvious traps

- o   If you do not know all of the answer choices
    - • use your English to eliminate wrong answers
    - • try to figure out the roots of the words

- o   If you don't know a word, staring at it will not help. Remember pacing is important. Guess after you have eliminated as many obviously wrong answers as possible.

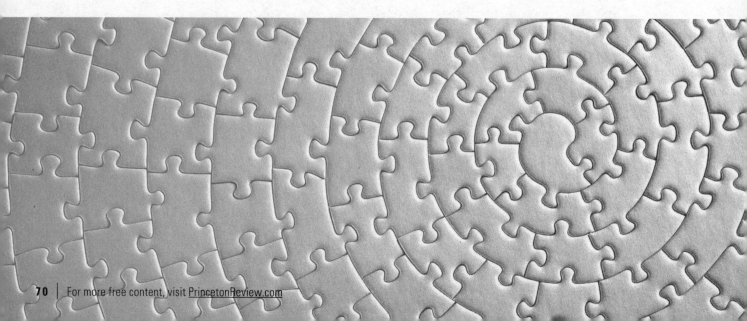

Chapter 4
Vocabulary Review

At this level, your basic French vocabulary should be good. The more French you read, the better you will acquire new words and feel comfortable with what you already know. The following vocabulary list should help you review. It organizes words into logical categories. This will make memorizing them easier. Look through each category and concentrate on the words you don't know or words that seem to be cognates but in fact have very different meanings.

BOOST YOUR VOCABULARY

If you really want to imprint new vocabulary words on your brain, passive reading is not enough. Critical reading with a dictionary at hand, as well as listening and watching French media, will increase your vocabulary significantly. Try one or more of the following techniques to help your learning.

Flashcards

Put the French word on one side, the English on the other. If you want to get fancy, color-code by category or make up a symbol. This way, you can mix up words in any order and regroup them in many different ways, such as where, when, and how the words can be used. On the French side, include part of speech, gender, and the word used in a sentence. Whenever you have a few minutes, pull out your cards and test yourself. Think of this as a game.

Mnemonics

If it works for you, think of a funny image or sound that corresponds to the word. The more outrageous, the easier it will be to remember. Make up your own mnemonics and add them to your flashcards.

Posters

Make a list of words and definitions and hang it on your wall. As you go about your day, glance at the poster and review a few words.

These are only a few of the ways you can work on your vocabulary. Anything you do to make it more creative or colorful (literally—use colored pens, colored index cards, stickers, or markers) will increase your ability to learn and remember vocabulary.

Vocabulary
Color-code your vocabulary list! Use three different highlighters to keep track of words you know, words you sort of know, and words you've never seen before. Assign a different color to each category so you know which words you need to work on.

VOCABULARY LIST

This section will help you review key vocabulary words. It is not the only vocabulary you need to know for the test, however. You will find suggestions for how to continue enriching your vocabulary. Pay particular attention to the commonly mixed-up words and false cognates.

Le Calendrier et le Temps
Une Année

un an	a year (with numbers, for age or a point in time)
une décennie	a decade
une année	a year (as in *l'année dernière*, last year)
un mois	a month
une quinzaine, quinze jours	a fortnight (two weeks)
une semaine	a week
un jour	a day
une journée	a day (as in *toute la journée*, all day long)
un siècle	a century
un calendrier	a calendar
un horaire	a schedule

The Calendar and the Time
A Year

> **Décade vs. Décennie**
> *Décade* means a period of ten days (or, more generally, any group of ten objects). It is sometimes informally used as a synonym for *décennie* to mean a period of ten years, similar to its meaning in English, but that usage is still considered incorrect.

Un Jour

le matin	the morning
la matinée	the morning (as in *tout la matinée*)
l'après-midi (m or f)	the afternoon
le soir	the evening
la soirée	the evening
la nuit	the night
l'aube (f)	daybreak
l'aurore (f)	dawn
le crépuscule	twilight
le lever du soleil	the sunrise
le coucher du soleil	the sunset
un jour férié	a holiday
un jour de congé	a day off
faire la grasse matinée	To sleep in (to sleep late)

A Day

> **Lundi vs. Le Lundi**
> Observe what happens when you use the definite article *le*. *Lundi* means "Monday." *Le lundi* means "on Mondays." Also, notice the following expressions: *Tous les lundis* means "every Monday." *Lundi en huit* means "a week from Monday," while *tous les deux lundis* means "every other Monday" and *tous les trois lundis* means "every third Monday," etc.

Une Heure

minuit	midnight
midi	noon
une montre	a watch
un réveil	an alarm clock
une horloge, une pendule	a clock
un minuteur	a timer (in the kitchen)
un chronomètre	a stop watch

An Hour

Les Expressions de Temps

Expressions of Time

Vocabulary

The expressions of time are very important to have memorized when choosing a tense or a mode of conjugation.

Never Forever, Ever!

The construction *ne* + verb + *jamais* means "never": *Il ne cesse pas de parler* means "He never stops talking." Without the preceding *ne*, *jamais* means "ever": *Si jamais je te manque, tu n'as qu'à me donner un coup de fil* ("If ever you miss me, all you have to do is call.") The common phrase *plus que jamais* means "more than ever" and the phrase *à jamais* means "forever."

être à l'heure	to be on time
être en retard	to be late
être en avance	to be ahead of schedule
tôt	early
tard	late
Quelle heure est-il?	What time is it?
avant	before
après	after
le lendemain	the day after
hier	yesterday
dès	since / from / as soon as
désormais	from now on / from then on
pendant	during
arriver de bonne heure	to arrive early
déjà	already
bientôt	soon
prochainement	shortly
toujours	always / still
ne…pas encore	not yet
ne…jamais	never
ne…plus	no longer
ne…plus jamais	never again
longtemps	for a long time
régulièrement	regularly
d'habitude	usually
habituellement	usually
autrefois	in the past / formerly
parfois	sometimes / on occasion
chaque jour	each / every day
hebdomadaire	weekly
se dépêcher	to hurry
se précipiter	to rush
Un instant!	Just a moment!
Ne quittez pas!	Please hold (on)!

Les Saisons (f)

le printemps

l'été (m)

l'automne (m)

l'hiver (m)

Seasons

spring

summer

autumn, fall

winter

Phrase Check
Au printemps means "in (the) spring." For pronunciation reasons, *en* is used in front of *hiver, été* and *automne* to translate "in." En *hiver;* en *été;* en *automne.*

La Nature et le Temps

la météo / le bulletin météo

le soleil

être bronzé

prendre un coup de soleil

attraper une insolation

Quel temps fait-il?

il fait beau

il fait chaud

avoir chaud

par beau temps

le nuage

la pluie

il pleut / pleuvoir

une averse

il pleut des cordes

être trempé(e)

être mouillé(e)

il fait mauvais

par mauvais temps

la neige

la glace

il neige

il fait froid

avoir froid

un ciel couvert

un orage

il y a des éclairs

le tonnerre

le brouillard

Nature and the Weather

the weather forecast

the sun, the sunshine

to be tanned

to get sunburnt

to get sunstroke

What's the weather like?

the weather is nice

it is hot

to be hot

in good weather

the cloud

the rain

it is raining / to rain

a downpour

it's raining hard

to be soaked

to be wet

the weather is bad

in bad weather

the snow

the ice

it is snowing

it is cold

to be cold

an overcast sky

a thunderstorm

there is lightning

thunder

the fog

Pleurer vs. Pleuvoir
A common mistake is to mix up *pleurer* (to cry) and *pleuvoir* (to rain).

la brume	light fog / a mist
le vent	the wind
une tempête	a storm
un ouragan	a hurricane
la rosée du matin	the morning dew
une rafale de vent	a gust of wind
une bourrasque	a squall
briller	to shine
souffler	to blow
il fait noir / sombre	it is dark
prédire	to predict

Le Plein Air / The Outdoors

dehors	outside
un arbre	a tree
un buisson	a bush
l'écorce (d'un arbre)	the bark (of a tree)
une feuille	a leaf
une prairie	a meadow
un champ	a field
l'herbe (f)	grass
le gazon / la pelouse	the lawn
une rivière	a river
un fleuve	a river flowing into the sea
la mer	the sea
une étoile	a star
la lune	the moon
un verger	an orchard
le jardin	the garden
une fleur	a flower
la floraison	(the) blooming or flowering, blossom time
le sol	the soil
la boue	the mud
la poussière	the dust
récolter	to harvest
glaner	to glean
ramasser	to gather, to pick up

Time to Glean!
To glean is the tradition of gathering crops left in the field after harvest. It is time-honored practice among the poor and protected by law. The Gleaners (*Des Glaneuses*) is a famous painting from 1857 by Jean-François Millet, and The Gleaners and I (*Les glaneurs et la glaneuse*) is a well-known documentary film from the year 2000 by Agnès Varda.

se promener / faire une promenade	to take a walk
se balader / faire une balade	to walk around
prendre l'air	to get some fresh air, to take a walk
faire une randonnée	to go hiking
tondre la pelouse	to mow the lawn

La Maison / The Home

un toit	a roof
un plafond	a ceiling
une cheminée	a chimney, a fireplace
le foyer	the hearth
un mur	a wall
une fenêtre	a window
un volet	a shutter
en haut	upstairs
en bas	downstairs
les toilettes / les WC	the restroom (toilet)
la salle de bains	the bathroom (bath)
une baignoire	a bathtub
prendre un bain	to take a bath
une douche	a shower
prendre une douche / se doucher	to take a shower
une serviette	a towel
un savon	a bar of soap
un lavabo	a bathroom sink
une glace / un miroir	a mirror
la chambre à coucher	the bedroom
un lit	a bed
une armoire	a wardrobe
un placard	a closet
un meuble	a piece of furniture
un tiroir	a drawer
un aspirateur	a vacuum cleaner
un climatiseur	an air conditioner
un rideau	a curtain
un oreiller	a pillow
un matelas	a mattress

une couverture	a blanket
un drap	a sheet
un plancher	a wooden floor
le sol	the floor
le salon / la salle de séjour	the living room
une chaise	a chair
un divan / un canapé	a couch
un tableau	a painting, a picture
un fauteuil	an armchair
ouvrir	to open
fermer	to close
se coucher	to go to bed
s'endormir	to fall asleep
se réveiller	to wake up
s'allonger	to lie down
avoir sommeil	to be sleepy
se lever	to get up
s'asseoir	to sit down
la salle à manger	the dining room
la cuisine	the kitchen
un évier	a kitchen sink
un four	an oven
un appareil ménager	a household appliance
un réfrigérateur	a refrigerator
une poubelle	a garbage can
un pot	a jar
une casserole	a pan
une poêle	a frying pan
un fourneau / une cuisinière	a stove
un cuisinier / une cuisinière	a cook
le grenier	the attic
la cave	the cellar
un coin	a corner
le sous-sol	the basement
un atelier	a studio, a workshop
le rez-de-chaussée	the ground floor
un / une concierge	a building superintendent / a custodian

une boîte à lettres	a mail box
le courrier	the mail
frotter	to rub
astiquer	to polish
balayer	to sweep
nettoyer	to clean
faire le ménage	to do the housework
faire la vaisselle	to wash the dishes
faire la cuisine	to cook
faire la poussière	to dust
ranger	to put away
monter	to go up / to bring up (stairs)
descendre	to go down / to bring down (stairs)
rester	to stay
se reposer	to rest
quitter (+ un nom)	to leave (a place or a person)
partir	to leave
bricoler	to fix

En Ville (f) — In Town

un immeuble	a building
un gratte-ciel	a skyscraper
un trottoir	a sidewalk
un passant / une passante	a passer-by
une rue	a street
un rond-point	a traffic circle
une zone piétonne	a pedestrian zone
un quartier	a neighborhood
flâner	to stroll
un endroit	a place
une gare	a train station
une piscine	a swimming pool
un gymnase, la gym	the gym
une banlieue	a suburb
habiter dans les environs de	to live on the outskirts of
habiter en banlieue	to live in the suburbs

False Cognates

Rester means "to stay," NOT "to rest." *Se reposer* means "to rest." *Quitter* means "to leave," NOT "to quit." Use *quitter* instead of *partir* when you mean it to be more permanent, or when the verb phrase requires a direct object. Examples: *Quitter son domicile; quitter son pays; quitter l'école. Abandonner* means "to quit."

Strolling Along

Flâner is a typical French word that defies strict translation, as do the related words *flânerie* (the act of strolling or idly wandering) and *flâneur* (an idle man-about-town or urban explorer). The female equivalent, *flâneuse,* is rare historically but becoming more widely used.

un stade	a stadium
un théâtre	a theater
assister à un concert	to attend a concert
une foule	a crowd
la boulangerie	the bakery
un boulanger / une boulangère	a baker
une pâtisserie	a pastry shop, a pastry
un pâtissier / une pâtissière	a pastry cook
une épicerie	a grocery store
un épicier / une épicière	a grocer
une fromagerie	a cheese store
une boucherie	a butcher shop
un boucher / une bouchère	a butcher
une charcuterie	a delicatessen
un charcutier / une charcutière	a pork butcher
une papeterie	a stationery store
une librairie	a bookstore
une bibliothèque	a library
un marché aux puces	a flea market
une quincaillerie	a hardware store
la boutique de bricolage	the do-it-yourself department
un tabac / un bureau de tabac	a shop selling tobacco items, stamps, newspapers
une banque	a bank
un kiosque à journaux	a newsstand
lécher les vitrines	to window-shop (literally, to lick the windows)
faire du lèche-vitrine	to go window-shopping

False Cognates

Assister à means "to attend," NOT "to assist." *Aider quelqu'un* means "to assist someone."

False Cognate

La librairie means "the bookstore," NOT "the library."

Faire les Courses (f)   ## Shopping for Food

la nourriture	food
la recette	the recipe
le pain	bread
un croissant	a croissant
les pâtisseries (f)	pastries
une tarte	a tart
une tartine	an open-faced sandwich
un gâteau	a cake

un chou à la crème	a cream-puff
un petit gâteau / un biscuit	a cookie
un biscuit salé	a cracker
un éclair	an éclair
les pâtes (f)	pasta
le riz	rice
le maïs	corn
les légumes (m)	vegetables
les épinards (m)	spinach
les haricots verts (m)	green beans
un oignon	an onion
un champignon	a mushroom
un poivron vert	a green pepper
les pommes de terre	potatoes
une pomme	an apple
les petits pois	peas
un avocat	an avocado
les fruits (m)	fruit
une fraise	a strawberry
une framboise	a raspberry
un ananas	a pineapple
une myrtille	a blueberry
une cerise	a cherry
une pêche	a peach
une poire	a pear
une noix	a walnut
une amande	an almond
une noisette	a hazelnut
une cacahuète	a peanut
le beurre de cacahuètes / beurre d'arachide	peanut butter
des raisins	grapes
des raisins secs	raisins
un pamplemousse	a grapefruit
un concombre	a cucumber
le fromage	cheese
le beurre	butter
le lait	milk

Avocado!?
The word *avocat* means "avocado" from a word that originated in Mexico. Watch out! It also means "lawyer" from the Latin word *advocatus.* Pay attention to the context when making a vocabulary choice on the SAT Subject Test in French.

la glace	ice cream
un œuf	an egg
la viande	meat
le jambon	ham
le veau	veal
un rôti	a roast
une boulette de viande	a meatball
le sel	salt
le poivre	pepper
la confiture	jam, preserves
le sucre	sugar
l'eau	water
une bière	a beer
le vin	wine
livrer	to deliver
commander	to order
vendre	to sell
acheter	to buy
faire les courses	to go shopping, to run errands
avoir besoin de	to need
avoir envie de manger	to feel like eating
l'argent (m)	money
retirer de l'argent	to withdraw money
rendre la monnaie	to give back the change
payer comptant	to pay cash
économiser	to save money

Au Restaurant (m) At the Restaurant

Check, Please!
The check is also sometimes called *la douloureuse*, or "the thing that causes pain." Similarly, in English one might say "What's the bad news?" or "What's the damage?"

un restaurant	a restaurant
le repas	the meal
le déjeuner	lunch
le petit déjeuner	breakfast
le dîner	dinner
un plat / un mets	a dish
le service est compris	service is included
et comme boissons	and for drinks?

un garçon, un serveur	a waiter
une serveuse	a waitress
un pourboire	a tip
l'addition (f)	the bill, the check
le couvert	table setting; cover charge
une serviette (de table)	a table napkin
une cuillère	a spoon
un couteau	a knife
une fourchette	a fork
une assiette	a plate
le verre	the glass
remplir	to fill
servir	to serve
se servir (de)	to use, to help oneself (with)
régler / payer l'addition	to pay the check
emporter	to take away
apporter	to bring
mettre le couvert	to set the table
débarrasser la table	to clear the table
se débarrasser de	to get rid of
fréquenter	to go to a place frequently
fréquenté	crowded, popular
mou / molle	soft
cru / crue	raw
cuit / cuite	cooked
bien cuit	well-done
à point	medium rare
saignant / saignante	rare
gras / grasse	greasy, fatty

Le Monde du Travail   The Working World

le chômage	unemployment
un(e) chômeur / chômeuse	an unemployed person
un ouvrier / une ouvrière	a worker
la médecine du travail	occupational medicine
un (e) médecin	a physician

un infirmier / une infirmière	a nurse
le droit	law
un(e) avocat(e)	a lawyer
un(e) juge	a judge
le monde artistique	the arts
un chanteur / une chanteuse	a singer
un acteur / une actrice	an actor, an actress
un metteur / une metteuse en scène	a film or stage director
une œuvre	a work
un chef-d'œuvre	a masterpiece
le commerce / les affaires	business
une femme / un homme d'affaires	a business woman / man
un(e) comptable	an accountant
un(e) patron / patronne	a boss
un / une cadre	an executive
l'informatique (f)	computer science
technologie (f) d'information (TI)	information technology (IT)
un ordinateur	a computer
la facture	the bill, the invoice
un facteur / une factrice	a mail carrier
l'usine (f)	the factory
l'outil (m)	the tool
un entretien	an interview
un syndicat	a union
embaucher	to hire
travailler	to work
être en grève / faire grève	to be on strike
renvoyer	to dismiss
mettre (quelqu'un) à la porte	to fire
licencier	to lay off
démissionner	to resign

Women Workers

In French, the words for professions have traditionally been gendered. This is changing: *boucher / bouchère* for "butcher," *boulanger / boulangère* for "baker," etc. But some professions, like *le médecin* ("doctor") and *le marin* ("sailor") have feminine forms that are already French words: *la médicine* denotes the practice of medicine, and *la marine* is the word for "navy." To avoid awkward ambiguity, such words keep the same form but can take either the masculine or feminine article: *Elle est médecin* ("She is a medical doctor"), *La médecin était rassurante* ("The doctor was reassuring").

False Cognate

Travailler means to work, not to travel.

Le Corps Humain

The Human Body

la tête	the head
la figure, le visage	the face
l'œil / les yeux (m)	the eye / the eyes
le nez	the nose
la bouche	the mouth
la lèvre	the lip
la dent	the tooth
la langue	the tongue
l'oreille (f)	the ear
le cou	the neck
l'épaule (f)	the shoulder
la poitrine	the chest
le bras	the arm
la main	the hand
le doigt	the finger
le coude	the elbow
l'ongle (m)	the nail
une articulation	a knuckle
le poignet	the wrist
la hanche	the hip
la jambe	the leg
le genou / les genoux	the knee / knees
les cheveux	the hair
la peau	the skin
le poumon	the lung
le cœur	the heart
le ventre	the belly
le talon	the heel
le poing	the fist
un coup de poing	a punch
le rein	the kidney
l'orteil	the toe
le dos	the back
un os	a bone
le sang	the blood
transpirer, suer	to sweat

respirer	to breathe
se faire mal à l'épaule	to hurt one's shoulder
avoir mal au ventre / à l'estomac	to have a stomachache
gros	fat
mince / grosse	slim, thin
maigre	skinny
être en forme	to be in shape
décontracté(e)	relaxed
muet / muette	mute
aveugle	blind
sourd(e)	deaf
se laver	to wash (oneself)
se laver la visage / les mains / etc.	to wash one's face / hands / etc.
se brosser les dents	to brush one's teeth
se peigner	to comb one's hair
se coiffer	to do one's hair
se raser	to shave
se maquiller	to put makeup on
du rouge à lèvres	lipstick
une crème	a cream
se sécher	to dry oneself

Les Vêtements (m) Clothes

au rayon femmes / hommes	in the women's / men's department
en solde	on sale
une robe	a dress
une robe du soir	a gown
une robe de chambre	a robe
un peignoir de bain	a bathrobe
une chemise de nuit	a nightgown
un chemisier	a woman's shirt
une chemise	a shirt
un tailleur	a woman's suit
un ensemble	a woman's suit, an outfit
un costume	a man's suit
un smoking	a tuxedo, dinner jacket

une jupe	a skirt
un pull / pullover	a sweater
un col roulé	a turtleneck sweater
un manteau	a coat
un imperméable	a raincoat
un parapluie	an umbrella
une chaussure / un soulier	a shoe
une botte	a boot
la semelle (d'une chassure)	the sole (of a shoe)
une chaussette	a sock
des collants (m)	tights
un pantalon	a pair of pants
un survêtement	a sweatsuit, a warmup suit
les sous-vêtements (m. pl.)	underwear
une manche	a sleeve
un bouton	a button
une poche	a pocket
un maillot de bain	a swimming suit / a bathing suit
une ceinture	a belt
un chapeau	a hat
une casquette	a cap
un foulard	a scarf
une écharpe	a winter scarf, a sash
une cravate	a tie
un nœud papillon	a bow tie (literally, a butterfly knot)
un collier	a necklace
une bague	a ring
une boucle d'oreille	an earring
un fil	a thread
la soie	silk
la laine	wool
le coton	cotton
le linge	linen
le cuir	leather
le caoutchouc	rubber
le velours côtelé	corduroy
la fourrure	fur

> **Did you know?**
> The word *maillot* by itself simply means "jersey." The *maillot jaune* ("yellow jersey") is worn by the rider in the Tour de France currently in the lead following each stage of the race.

l'aiguille	the needle
la taille	height, size, waist
la pointure	shoe size
le cintre	the hanger
essayer	to try on
porter	to wear
mettre	to put on
froisser	to wrinkle
repasser	to iron
le repassage	ironing
déchirer	to tear
coudre	to sew
la couture	sewing
le tricot	knitting
tricoter	to knit
rétrécir	to shrink
aller bien	to suit / to go well
être à la bonne taille	to fit
avoir de l'allure	to have style
propre	clean
une tache	a stain
taché(e)	stained
à la mode	in style, fashionable
décontracté(e)	casual
démodé(e)	out of style
assorti(e) à	matching
uni(e)	solid color
à rayures	striped
imprimé(e)	printed
écossais(e)	plaid
à fleurs	floral
à pois	polka-dotted
à carreaux	checked
délavé(e)	faded, washed-out

Vocabulary

Allure means "appearance," but it also means "speed" or "pace." *Il va à toute allure!* "He is going at top speed!"

Tache vs. Tâche

Une tache means "a stain." *Une tâche* means "a task."

Les Voyages/
Les Transports

Travel/
Transportation

un voyage	a trip
faire un voyage	to go on a trip
faire ses valises	to pack one's suitcases
être en vacances	to be on vacation
l'itinéraire	the itinerary, the route
la route	the way / the road
un vélo, une bicyclette	a bicycle
une voiture	a car, a carriage, a wagon
une voiture d'occasion	a secondhand car
une ceinture de sécurité	a seatbelt
une autoroute	a highway
un bouchon / un embouteillage	a traffic jam
l'heure de pointe / d'affluence	rush hour / peak hour
un feu rouge	a red light
un feu vert	a green light
rouler	to move forward, to roll, to drive
conduire	to drive
doubler une voiture	to pass a car
klaxonner	to honk
interdiction de stationner	no parking
tourner à gauche / à droite	turn left / right
défense de tourner à gauche	no left turn
se garer	to park
démarrer	to start driving, to start a car
un permis de conduire	a driving license
l'essence	gas
faire le plein	to fill up the tank
tomber en panne	to break down (as a car)
avoir une panne d'essence	to run out of gas
une roue	a wheel
un pneu	a tire
un pneu crevé	a flat tire
un volant	a steering wheel
un frein	a brake

Vocabulary
Un bouchon also means "a cork." *Un embouteillage* comes from the word *une bouteille*, "a bottle." The French words, therefore, imply a bottleneck.

un rétroviseur	a rearview mirror
un phare	a headlight
feu (m) / phare (m) arrière	tail light
une station-service	a gas station
s'arrêter	to stop
reculer	to back up
un train	a train
le chemin de fer	the railroad
une gare	a train station
un guichet	a ticket booth
demander un renseignement	to ask for information
composter	to punch in (tickets)
rater (le train)	to miss (the train)
une correspondance	a train connection, a transfer
le prochain arrêt	the next stop
un contrôleur	a ticket inspector
changer	to transfer
monter	to get on
descendre	to get off
un bateau	a boat
une voile	a sail
une bouée de sauvetage	a life preserver
un gilet de sauvetage	a life jacket
avoir le mal de mer	to be seasick
une croisière	a cruise
un avion	a plane
enregistrer les bagages	to check in (one's luggage)
les bagages à main	carry-on luggage
décoller	to take off
le décollage	takeoff
atterrir / se poser	to land
l'atterrissage	the landing
une escale	a stop, a stopover
une aile	a wing
avoir le mal de l'air	to feel airsick
voler	to fly
un vol	a flight

l'embarquement	boarding
la douane	customs
un billet	a ticket
un aller simple	a one-way ticket
un aller-retour	a roundtrip ticket
une agence de voyages	a travel agency
traverser	to cross
transporter	to transport
proche	near
loin	far
le décalage horaire	the time difference, jet lag
une fusée	a rocket
complet	full
il y a de la place	there is room
une place libre	an empty seat
annulé(e)	cancelled

Les Accidents et les Urgences

Accidents and Emergencies

le dégât	the damage
la faute	the mistake, the fault
grave	serious
le témoin	the witness
une blessure	an injury
une brûlure	a burn
l'assurance (f)	the insurance
la prison	the jail
un incendie	a wildfire, a fire
un feu	a fire
une piqûre d'insecte	a sting / an insect bite
enfermer	to lock up
se couper	to cut oneself
brûler	to burn
saigner	to bleed
se casser (la jambe)	to break (one's leg)
être témoin de	to witness

assurer	to ensure, to assure
arrêter	to stop, to arrest
renverser quelqu'un	to hit somebody (with a vehicle)
soutenir	to hold up, to support
secourir, aider	to help
	to save / to rescue
avoir tort	to be wrong
avoir raison	to be right
échapper à	to escape (from)
attraper	to catch
éviter	to avoid
blesser	to injure
assommer	to knock out (a person)
faire tomber	to knock down (something)
tomber	to fall
glisser	to slip
faire un plâtre / plâtrer	to put a cast on
faire un pansement	to put a bandage / a dressing on
s'étrangler	to choke
la réanimation	resuscitation
sortir indemne	to come out unharmed
heureusement	fortunately
malheureusement	unfortunately

Aidez-moi!
You call for help in French by yelling *"Au secours!"*

False Cognates
Blesser means "to hurt"; *se blesser* means "to get hurt," NOT "to bless." *Sauver* means "to save" or "to rescue." If you mean "to save money," you must use the word *économiser*, and *se sauver* means "to run away."

La Maladie

Illness

un rhume	a cold
une angine	a throat infection
des vertiges	dizzy spells
la nausée	nausea
une crampe	a cramp
la douleur	pain
une baisse de tension	a drop in blood pressure
la rougeole	measles
la varicelle	chicken pox
la chirurgie	surgery
la salle d'attente	the waiting room

un rendez-vous	an appointment
une ordonnance	a prescription
un comprimé	a pill
un cachet	a tablet
prendre des médicaments	to take medicines or medication
une analyse de sang	a blood test
avaler	to swallow
avoir mal au cœur	to feel nauseated
avoir des boutons	to have a rash
être enrhumé(e)	to have a cold
avoir de la fièvre	to have a fever
avoir la grippe	to have the flu
avoir de la tension	to have high blood pressure
avoir des palpitations	to have palpitations
s'évanouir	to faint
vomir	to throw up
éternuer	to sneeze
tousser	to cough
avoir mal à la gorge	to have a sore throat
avoir mal à la tête	to have a headache
le traitement	the treatment
soigner	to treat
se soigner	to take care of oneself
vacciner contre	to vaccinate against
faire une piqûre	to give a shot
faire une radio	to take an X-ray
aller / se porter bien / mal / mieux	to be well / ill / better
être en bonne santé / bien portant	to be in good health
être en pleine forme	to be in top shape
déprimé(e)	depressed
malade	sick, ill

L'émotion (f)   Emotion

la confiance	confidence or trust
le plaisir	pleasure
la hâte	haste

Avoir and Emotions

Many expressions with *avoir* describe an emotion:

avoir confiance (en)	to trust
avoir peur (de)	to be afraid
avoir honte (de)	to be ashamed of
avoir de la peine	to be sad
avoir hâte (de)	to be eager to, to be impatient to

la honte		shame
la méfiance		mistrust
l'agrément (m)		pleasure; approval
	un caprice	a whim
	une larme	a tear
	un baiser	a kiss
	combler (quelqu'un)	to gratify / to satisfy
	être d'accord	to agree

"Félicitations!"
You congratulate someone in French by saying *"Félicitations!"* or *"Je te félicite!"*

s'occuper (de)	to take care of
éprouver	to feel, to experience
étonner	to astonish
s'étonner de	to be amazed by
estimer	to hold in esteem; to estimate
tolérer	to tolerate
surprendre	to surprise
se méfier (de)	to distrust
faire de la peine (à quelqu'un)	to hurt someone's feelings
avoir de la peine	to feel bad

The verb *manquer* has a few meanings:

Tu me manques, or *vous me manquez.* — I miss you.

Il a manqué le train et son rendez-vous. — He missed the train and his appointment.

Elle a manqué son gateau. — She ruined her cake.

tromper	to trick, to deceive
se tromper	to make a mistake
changer d'avis	to change one's mind
s'amuser	to have fun
rire	to laugh
sourire	to smile
pleurer	to cry
s'embêter / s'ennuyer	to be bored
s'énerver	to get upset / annoyed
jurer	to swear
j'en ai marre / j'en ai assez	I am fed up, I have had enough
taquiner	to tease
se quereller	to quarrel
se disputer	to have an argument / to argue
se réconcilier avec	to make up with
se réjouir de	to be delighted by
prévoir	to predict
se souvenir de	to remember

False Cognate
Crier means "to shout," NOT "to cry."

A great idiom (very colloquial) for expressing frustration is *J'en ai ras-le-bol!* which means roughly, "I've had it up to here!"

soutenir	to give support
rompre (avec)	to break up (with)
se fâcher (avec)	to get upset (at)
se douter de quelque chose	to suspect something
sembler	to seem
craindre	to fear, to be afraid of
menacer	to threaten
avoir le coup de foudre pour	to fall in love at first sight
tomber amoureux / amoureuse de	to fall in love (with)
s'entendre	to get along
plaindre	to feel sorry for
en vouloir à	to be angry at, to have a grudge against
Ne t'en fais pas!	Don't worry!
Ça va s'arranger!	It's going to get better!
profiter de	to take advantage of
convaincre	to convince
ennuyeux / ennuyeuse	boring
ennuyé(e)	bored, embarrassed, in trouble
joyeux / joyeuse	joyful
heureux / heureuse	happy
content(e)	glad, pleased, happy, content
de bonne humeur	in a good mood
de mauvaise humeur	in a bad mood
triste	sad
fier / fière	proud
énervé(e)	on edge, annoyed
énervant(e)	irritating
comblé(e)	fortunate, happy
méchant(e)	mean, nasty
bassement	meanly, nastily
malheureux / malheureuse	unhappy
savant(e)	learned, knowledgeable
en colère, fâché(e)	angry
honteux / honteuse	shameful, ashamed
sage	wise

It Seems to Me…

Avoir l'air means "to appear" or "to look."

Elle a l'air fatigué.
   She looks tired.

Sentir means "to smell" (having an odor or noticing an odor).

Elle sent quelque chose de bon dans le four.
   She can smell something nice in the oven.

Ce poulet sent bon.
   This chicken smells good.

Se sentir means "to feel."

Comment te sens-tu aujourd'hui?
   How do you feel today?

Je me sens seul.
   I feel lonely.

Ressentir (+ noun) means "to feel" (a pain or an emotion).

Vocabulary
If you want to tell someone to be happy, good, proud, etc., use the imperative of the verb *être* plus an adjective.
Soyez sages! Be good!
Sois confiant! Be confident!
Sois fier! Be proud!
Sois content! Be happy!

profond(e)	profound or deep
inquiet / inquiète	worried
préoccupé(e)	worried
déçu(e)	disappointed
tendu(e)	uptight, tense
ravi(e)	delighted
étonné(e)	astonished
ému(e)	moved, touched
fou / folle	crazy
dévoué(e) à	devoted to
exquis(e)	exquisite
bouleversé(e)	overwhelmed
vaniteux / vaniteuse	vain

> Work on your memorization: Regroup the verbs, nouns, and adjectives that carry the same meaning. Example: *la dévotion; se dévouer; dévoué.*

Les Expressions de Quantité
Expressions of Quantity

le numéro	specific number (as in digits)
le nombre	number (as in quantity)
le compte	count, account
la somme	sum
les chiffres	individual numbers / digits
évaluer	to evaluate
l'augmentation (f)	increase / raise
la croissance	growth
la subvention	the subsidy
le manque	lack
rien	nothing
tout	everything
tout le monde	everybody
beaucoup de	a lot of, many
un peu de	a little of, a few
peu de	little / few
trop de	too many, too much
moins de / moins que	less / fewer, less than / fewer than
quelques	some, a few
aucun / aucune	none, not any

ne ... guère	not much, not often
un tas de	a stack of, many
plein de	full of
le taux	the rate
les frais (m,pl.)	expenses, costs

L'école (f) — School

une bourse d'études	a scholarship
une sortie scolaire	a field trip
une moyenne	a grade point average
un carnet de notes	a report card (elementary school)
un bulletin scolaire	a report card (secondary school)
une interrogation	a quiz, a test
un dossier	a file
un débouché	a career prospect
une agrafeuse	a stapler
la colle	glue
un rapporteur	a protractor
un panneau d'affichage	a bulletin board
une bonne note	a good grade
une erreur	a mistake
feuilleter	to leaf through
permettre	to permit, to allow
traduire	to translate
écrire	to write
enseigner	to teach
parler couramment	to speak fluently
une dissertation	an essay, a paper
admettre	to admit
noter	to grade
suivre / prendre des cours	to take classes
souligner	to underline
faire une erreur / se tromper	to make a mistake
corriger	to correct
constater une erreur	to notice a mistake / be wrong
passer un examen	to take an exam

The French school system is quite different from that of the U.S. By high school (*le lycée*), students have been divided into categories, each of which has a learning specialty: sciences, languages, economics, literature, etc. To graduate from *le lycée*, students must pass a comprehensive exam in their specialty, *le baccalauréat (le bac)*.

False Cognate

Passer un examen means "to take an exam," NOT "to pass an exam."

rater	to flunk / to fail
sécher sur un sujet	to draw a blank in
sécher un cours	to skip a class
fair l'école buissonnière	to skip school
échouer à	to fail
être reçu(e) à un examen	to pass an exam
coller un(e) élève	to give a detention to a student
recaler	to fail a student
être recalé(e) à un examen	to fail a test
doué(e)	gifted
futé(e)	smart
perturbateur / perturbatrice	disruptive

Les Sports (m) — Sports

le gymnase / la gym	the gym
aller au gymnase / à la gym	to go to the gym
faire de la gymnastique	to do gymnastics / to exercise or work out
l'escrime (f)	fencing
l'équitation (f)	horseback riding
la natation	swimming
le parapente	parasailing
l'entraînement (m)	practice, training
l'haltérophilie (f) / la musculation (f)	weightlifting
le vestiaire	the locker room
un but	a goal
la course	the race
le filet	the net
le cerceau	the hoop
une piste	a trail, a track, a rink
un terrain	a ground, a field, a course
un sifflet	a whistle
un arbitre	a referee, an umpire
une médaille	a medal
un exploit	a feat
le football	soccer
le football américain	football

la Coupe du Monde	the World Cup
le poids	weight
tenter	to attempt, to tempt
atteindre	to reach
étendre le bras	to stretch out one's arm
entraîner	to train, to coach
s'entraîner	to practice, to train
attraper	to catch
lancer	to throw
accomplir	to achieve
sauter	to jump
s'assouplir	to limber up, to become supple
repousser	to push back
monter	to go up
escalader, grimper	to climb
être ex aequo / faire match nul	to tie (as in scoring)
souple	flexible
vif / vive	quick, lively
un coup déloyal(e)	a foul

Les Faux Amis: words that look like an English word but mean something different!

Les Faux Amis			Common Mix-Ups	
la librairie	bookstore	and	*la bibliothèque*	the library
la gare	the train station	and	*la station service*	the gas station
le billet	the ticket, bill (money), note	and	*la facture*	the bill
décevoir	to disappoint	and	*tromper*	to deceive
crier	to shout, to scream	and	*pleurer*	to cry
une course	an errand	and	*un cours* *une classe*	a class, a course of study
une course	a race	and	*la race*	the race, the ethnicity
le couvert	the table setting, the cover charge	and	*la couverture*	the cover, the blanket
blesser	to wound, to hurt	and	*bénir*	to bless
l'éditeur	the publisher	and	*le rédacteur*	the editor
le spectacle	the show, the play	and	*les lunettes*	the eyeglasses
l'agrément	the pleasure, the approval	and	*l'accord*	the agreement
le stage	the training course, the internship	and	*la scène*	the stage
la droguerie	hardware store	and	*la pharmacie*	drugstore
la location	the rental	and	*le lieu/l'éndroit*	the location
passer un examen	to take an exam	and	*réussir un examen*	to pass an exam
travailler	to work	and	*voyager*	to travel

Only two or three questions on Part A will have tricky mix-ups.

Vocabulary
Vocabulary questions on Part C will often have mix-ups. Usually you will be given four words that are close in meaning or look alike.

Les Faux Amis			Common Mix-Ups	
actuellement	at present, now	and	en fait	actually
finalement	eventually	and	éventuellement	possibly
exiger	to demand	and	demander	to ask
se reposer	to rest	and	rester	to stay
prendre sa retraite	to retire	and	retirer	to withdraw, to remove
sensible	sensitive	and	raisonnable	sensible
un nom de famille	a surname	and	un surnom	a nickname
le médicament	the medicine	and	le médecin	the doctor
empêcher	to prevent	and	prévenir	to warn
résumer	to sum up	and	recommencer	to resume

French words that look and sound similar but have different meanings			
pleurer	to cry	pleuvoir	to rain, it's raining
tromper, se tromper	to deceive, to be wrong	tremper	to soak
vouloir	to want	en vouloir à	to be angry at
douter	to doubt	se douter de	to suspect

Summary

Use the study techniques that work best for you and review the following categories of vocabulary:

- *Le calendrier et le temps*
- *Les expressions de temps*
- *La nature*
- *Le plein air*
- *La maison*
- *En ville*
- *Faire les courses*
- *Au restaurant*
- *Le monde du travail*
- *Le corps humain*
- *Les vêtements*
- *Les voyages / Les transports*
- *Les accidents et les urgences*
- *La maladie*
- *L'émotion*
- *Les expressions de quantité*
- *L'école*
- *Les sports*

Chapter 5
Grammar Review

Grammar is tested in Parts B and C of the SAT Subject Test in French. Part B tests only grammar, while Part C tests both grammar and vocabulary. The same points of grammar are tested in Parts B and C. The French Subject Test contains questions about very specific aspects of French grammar. Therefore, grammar is one of the easiest test topics on which to improve. If you can remember and master a few rules, you'll easily get more points. This chapter will explain exactly what you need to know. First, look at the point-by-point summary of the question types you can expect. Then, keep the question style in mind as you review your French grammar. Not all that you have learned in school will be included in the test, but you may find it helpful to go back to your textbooks for more examples on the topics we suggest. We focus on the grammatical topics and difficulties most often encountered on the SAT: pronouns, verbs, prepositions, and adverbs.

PART B: GRAMMAR

Part B will consist of approximately 15 to 20 questions, arranged in order of difficulty. The first third of the questions will be considered easy, the next third will be of intermediate difficulty, and the final third will be the most challenging.

In these questions, there will be a sentence with a blank. You will choose the answer that is grammatically correct.

Become familiar with these directions that appear on the real test:

SAT difficulty is determined by the percentage of students who are expected to get the question wrong. You may find some of the difficult questions quite easy. You may also find some of the easy questions to be challenging. It is important to identify and remember your own Personal Order of Difficulty (POOD) and Pacing as you work through this section.

Part B

Directions: Each of the following sentences contains a blank. From the four choices given, select the one that can be inserted in the blank to form a grammatically correct sentence and fill in the corresponding circle on the answer sheet. Choice (A) may consist of dashes that indicate that no insertion is required to form a grammatically correct sentence.

Jean-Claude est venu avec -------.

(A) ils
(B) leur
(C) eux
(D) soi

The correct answer is (C).

PART C: COMPLETE THE PARAGRAPH

Part C tests both grammar and vocabulary. In this section, there are approximately 12 to 20 questions in no clear order of difficulty.

On this part of the test, several questions are combined in one paragraph. You may have three or four mini-paragraphs with three to five blanks within each, or you may have one long paragraph. You are asked to select the answers that best complete the sentences on the basis of either vocabulary or grammar.

Become familiar with these directions:

Part C

Directions: The paragraph below contains blank spaces indicating omissions in the text. For some blanks it is necessary to choose the completion that is most appropriate to the meaning of the passage; for other blanks, to choose the one completion that forms a grammatically correct sentence. In some instances, choice (A) may consist of dashes that indicate that no insertion is required to form a grammatically complete sentence. In each case, indicate your answer by filling in the corresponding circle on the answer sheet. Be sure to read the paragraph completely before answering the questions related to it.

This section combines the characteristics of Parts A and B. The small differences between the two are discussed at the end of this chapter.

KNOW WHAT YOU ARE LOOKING FOR

All the grammar questions on the SAT Subject Test in French will fall into one of the following four categories.

1. pronouns
2. verbs
3. prepositions
4. odds and ends

The best way to improve in these areas is to learn the grammatical rules that are tested again and again. These rules are covered in the following grammar review.

GRAMMAR REVIEW

Grammar is a great area to focus your attention for this test. Why? Because to do well on the grammar review you need to review only a limited number of rules. Those rules will lead you to the right answer again and again. Unlike vocabulary, where luck determines whether the words you've learned will show up, grammar rules—and therefore, the content of these test questions—stay the same.

> **Good News**
> Only a minuscule number of grammar questions (around two) will test you on whether a noun is masculine or feminine.

You'll be tested primarily on three things: pronouns, verbs, and prepositions. Each question will address only one grammatical point. We'll cover each of these categories, giving you the rules that get you right answers. We'll also give practice questions for each category. Finally, we'll cover some odds and ends that occasionally show up on the test.

BASIC TERMS

You won't be tested on this material directly, but take a quick look through to make sure that you understand what the following terms mean. We'll be using them in this grammar review.

Parts of Speech

None of this terminology is needed for the test. Understanding these terms, however, will help you comprehend the explanations in the grammar review that follows.

1. **Noun**—a person, place, thing, quality, or action. It can be either a subject or an object
2. **Verb**—the action that is being performed by the subject
3. **Pronoun**—a word that takes the place of a noun
4. **Preposition**—a word that expresses the relationship of one word to another in terms of direction, motion, or position
5. **Adjective**—a descriptive word that gives more information about a noun
6. **Adverb**—a word that modifies a verb, an adjective, or another adverb
7. **Article**—a small word that gives a little information about a noun

Sentence Structure

1. **Subject**—the person or thing in the sentence that is performing the action
2. **Compound subject**—two or more subjects joined by *and, or,* or *but*
3. **Object**—the person or thing that is on the receiving end of the action
4. **Direct object**—the word or phrase that receives the direct action of the verb. These do not take a preposition to be objects.
5. **Indirect object**—a word or phrase that precedes the direct object and answers the questions "to whom" or "for whom" the action of the verb is done. These take prepositions in English (though sometimes, the preposition is elided, as in "Give [to] me the book"). In French, an indirect object will take a preposition if it follows the verb, but it will not take one if it precedes the verb.
6. **Infinitive**—the form of a verb in English that uses "to," as in "to go" or "to speak." In French, the infinitive is a single word: *aller, parler,* etc.
7. **Auxiliary verb**—a helper verb, either *avoir* or *être,* that loses its own meaning to help form the compound past tense for other verbs, such as the *passé composé.* It is followed by the past participle of the conjugated verb.
8. **Semi-auxiliary verb**—a verb, such as *aller* or *venir,* that helps express a different aspect of the verbal action, such as the near future or the recent past
9. **Past participle**—in the past tense, the form of the verb that teams up with the auxiliary or "helper" verb

Mom and Dad	gave	me	a car	for graduation.
compound subject	verb	indirect object	direct object	prepositional phrase
They	**baked**	**a**	**delicious**	**cake.**
subject pronoun	verb	article	adjective	direct object

PRONOUNS

A quarter of all grammar questions on the SAT French test will challenge your knowledge of pronouns. Unlike English, which uses mainly subject and object forms of pronouns (he and him, for example), French uses four important forms of pronouns: subject pronouns, direct object pronouns, indirect object pronouns, and stressed pronouns.

What Is a Pronoun?

A pronoun takes the place of a noun. It stands in for the full name or description of a person, place, or thing. In French, a pronoun will take different forms depending on the identity of the noun it replaces (including number—singular or plural—and gender) and the pronoun's role in the sentence. Half of the pronoun questions on the test ask you to choose among subject pronouns, direct or indirect object pronouns, reflexive pronouns, and stressed pronouns.

The following are the pronouns you should know. **You're most likely to be tested on third-person singular and plural,** since these are the forms that change the most.

Subjects	Objects		Reflexive	Stressed
	Direct	**Indirect**		
je	*me (m')*	*me (m')*	*me (m')*	*moi*
tu	*te (t')*	*te (t')*	*te (t')*	*toi*
il, elle	*le, la (l')*	*lui*	*se, (s')*	*lui, elle*
nous	*nous*	*nous*	*nous*	*nous*
vous	*vous*	*vous*	*vous*	*vous*
ils, elles	*les*	*leur*	*se (s')*	*eux, elles*

Because this is a multiple-choice test, you will be asked which of four pronouns goes into the blank. Notice that some pronouns are always the same: *nous* and *vous*.

nous or *vous* can be:
- subject
- direct object
- indirect object
- reflexive
- stressed

There are two kinds of pronoun questions on the test: one asks you to choose among the five main kinds of pronouns (subject, direct object, reflexive, indirect object, and stressed), and the other asks you to choose among relative pronouns like *qui, que, dont,* and *lequel*. Relative pronouns introduce dependent or subordinate clauses that modify a noun in the sentence.

Once you recognize each of these four main types of pronouns, you will find it easy to use Process of Elimination on the answer choices.

1. Subject Pronouns

Subject pronouns replace the subject of the sentence.

Jean a montré son dessin à Edith.
Jean showed his drawing to Edith.

Il a montré son dessin à Edith.
He showed his drawing to Edith.

je or *j'*	=	I	*nous*	=	we
tu	=	you (informal singular)	*vous*	=	you (plural or formal singular)
il	=	he or it	*ils*	=	they (masculine)
elle	=	she or it	*elles*	=	they (feminine)

These pronouns are usually the wrong answer choices. Why? Because these are the pronouns with which everyone is most familiar and comfortable.

2. Direct Object Pronouns

These pronouns replace the direct object of a sentence. The direct object answers the question "what?"

*Jean a montré **son dessin** à Edith.*
Jean showed **his drawing** to Edith.

*Jean **l'a** montré à Edith.*
Jean showed **it** (the drawing) to Edith.

Notice in these examples that, when a noun is used for the direct object, it usually follows the verb. When a pronoun is used as a direct object, it precedes the verb.

me or *m'*	=	me	*nous*	=	us
te or *t'*	=	you (informal singular)	*vous*	=	you (plural or formal singular)
le or *l'*	=	him or it	*les*	=	them (person or thing both masculine and feminine)
la or *l'*	=	her or it			

3. Indirect Object Pronouns

These pronouns replace the indirect object of a sentence. The indirect object answers the questions "to what?" or "to whom?" Notice that the pronoun replaces both the indirect object and the preposition that goes with it.

*Jean a montré son dessin **à Edith**.*

Jean showed his drawing **to Edith**.

*Jean **lui** a montré son dessin.*

Jean showed **her** his drawing.

me or *m'*	=	me	*nous*	=	us
te or *t'*	=	you (informal singular)	*vous*	=	you (plural or formal singular)
lui	=	him or her	*leur*	=	them (person or thing, masculine and feminine)

Pay particular attention to the following verbs:

The verbs *écouter* (to listen to), *regarder* (to look at), and *attendre* (to wait for) are verbs that always take a **direct object** in French.

Il m'écoute.

He listens (to) me.

Je l'ai regardé.

I looked (at) him.

Nous les attendons.

We are waiting (for) them.

Conversely, the verbs *téléphoner à* (to call on the phone), *répondre à* (to answer), *demander à* (to ask), and *rendre visite à* (to visit someone), take an **indirect object** in French, unlike in English.

Ton père téléphone à ses parents.

Your father is calling his parents.

Ton père leur téléphone.

Your father is calling them.

Ton père te téléphone.

Your father is calling you.

Sa mère lui demande de nettoyer sa chambre.

Her mother is asking her to clean her room.

Cette semaine, il rend visite à son grandpère.
> He is visiting his grandfather this week.

Cette semaine, il lui rend visite.
> He is visiting him this week.

The direct and indirect object pronouns are placed before the verb even when you use the negative form.

*Je ne **te** donne pas mon nouveau pull.*
> I will not give you my new sweater.

*Il ne **leur** parle pas.*
> He does not speak to them.

The direct and indirect pronouns are also placed before the verb in compound tenses.

*Je **leur** ai parlé.*
> I spoke to them.

*Il ne **m'**aurait pas écouté.*
> He would not have listened to me.

However, when the sentence is constructed with an infinitive, the pronoun is placed before the infinitive. This is the case with the near future tense, as well as when the verbs *vouloir, pouvoir, devoir,* and *préférer* are followed by an infinitive.

*Je vais **te** voir demain.*
> I am going to see you tomorrow.

*Je voudrais **les** manger.*
> I would like to eat them.

*Je préfère **lui** dire plus tard.*
> I prefer to tell him later.

The place of the negation does not change when there is an infinitive construction and a pronoun.

*Je ne vais pas **te** voir demain.*
> I am not going to see you tomorrow.

*Je ne voudrais pas **les** manger.*
> I would not like to eat them.

*Je ne préfère pas **lui** dire plus tard.*
> I prefer not to tell him later.

4. Reflexive Pronouns

The reflexive pronoun shows that the action is being performed both by and to the subject. In other words, the direct or indirect object is the same as the subject. Only certain verbs have reflexive forms. Most often reflexives will show up as incorrect answer choices.

> *Tu te laves.*
> You wash yourself.

> *Tu te laves les mains.*
> You wash your hands.

In French, when one speaks of doing something to one's own body, instead of using the possessive pronoun, one uses the reflexive pronoun and a direct object. Notice the difference between the French and English versions of these expressions:

> *Il se brosse les dents.*
> He is brushing his teeth.

> *Elle s'est cassé la jambe.*
> She broke her leg.

me / m'	myself	*nous*	ourselves
te / t'	yourself (informal singlular)	*vous*	yourselves or yourself (plural or formal singular)
se / s'	himself/herself/itself	*se / s'*	themselves

You might also see *moi-même, toi-même, lui-même/elle-même, soi-même* (oneself), *nous-mêmes, vous-même(s), eux-mêmes / elles-mêmes.* They would be used as stressed pronouns would be.

> *Tu te coupes **toi-même** les cheveux!*
> You cut your hair **yourself**!

All reflexive verbs take the auxiliary *être* in the compound tenses. If the verb has no direct object (preceding or following), the past participle always agrees with the subject:

> *Elles se sont dépêch**ées**.*
> They hurried.

> *Elle s'est coup**ée**.*
> She cut herself.

However, there is no agreement of the past participle when the body part, or direct object, comes after the reflexive verb. We'll talk more about this later in the review.

> *Elles se sont lavé les mains.*
> They washed their hands.

> **Pronouns**
> Reflexive pronouns are used in French in situations in which they are not used in English. For example, *Je me lave les mains* (I wash my hands).

Pronoun Order

If the sentence contains both a direct and an indirect pronoun, order the pronouns as shown in the chart below.

Indirect Object	before	Direct Object	before	Indirect Object
me		*le*		*lui*
te		*la*		
nous	before	*l'*	before	
vous		*les*		*leur*

*Tu donnes le cadeau à ta sœur. Tu **le lui** donnes maintenant.*
> You are giving the present to your sister. You are giving **it to her** now.

Est-ce que tu écris cette lettre à ton frère? Oui, je la lui écris.
> Are you writing this letter to your brother? Yes, I am writing **it to him**.

*Je vous prête mes livres. Je **vous les** prête.*
> I lend my books to you. I lend **them to you**.

Pronoun Order with Commands

In negative commands, the order of pronouns follows the same rule:

*Ne **le lui** rends pas!*
> Don't give **it** back **to him**!

*Ne **me les** donne pas!*
> Don't give **them to me**!

In affirmative commands, *me* becomes *moi*, and *te* becomes *toi* (when the command is a reflexive verb). The direct or indirect pronoun (*moi, nous...*) is placed after the verb with a hyphen between the two words.

*Appelle-**moi** ce soir!*
> Call **me** tonight.

*Répondez-**nous** tout de suite.*
> Give **us** an answer right away.

When the command contains a direct pronoun and an indirect pronoun, both pronouns come after the verb. Follow the order below:

Direct Object	before	Indirect Object
le		*moi*
		toi
la	before	*lui*
les		*nous*
		vous
		leur

*Donne-**les-moi**!*
> Give **them** **to me**!

*Rends-**le-lui**!*
> Give **it** back **to her**!

Pronouns *y* and *en*

These are adverbial pronouns. Y replaces a place.

*Il va **à Paris**. Il **y** va.*
> He goes **to Paris**. He goes **there**.

*Il est **chez lui**. Il **y** est.*
> He is **at home**. He is **there**.

*Il aime passer ses étés **en France**. Il aime **y** passer ses étés.*
> He likes to spend his summers **in France**. He likes to spend his summers **there**.

Y also replaces a thing introduced by a verb followed by *à, au, aux, à l'*, and *à la*. You can find a list of verbs that are followed by *à, au, aux, à l'*, and *à la* on page 151.

*Je participe **à la réunion**. J'**y** participe.*
> I participate **in the meeting**. I participate **in it**.

*Fais attention **au chien**! Fais-**y** attention!*
> Be careful **with the dog**! Be careful **with him**!

En replaces an undetermined quantity, introduced by *du, de la, de l', des* or *beaucoup de, assez de*, and other adverbs of quantity.

*Je mange **de la viande**. J'**en** mange.*
> I eat **meat**. I eat **some**.

*J'ai **beaucoup de livres**. J'**en** ai beaucoup.*
> I have **a lot of books**. I have a lot of **them**.

En is used even when the quantity is expressed.

> *Tu as **combien de chats?** J'en ai deux.*
>> **How many cats** do you have? I have two (of them).

> *Vous avez **une maison de campagne**? J'en ai une.*
>> Do you have **a countryside house**? I have one.

En also replaces a thing introduced by a verb followed by *de, du, de l', de la,* and *des.* You can find a list of verbs that are followed by *de, du, de l', de la,* and *des* on page 151.

> *Il parle **de son sujet préféré**. Il **en** parle.*
>> He is speaking **about his favorite subject.** He is speaking about **it**.

> *J'ai besoin **d'un stylo**. J'en ai besoin.*
>> I need **a pen**. I need **it**.

> *Je viens **de l'aéroport**. J'en viens.*
>> I come **from the airport**. I come **from there**.

Y and *en* are placed before the verb except when the sentence construction has an infinitive, then *y* or *en* are placed before the infinitive.

> *Je vais **y** aller.*
>> I am going to go **there**.

> *Je peux **en** avoir besoin.*
>> I might need **it**.

Remember that *y* comes before *en*, and that indirect objects always precede both.

> *Il **y** a beaucoup de fraises au marché ce matin. Il **y en** a beaucoup.*
>> **There** are lots of strawberries at the market this morning. **There** are lots **of them**.

> *Il rend visite à sa tante à l'hôpital. Il **lui y** rend visite tous les jours.*
>> He visits his aunt at the hospital. He visits **her there** every day.

> *Nous rencontrons souvent nos amis au cinéma. Nous **les y** rencontrons souvent.*
>> We often meet our friends at the movies. We meet **them there** often.

> *Tu **m'y** retrouves à six heures.*
>> You'll meet **me there** at six o'clock.

These pronouns are often seen in commands. In affirmative commands, they will come after other pronouns (separated by a hyphen). In commands with reflexive verbs, if *toi* comes before *y* or *en*, it will elide into *t'y* or *t'en*.

> *Achète-**lui-en**!*
>> Buy **him/her some**!

*Ne **leur en** prête pas!*
  Don't lend **them any**!

*Occupe-**t'en** tout de suite!*
  [**You**] Take care **of it** right away!

*Occupons-**nous-en** toute de suite!*
  Let's take care of it right away!

*Si tu aimes quelque chose, tiens-**t'y** de toute ta force.*
  If you love something, hold onto it with all **your** might.

5. Stressed Pronouns

Stressed pronouns are used only to replace nouns representing people or animals.

moi	=	me or I	*nous*	=	us or we
toi	=	you	*vous*	=	you (plural or formal)
lui	=	him or he	*eux*	=	them or they (masculine or including both masculine and feminine)
elle	=	her or she	*elles*	=	them or they (feminine)

Uses of the Stressed Pronoun

A. After a preposition such as *à, pour, avec, sans, chez.*

*Elle pense à **sa sœur**. Elle pense à **elle**.*
  She thinks of **her sister**. She thinks of **her**.

*Je travaille pour **mes patrons**. Je travaille pour **eux**.*
  I work for **my bosses**. I work for **them**.

*Je vis avec **mon père**. Je vis avec **lui**.*
  I live with **my father**. I live with **him**.

*Tu vas au cinéma sans **ton frère**. Tu vas au cinéma sans **lui**.*
  You go to the movies without **your brother**. You go to the movies without **him**.

*Tu peux rester chez **mes tantes**. Tu peux rester chez **elles**.*
  You can stay at **my aunts'** house. You can stay at **their** house.

B. To reinforce a subject pronoun. There is no real English equivalent.

***Moi**, je parle très bien le français.*
  [Myself], I speak French very well.

***Vous**, vous êtes parfait!*
  [Yourself], You are perfect!

C. After the expressions *c'est* and *ce n'est pas* and, of course, their various conjugated forms.

> *C'est **ton frère** qui est avec cette fille? Non, ce n'est pas **lui**.*
> Is it **your brother** who is with this girl? No, it is not **(he)**.

D. Before and after *et* and *ou*.

> ***Toi** et **lui**, vous allez bien vous amuser.*
> **You** and **he** are going to have fun.

E. In short sentences with no verb.

> *Qui a demandé un chocolat? **Moi**.*
> Who asked for a chocolate? **Me**. (I did.)

6. Demonstrative Pronouns

The demonstrative pronoun *celui* (this / the one) is used instead of *ce* + noun or *le* + noun.

It agrees in gender and number with the noun it replaces: *celui, celle, ceux, celles.*

There are a few combinations to keep in mind:

a. In a composed form
   celui-ci, celui-là, ceux-ci, celles-ci, celle-là...
   *Voilà les robes blanches. Ce sont **celles**-ci que j'aime.*
   Here are the white dresses. **These** are the ones I like.

> In composed form, combinations ending with *-ci* generally mean "these" and combinations ending with *-là* generally mean "those."

b. With the preposition *de*
   *Ce ne sont pas mes sandales. Ce sont **celles** de Sophie.*
   These are not my sandals. **These** are Sophie's.

c. With *qui*, *que*, or *dont*. (See the use of these relative pronouns in the next section.)
   *J'aime les robes blanches, surtout **celles** qui sont à la mode.*
   I like white dresses, especially the trendy **ones**.

d. *Ce* is the neutral simple form and is used with the verb *être*.
   ***C'est** toujours bon de se revoir!*
   It's always nice to see each other again.

e. *Ceci* and *cela* are the compound neutral forms, with the general sense of "this" and "that," respectively.
   ***Cela** me donne une idée.*
   This gives me an idea.

7. Interrogative Pronouns

The interrogative pronoun *lequel* (which one) is sometimes used in questions to replace *quel* + noun.

> **Quel livre** *préfères-tu?*
> > **Which book** do you prefer?

> **Lequel** *préfères-tu?*
> > **Which one** do you prefer?

It agrees in gender and number with the noun it replaces: *lequel, laquelle, lesquels, lesquelles.*

See the table below for the forms combining these pronouns with prepositions *à* and *de*:

of (which one)	about (which one)
à + laquelle = à laquelle	*de + laquelle = de laquelle*
à + lequel = auquel	*de + lequel = duquel*
à + lesquels = auxquels	*de + lesquels = desquels*
à + lesquelles = auxquelles	*de + lesquelles = desquelles*

> *J'ai deux frères.* **Duquel** *me parles-tu? (= de quel frère?)*
> > I have two brothers. **Which one** are you talking about?

> *Il y a plusieurs classes à choisir pour ce niveau.* **Auxquelles** *voulez-vous participer?*
> *(= à quelles classes?)*
> > There are several classes to choose from at this level. **Which ones** do you want to attend?

Lequel, laquelle, lesquels, lesquelles can also be used after prepositions like **sur, pour, dans, avec, sans**...etc.

> *Je travaille* **sur le dossier de mon client**. *Le dossier* **sur lequel** *je travaille...*
> > I work on my clients file. The file I am working on....

> *Je cuisine* **pour les amis de ma fille**. *Les amis* **pour lesquels** *je cuisine...*
> > I cook for my daughter's friends. The friends whom I cook for....

Let's practice our pronoun skills.

Paul voulait ------- faire peur.

(A) elle
(B) la
(C) lui
(D) les

Here's How to Crack It

Does the missing pronoun here serve as a subject or object? It serves as an object, so we can eliminate (A). *Elle* serves only as a subject pronoun or a stressed pronoun. We won't use a stressed pronoun because a preposition is not being used.

Does the verb *faire peur* take a direct or indirect object? Indirect. In English, "to frighten someone" takes a direct object, but in French the expression is *faire peur* **à** *quelqu'un*.

Often, three choices will refer to one person, the fourth to more than one person. In most cases, the one that is different will be wrong.

Let's cross out (D) *les,* which is a direct object pronoun as well as the only plural pronoun.

So, which choice is an indirect object pronoun?

Lui, (C), is the indirect pronoun for third person singular. It is the right answer. *La,* (B), is the direct object pronoun.

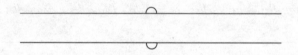

Je suis allé au concert sans -------.

(A) leur
(B) tu
(C) le
(D) eux

Here's How to Crack It

What type of pronoun would come after *sans*? A stressed pronoun must follow a preposition. Which of the answer choices is a stressed pronoun? Only (D). *Eux* is the stressed pronoun meaning "them." Choice (A) is an indirect object pronoun. Choice (B) is a subject pronoun. Choice (C) is a direct object pronoun. Choice (D) is the correct answer: *Je suis allé au concert sans eux.*

More Types of Pronouns

You also want to be familiar with some other types of pronouns that may show up. The following are most likely to appear on the real test as incorrect answer choices.

Possessive Pronouns

Possessive pronouns agree in gender and number with the noun that they replace.

Ce livre est à Nathalie.
    This book is Nathalie's.

C'est le sien.
    It is hers.
    (use of possessive pronoun)

Cette montre est à Pierre.
    This watch is Pierre's.

C'est la sienne.
    It is his.

Singular Pronouns

le mien / la mienne
le tien / la tienne
le sien / la sienne

le nôtre / la nôtre
le vôtre / la vôtre
le leur / la leur

Ce livre est à toi.
    This book is yours.

C'est le tien.
    It is yours.

Plural pronouns

les miens / les miennes
les tiens / les tiennes
les siens / les siennes

les nôtres
les vôtres
les leurs

Ces chaussures sont à elles.
    These shoes are theirs.

Ce sont les leurs.
    They are theirs.

Possessive pronouns must always be used with an article (*le, la, les*).

In French, the possessive adjectives *sa* and *son* and the possessive pronouns *sien* and *sienne* denote the gender of the thing possessed, not of the person possessing it: *Sa voiture est bleue* can mean either "His car is blue" or "Her car is blue"; *Cette voiture est la sienne* can mean "That car is his" or "That car is hers."

Person	Singular		Plural	
	Masculine	**Feminine**	**Masculine**	**Feminine**
je	*le mien*	*la mienne*	*les miens*	*les miennes*
tu	*le tien*	*la tienne*	*les tiens*	*les tiennes*
il, elle	*le sien*	*la sienne*	*les siens*	*les siennes*
nous	*le nôtre*	*la nôtre*	*les nôtres**	
vous	*le vôtre*	*la vôtre*	*les vôtres**	
ils, elles	*le leur*	*la leur*	*les leurs**	

*These represent both the masculine and the feminine forms.

Still More Types of Pronouns

About half of the pronoun questions revolve around the use of other types of pronouns (adverbial pronouns, demonstrative pronouns, relative pronouns, indefinite pronouns, etc.). Don't worry—you don't need to know the terminology, just the roles and usage of these pronoun types.

Example:

> Je n'ai pas le temps de faire les courses ------- ma mère m'a demandé de faire.
>
> (A) qui
> (B) que
> (C) dont
> (D) lesquelles

Which pronoun is correct?

Let's take a look at each in turn and see what rules govern their use.

Qui—Who or Which or That

Qui is the equivalent of the English "who," except that *qui* can also be used to refer to things ("that" or "which"). *Qui* refers to a noun in the main clause of the sentence, and it serves as the subject of the dependent clause that follows.

> **Qui vs. Que**
> Don't use your ear to determine if **qui** or **que** is right. Learn a few rules that will help you choose: 1. Is the noun before the blank the subject or object of the phrase? 2. Is the pronoun preceded by a preposition?

> *la dame **qui** danse là-bas . . .*
>   the lady **who** is dancing over there . . .

> *la table **qui** est cassée . . .*
>   the table **that** is broken . . .

Qui can also be used with a preposition. In this case, it can only refer to a person.

> *l'homme sans **qui** je n'aurais rien accompli . . .*
>   the man without **whom** I would have accomplished nothing . . .

Ce qui—What

Ce qui is used as the subject of the sentence or clause.

> *Qu'est-ce qui se passe?*
>> **What** is happening?

> *Je ne sais pas ce qui la fait pleurer!*
>> I do not know **what**'s making her cry!

Que—Whom or That

Que is used in a number of ways in the French language. On the SAT French Test, however, it usually shows up as a relative pronoun. If referring to a person, it is the equivalent of "whom"; if referring to a thing, it equates to "that" or "which." The person or thing referred to is the direct object of the action in the dependent clause that follows. **Que is never used with a preposition.**

> *l'enfant que j'ai puni . . .*
> (i.e., *j'ai puni l'enfant*)
>> the child **whom** I punished . . .

> *la bicyclette que j'ai reçue pour mon anniversaire . . .*
> (i.e., *j'ai reçu la bicyclette pour mon anniversaire*)
>> the bicycle **that** I received for my birthday . . .

Ce que—What

Ce que is used as a direct object in a sentence or clause.

> *Je ne comprends pas ce qu'il dit.*
>> I do not understand **what** he is saying.

> *Je préfère ce que tu viens d'acheter.*
>> I prefer **what** you just bought.

When Do You Use *Qui* and When Do You Use *Que*?

Unless there is a preposition involved, this is similar to the English use of "who" or "whom" (if the noun referred to is a person). In English, one test is to see if the "who" or "whom" would be replaced by "he" or "him."

> the man _____ is smoking over there . . .
>> "He" is smoking, so you would use "who."

> the woman _____ I hugged . . .
>> I hugged "her," so you would use "whom."

If you understand "who/whom" in English, you may want to translate and decide if "who" or "whom" is correct. If "who" is correct, use *qui;* if "whom" is correct, use *que.*

*l'homme **qui** fume là-bas . . .*
the man **who** is smoking over there . . .

*la femme **que** j'ai embrassée . . .*
the woman **whom** I hugged . . .

If there is a preposition before the blank, you use *qui* if referring to a person, and the correct form of *lequel* if referring to a thing or a person. You never use *que* immediately following a preposition.

What If a Preposition Is Involved?

If a preposition is involved and the pronoun refers to a person, use *qui* or the correct form of *lequel.*

*l'homme **à qui** j'ai donné de l'argent . . .*
the man **to whom** I gave money . . .

*l'ami **pour lequel** j'ai acheté un chapeau . . .*
the friend **for whom** I bought a hat . . .

*la jeune fille **pour laquelle** j'ai fait une robe . . .*
the girl **for whom** I made a dress . . .

*Lequel, laquelle, lesquels,* and *lesquelles,* are always used after the prepositions *entre, sans, parmi,* and *avant.*

Lequel is used with a preposition if the pronoun refers to people or things. The form of *lequel* agrees in gender and number with the person(s) or thing(s) it refers to.

*l'argent **avec lequel** j'ai payé la facture . . .*
the money **with which** I paid the bill . . .

Quoi—Which or What

Quoi is used to refer to things only. It is usually used with a preposition when asking a question.

*À **quoi** pensez-vous?*
What are you thinking of?

*De **quoi** parlez-vous?*
What are you talking about?

De quoi is also used in many idiomatic expressions, such as:

avoir de quoi faire
to have a lot to do

avoir de quoi manger
to have something to eat

avoir de quoi vivre
to have enough to live on

Merci beaucoup! Il n'y a pas de quoi!
> Many thanks! Don't mention it!

Quoi can be used in questions without a preposition in the expression *C'est quoi?* ("What is it?"). This is essentially a shortened version of *Qu'est-ce que c'est?*

Ce à quoi—What

Ce à quoi is used to emphasize an idea, but it is mostly avoided otherwise.

> *Ce à quoi il faut toujours faire attention, c'est l'utilisation des pronoms.*
> **What** you must always pay attention to is the use of pronouns.

Avec quoi—With What

> *Je voudrais savoir avec quoi il a fait cela.*
> I would like to know **with what** he did this.

Sans quoi—Otherwise, If Not

> *Si tu fais tes devoirs tu pourras sortir; sans quoi tu resteras ici.*
> If you do your homework, you can go out; **otherwise**, you'll stay here.

Dont—Of Whom or Of Which

Dont is correct only if the verb in the clause it introduces is one that takes *de* as a preposition. *Dont* is always placed directly after the noun it replaces.

> *Le livre dont j'ai besoin est dans ma chambre.*
> The book **that** I need is in my room.

> *L'ami dont elle a parlé viendra chez nous ce soir.*
> The friend **of whom** she spoke will come to our house this evening.

When it is separated by a preposition, use *duquel, de laquelle, desquels, desquelles*.

> *L'homme à côté duquel le chien attend nous a salués.*
> The man next to **whom** the dog waits greeted us.

> *Les gens à côté desquels nous étions assis n'ont pas arrêté de parler.*
> The people next to **whom** we were sitting did not stop talking.

Dont can be the complement of a noun or an adjective.

> *C'est le magasin dont je suis le directeur (Etre directeur de).*
> This is the store of which I am the manager (To be the manager of).

> *C'est une réunion dont je suis content (Etre content de).*
> It is a meeting I am happy about (To be happy about).

> *La façon de...* ("the way of..."), or *la manière de...* ("the manner of...") also use *dont*. *J'aime la la façon dont elle cuisine* ("I like the way she cooks").

Dont can also be used as a preposition, in the sense of "among which" or "including."

> *J'ai un tas d'intérêts, dont le cinéma et le jardinage.*
>> I have a lot of interests, including movies and gardening.

> *Ils ont acheté dix barres chocolatées, dont trois aux amandes.*
>> They bought ten chocolate bars, including three with almonds.

Ce dont—What

Ce dont is used as an object if the verb phrase in the clause that follows takes the preposition *de.*

> *Il ne comprend pas **ce dont** j'ai besoin.*
>> He does not understand **what** I need.

> *J'ai oublié **ce dont** elle m'a parlé.*
>> I forgot **what** she talked to me about.

Now let's go back to our example first given on page 120.

———————○———————

> Je n'ai pas le temps de faire les courses ------- ma mère m'a
> demandé de faire.
>
> (A) qui
> (B) que
> (C) dont
> (D) lesquelles

Here's How to Crack It

Is a preposition involved? No. Get rid of (D) *lesquelles*. You can also get rid of (A) *qui*, because *qui* can only refer to a thing (like *courses*) if it is the subject of the clause that follows. But the subject of that clause is *ma mère* so the pronoun here must be the object of the clause.

Does *faire* take *de* as a preposition? No. Eliminate (C) *dont*. The answer must be (B) *que*.

———————○———————

———————○———————

> Voilà l'ami ------- j'ai passé l'été.
>
> (A) chez qui
> (B) à qui
> (C) que
> (D) dont

Here's How to Crack It

Can *de* be used as a preposition following *passer l'été*? No. Eliminate (D).

Can *passer l'été* be used without a preposition? No. Eliminate (C) *que*. The relative pronoun *que* is used only for the direct object of the clause that follows, but the object of *j'ai passé* is *l'été*.

You can use *à* with *passer l'été*, but in that case it would be used with a place, not with a person. Eliminate (B).

Can *passer l'été* be used with *chez*? Yes. *Passer l'été chez* means "to spend the summer at the home of." Choice (A) is the right answer.

───────○───────

Où—Where

*Voilà la bibliothèque **où** j'ai passé beaucoup de temps.*
There is the library **where** I spent a lot of time.

*J'ai vu l'hôpital **où** je suis né.*
I saw the hospital **where** I was born.

Où can in many cases be replaced by *dans lequel* (*laquelle/lesquels/lesquelles*).

Où means **when** after the expressions *au moment, à l'époque, au temps,* and *le jour.* Use this carefully and only when it could be replaced by *pendant lequel.*

*Les jours **où** il n'y avait plus de pain, ils mangeaient du riz.*
On the days **when** there was no more bread, they ate rice.

> *Où* and *dans lequel* sometimes mean the same thing. You'll never be asked to choose between the two.

D'où—from where, hence

Il n'importe pas d'où est survenue l'erreur.
It doesn't matter where the error arose from.

Des chercheurs expliquent d'où vient le bruit quand on se fait craquer les articulations.
Researchers have explained where the sound comes from when you crack your knuckles.

Le sujet est épineux, d'où mon hésitation à en parler.
The subject is very thorny, hence my hesitation to speak about it.

Chacun—Each One

Chacun son tour!
> Wait your turn!

À chacun son goût. (or, *Chacun son goût.*)
> To each his own.

On a trois euros chacun.
> We each have three euros.

Quelques-uns/unes (de)—Some (Of)

Quelques-uns *de ces livres sont à lire avant la fin du semestre.*
> **Some of** those books are to be read before the end of the semester.

Je peux goûter ces bonbons?
> May I taste these candies?

> *Oui, prends-en* **quelques-uns.**
> Yes, take **some of** them.

Aucun/Aucune—Not One, None

Je n'en aime ***aucun!***
> I like **none** of them!

Aucun and *aucune* are always used with *ne.*

Aucune *de ces réponses n'est correcte.*
> **None** of these answers is correct.

Aucun, personne, and *rien* must be used with *ne* in a sentence. *Ne* immediately precedes the verb, and the negative pronoun (*aucun, personne,* or *rien*) will come before the verb if it's the subject or after the verb if it's the object.

Quelqu'un—Someone

Quelqu'*un a volé ma moto!*
> **Someone** stole my motorcycle!

Personne—No One

Est-ce que quelqu'un a vu le voleur?
> Did anyone see the thief?

Non, **personne** *ne l'a vu.*
> No, **no one** saw him.

Like *aucun, personne* is used with *ne. Personne* can be used without the *ne* only if it is a one-word answer to a question.

Qui a cassé ce vase?
Who broke this vase?

Personne*.*
No one.

Quelque chose—Something

*Je vous ai acheté **quelque chose** à la pâtisserie.*
I bought you **something** at the pastry shop.

Ne...rien—Nothing

Est-ce que tu as acheté quelque chose à la pâtisserie?
Did you buy something at the pastry shop?

*Non, je **n'ai rien** acheté.*
No, I did **not** buy **anything**.

────────────○────────────

Avez-vous des stylos? -------.

(A) Oui, lesquels.
(B) Oui, j'ai quelques.
(C) Non, je n'en ai aucun.
(D) Non, je n'ai pas.

Here's How to Crack It

(A) *lesquels* cannot stand by itself in a sentence unless it is itself a question (*Apporte-moi les stylos. Lesquels?*). Eliminate it.

(B) *quelques*, meaning "some," is an adjective and can only be used to modify a noun (*j'ai quelques stylos* or *j'en ai quelques-uns*). Eliminate it.

(C) *aucun* is used with *ne*. This is correct.

(D) By itself, *je n'ai pas* does not work. It lacks a reference to what it is that I do not have. To be correct, you would need to say either *je n'en ai pas* or *je n'ai pas de stylos*.

────────────○────────────

> **No Way!**
> All three negattive pronouns (*aucun, personne,* and *rien*) can be used in their negative senses as one-word answers to questions: *Qu'est-ce que tu veux ? Rien.* (What do you want? Nothing.)

Qui va chercher le paquet à la poste? ------- vais.

(A) A quoi
(B) J'y
(C) Personne
(D) J'en

Here's How to Crack It

(A), *A quoi* does not work and makes no sense. It refers to things and is usually used with a preposition.

(B) is correct. The *y* replaces the expression *à la poste.*

(C) has two problems. First, *personne* needs to be used with *ne.* Second, *personne* takes the third person singular form of the verb (in this case, *va*).

(D) *En* is used to show either possession or to replace a noun that works with a verb that takes *de.* Here the verb is *aller* and it takes the preposition *à.* So *en* is not correct.

Quand + Futur—When

In sentences expressing a likely or certain outcome, a clause introduced by *quand* or similar expression of time will take the future tense. A sentence with similar meaning in English would have "when" with the present tense.

> *Quand j'irai à l'école, je serai entouré de mes copains.*
> When I go to school, I'll be surrounded by my pals.

> *Lorsque mes parents arriveront demain, j'irai les chercher à l'aéroport.*
> When my parents arrive tomorrow, I will go pick them up at the airport.

> *Une fois que mes études seront terminées, je gagnerai beaucoup d'argent.*
> Once my studies are done with, I will make lots of money.

> *Dès que les fleurs seront livrées, il faut les mettre dans l'eau.*
> As soon as the flowers arrive, it's necessary to put them in water.

An/Année, Jour/Journée, Soir/Soirée

Notice that there are four periods of time with both a masculine and feminine form:

> *un an — une année* (year)
> *un jour — une journée* (day)
> *un matin — une matinée* (morning)
> *un soir — une soirée* (evening)

Let's learn the difference in meaning and the constructions used.

In general, the masculine forms are quantity words. They represent countable units of time and are used with cardinal numbers or to express a frequency.

> *Elle y travaille depuis cinq ans.*
> She's been working there for five years.

> *On a mis deux jours à achever l'ouvrage.*
> We took two days to finish the work.

> *Je travaille tous les matins.*
> I work every morning.

> *Je rentre chez moi vers 18 heures le soir.*
> I get back home around 6 o'clock in the evening.

The masculine words are also used with adverbs of time.

> *Hier matin.*
> Yesterday morning.

> *Demain soir.*
> Tomorrow night.

The feminine forms are quality words; they put the emphasis on the actual length of time. They are used with ordinal numbers or adjectives.

> *J'ai travaillé toute la matinée.*
> I worked all morning.

> *C'est trop tard dans l'année pour planter des bulbes.*
> It's too late in the year to plant flower bulbs.

> *J'ai passé la journée à faire des courses.*
> I spent the day running errands.

The feminine form is used with undefined quantities.

> *Combien d'années? Des centaines d'années. Plusieurs années.*
> How many years? Hundreds of years. Several years.

Note the difference between *tous les jours* (every day) and *toute la journée* (all day), or *tous les ans* (every year) and *toute l'année* (all year).

DRILL 1: PRONOUN QUESTIONS

Answers can be found in Part IV.

1. ------- est arrivé à Paul hier?

   (A) Quel
   (B) Quoi
   (C) Qu'
   (D) Qu'est-ce qui

2. C'est -------.

   (A) eux
   (B) il
   (C) lui
   (D) le

3. C'est grâce à ------- que nous avons pu venir.

   (A) eux
   (B) les
   (C) leur
   (D) ils

4. La chose la plus difficile est de ------- réveiller le matin.

   (A) lui
   (B) il
   (C) le
   (D) moi

5. ------- a sorti la poubelle.

   (A) Il n'
   (B) Personne n'
   (C) Aucun
   (D) Qui

6. Le livre ------- je suis l'auteur est une histoire d'Amérique pendant le 19ème siècle.

   (A) lequel
   (B) dont
   (C) que
   (D) qui

7. La femme ------- Isabelle est assise est le chef de la compagnie.

   (A) à côté de laquelle
   (B) à côté auquel
   (C) à côté qui
   (D) à côté

8. J'ai interviewé beaucoup de célébrités, mais ------- ne me fait cet effet.

   (A) personne
   (B) jamais
   (C) quelque chose
   (D) aucun

9. ------- d'extraordinaire est arrivé aujourd'hui. J'ai reçu mon doctorat.

   (A) Quelqu'un
   (B) Quelques fois
   (C) Quelque chose
   (D) Aucun

10. On comprend très bien ------- les citoyens avaient peur pendant la première guerre mondiale.

    (A) quoi
    (B) d'où
    (C) qui
    (D) ce dont

VERBS

There are three areas that verb questions tend to test: use of the subjunctive, agreement of the past participle, and tense choice.

> Roughly 4–5 questions on Parts B & C will test the use of the subjunctive. Knowing these rules can help you snag several crucial points!

Know the Subjunctive

About 25 percent of the grammar questions on the test deal with verb use. Over half of them ask you to decide whether or not to use the subjunctive.

What Is the Subjunctive?

Like the indicative, the subjunctive is not a tense; it is a mode or mood. While it is not often used in English, it is used very frequently in French. This is why it is always found on the SAT Subject Test in French.

When Do You Use the Subjunctive?

In French and on the SAT French, you will use the subjunctive in phrases that follow expressions of doubt, suggestion, preference, desire, improbability, or emotion. The subjunctive is also used with certain conjunctions. All phrases that require use of the subjunctive will contain the word *que*.

Expressions That Take the Subjunctive

Doubt or Uncertainty

Je doute qu'il réussisse son examen.
I doubt that he will pass his exam.

J'ai peur qu'il rate son examen.
I am afraid that he will fail his exam.

Je ne crois pas que vous ayez raison.
I don't believe that you are right.

Il est douteux qu'elle vienne ce weekend.
It's doubtful that she will come this weekend.

C'est possible que j'aie tort.
I may be wrong. (**It is possible that** I am wrong.)

You must use the **indicative mode** with verbs expressing an opinion, such as *penser que, croire que, espérer que, être sûr que, être certain que* when they are used in the affirmative form.

Je crois que vous avez raison.
I believe you are right.

Nous pensons que tes parents seront contents de te revoir.
We think your parents will be happy to see you again.

J'espère que vous allez bien.
I hope you are well.

Compare the above examples to the following examples, which display these verbs used in the negative form. The negative form makes a difference since it requires the subjunctive!

*Je ne crois pas qu'il **ait** raison.*
I don't think he's right.

*Nous ne pensons pas que tes parents **soient** contents.*
We don't think your parents are happy.

132 | For more free content, visit PrincetonReview.com

SAT Subject Test French Prep

Suggestion or Preference

Je préfère que vous rentriez tout de suite.
> **I prefer that** you return at once.

Je tiens à ce que tu sois à l'heure.
> **I insist that** you be on time.

Il vaut mieux que vous ne sortiez pas ce soir.
> **It is better that** you do not go out tonight.

Il est important que vous étudiiez l'emploi du subjonctif.
> **It is important that** you study the use of the subjunctive.

Il faut que je prenne un rendez-vous chez le dentiste.
> **It is necessary that** I make an appointment at the dentist's.

All phrases that require use of the subjunctive will contain the word *que*.

Desire

Je veux que tu travailles plus sérieusement.
> **I want** you to work more seriously.

Je souhaite que tout se passe bien.
> **I wish that** everything goes well.

Je désire qu'il soit heureux.
> **I want** him to be happy.

Improbability

Il est peu probable qu'il neige demain.
> **It is unlikely that** it will snow tomorrow.

Emotion

Je suis étonné qu'il ne soit pas encore là.
> **I am surprised** that he is not yet here.

Je suis content que tout se soit bien passé.
> **I am happy that** everything went well.

Je regrette que le temps passe si vite.
> **I am sorry that** time goes by so quickly.

The subjunctive is used with expressions of doubt, preference, or emotion.

Superlative

Cet homme est le seul qui sache encore travailler de ses mains.
> **This man is the only one who** still knows how to work with his hands.

C'est la meilleure nouvelle que vous puissiez lui donner.

It is the best news that you can give him.

Expressions That DO NOT Take the Subjunctive

The following expressions do not take the subjunctive when they are used in the **affirmative form only**:

> **Pay Attention to Probability vs. Improbability**
>
> "It's likely it will rain tomorrow" would use the indicative in French. "It is unlikely to be beautiful tomorrow" would take the subjunctive.

il est probable que	it is likely
espérer	to hope
se demander	to wonder
croire	to believe
penser	to think
se douter que	to suspect

Il est probable qu'il neigera demain.

It is probably going to snow tomorrow.

Je me demande s'il viendra.

I wonder if he will come.

Beware of *ne* used as an expletive after *avant que, de peur que, de crainte que, avoir peur que, craindre que,* and *à moins que*. **It is not a negative form, but only substantiates an already-negative main clause, such as in expressions of fear, warning, or doubt.**

Je vais aller me promener avant qu'il ne pleuve.

I will go for a walk before it rains.

Je crains qu'il ne pleuve.

I am afraid it might rain.

Conjunctions That Take the Subjunctive

pour que, de manière (à ce) que	so that
de sorte que, afin que	so that
quoique, bien que	although
pourvu que, à condition que	provided that, so long as
à moins que	unless
jusqu'à ce que	until
en attendant que	waiting for
avant que (but not *après que*)	before
de crainte que, de peur que	for fear that
sans que	without
malgré que	even though, in spite of
pour autant que	as far as

Conjunctions That DO NOT Take the Subjunctive

après que	after
dès que, aussitôt que	as soon as
pendant que	during
parce que	because
puisque	since
étant donné que	given that / with the understanding that
tandis que	while / whereas

So Now What?

You won't have to construct the subjunctive of a given verb; you only need to recognize it among the four answer choices. In addition to the present subjunctive, you may also see the past of the subjunctive. You'll recognize it because the auxiliary or helper verb (*avoir* or *être*) will be in the subjunctive. Note that with *avoir*, *il a* becomes *qu'il ait* and with *être*, *il est* becomes *qu'il soit*.

Present Tense

Certain:	*Je sais qu'il vient ce soir.*
	I know that he is coming tonight.
Uncertain:	*Je doute qu'il vienne ce soir.*
(Pres. Subj.)	I doubt that he is coming tonight.

Past Tense

Certain:	*Je sais qu'il est venu hier.*
	I know that he came yesterday.
Uncertain:	*Je doute qu'il soit venu hier.*
(Past Subj.)	I doubt that he came yesterday.

Now you try it:

Jean-Paul ne m'a pas téléphoné; j'ai peur qu'il
------- oublié notre rendez-vous.

(A) a
(B) avait
(C) ait
(D) aura

Here's How to Crack It

Does the expression *J'ai peur que* . . . take the subjunctive? Yes! It shows doubt, fear, or uncertainty. If you recognize that (A) *a* is the present indicative, (B) *avait* is the imperfect, and (D) *aura* is the future, then by process of elimination you can infer that (C) must be in the subjunctive. The answer is (C).

———————◯———————

Try another one:

———————◯———————

Ma mère m'a grondée quand elle ------- ma robe déchirée.

(A) voit
(B) a vu
(C) voie
(D) ait vu

Here's How to Crack It

Does the expression *Ma mère m'a grondée quand* . . . take the subjunctive?

No. The verb in this case (*voir*) is an actual event. Eliminate (C) and (D). This sentence requires the past, so the answer is (B). Also, note that we have *quand* here and not *que*.

———————◯———————

———————◯———————

Détruisez les preuves avant qu'il n'------- ce que nous avons fait.

(A) apprendra
(B) apprenne
(C) apprendrait
(D) apprend

Here's How to Crack It

Is *avant que* a conjunction that takes the subjunctive?

Yes. The answer is (B). Choice (A) is the future. Choice (C) is the conditional. Choice (D) is the present indicative.

———————◯———————

Tense

You remember all those fancy verb tenses you learned in French class: the *passé simple*, the future perfect, the pluperfect subjunctive? Well, for the purposes of this test, you can forget them.

For the French Subject Test, you need to recognize the present, the imperfect, the *passé composé*, the *plus-que-parfait*, the future, the conditional, the past of the conditional, and you must know when to use them. The subjunctive, actually a mode or mood rather than a tense, is the verb form most frequently tested. The conditional, also a mode or mood, is the next most frequently tested verb form.

English	French
Present	*Présent*
Past	*Passé Composé*
Imperfect	*Imparfait*
Past Perfect	*Plus-que-parfait*
Future	*Futur simple*
Conditional	*Conditionnel*
Past Conditional	*Conditionnel Passé*

Le Présent

This is pretty straightforward. It's the form of the verb you're most used to seeing.

> *Il part.*

L'Imparfait

The imperfect tense is a form of the past that indicates something was ongoing: either something that went on for a period of time in the past or something that happened repeatedly in the past.

présent	*imparfait*
Il part.	*Il partait.*

Le Passé Composé

This tense indicates that a past action (or state) is now complete. It is made up of an auxiliary verb (either *avoir* or *être* in the present tense) and a past participle. It indicates something that started and ended in the past and is now over. The auxiliary verb is *avoir* for most verbs, but *être* for reflexive verbs and for certain verbs implying motion. This will be covered later in the chapter.

présent	*passé composé*
Il part.	*Il est parti.*

The *Passé Composé* vs. the *Imparfait*
Notice the difference between the *passé composé* and the *imparfait*. The *passé composé* describes a one-time action that is now complete, while the *imparfait* describes an action that was ongoing in the past.

Le Plus-Que-Parfait (Past Perfect)

The past perfect indicates that something happened in the past prior to another action in the past. It is made up of an auxiliary verb (*avoir* or *être* in the imperfect tense) and a past participle.

présent	*plus-que-parfait*
Il part.	*Il était parti avant qu'il ait plu.*

Le Futur

This indicates that something will happen.

présent	*futur*
Il part.	*Il partira.*

Le Conditionnel

The conditional mode or mood is used to describe what people would do or what would happen if a set of conditions were met. In most cases it is used with another clause starting with *si*.

présent   *conditionnel*

Il part.   *Si cela arrivait, il partirait.*

                                        Il partirait si cela arrivait.

The conditional is also used as a polite way to request things.

Je voudrais une baguette, s'il vous plaît, madame.
I would like a baguette please, madame.

Use of the Conditional

Almost half of the questions that relate to verb sequence test you on the use of the conditional. The conditional is used in a sentence if there is a clause that begins with *si* and uses the imperfect tense.

si + imparfait → conditionnel

Si j'avais le temps, je le ferais moi-même.
If I had the time, I would do it myself.

If the past imperfect is used, then the past conditional will be used.

si + plus-que-parfait → conditionnel passé

Si j'avais eu le temps, je l'aurais fait moi-même.
    If I had had the time, I would have done it myself.

Présent	Aujourd'hui, il fait ses devoirs.
Imparfait	Quand il était petit, il faisait ses devoirs.
Passé composé	Hier il a fait ses devoirs.
Plus-Que-Parfait	J'avais déjà fini mes devoirs quand il est parti.
Futur	Demain, il fera ses devoirs.
Conditionnel	S'il avait des devoirs, il les ferait.

Sequence of Tenses

In questions with several verbs, the tenses and mode must follow a logical sequence.

- Sentences with a *si* clause*:*

Si clause	Result
imparfait	*conditionnel présent*
Si j'avais de l'argent	*j'achèterais un bateau.*
plus-que-parfait	*conditionnel passé*
Si j'avais eu de l'argent	*j'aurais fait ce voyage en Afrique.*

- Conjunctions referring to time such as *quand, une fois que, après que, lorsque, aussitôt que,* and *dès que* often require the use of the *futur antérieur* (future perfect) instead of the *futur simple*. You must consider whether:

1. In the sequence of future events, one action must be finished before the other can take place.

   Je pourrai répondre à ta question quand j'aurai parlé à mon frère.

   I will be able to answer your question when I have talked to my brother.

2. In the future, the actions in both clauses will take place at the same time.

   Je vous appellerai quand il arrivera à la maison.

   I will call you as soon as he arrives.

Je sortirai aussitôt que mon travail -------.

(A) finira
(B) serait fini
(C) sera fini
(D) finirait

Here's How to Crack It

What tense is correct? It is not a *si* clause or any form of politeness; therefore, it cannot be conditional mode. Eliminate (B) and (D). The conjunction *aussitôt que* indicates that one action has to take place before the other. Eliminate (A). Choice (C) is the correct answer.

Si j'étais riche, je ------- un yacht.

(A) m'achète
(B) m'achèterai
(C) m'achetais
(D) m'achèterais

Here's How to Crack It

What tense is correct here? Because *si* is used with the imperfect, the following verb must be the conditional.

How do we recognize the conditional? It combines the structure of the future with the endings of the imperfect (*ais*, *ait*, etc.). Choice (D) is the correct choice.

Avant d'entrer au restaurant, il m'a demandé si j' ------- assez d'argent pour payer le dîner.

(A) ai
(B) avais
(C) ai eu
(D) aurai

Here's How to Crack It

What tense is correct here? Choice (A) cannot be correct. It is the present tense, and the previous clause, *il m'a demandé*, tells us the action is in the past. Since (D) is the future, we can eliminate it as well.

Do we use the imperfect or the past? Choice (C) implies that having enough money was an event or action that occurred once prior to the question. Because we have the phrase, *avant d'entrer*, we know that the state of having money is an ongoing one, preceding and presumably continuing throughout dinner. Choice (B) is the correct answer.

> It is important that you recognize what each tense or mood looks like when you see it. Usually the ending of the verb will give you a clue.

Make sure you can identify which tense (or mood) is which.

Présent	Imparfait	Passé composé	Plus-que-parfait
je donne	je donnais	j'ai donné	j'avais donné
tu donnes	tu donnais	tu as donné	tu avais donné
il donne	il donnait	il a donné	il avait donné
nous donnons	nous donnions	nous avons donné	nous avions donné
vous donnez	vous donniez	vous avez donné	vous aviez donné
ils donnent	ils donnaient	ils ont donné	ils avaient donné
Futur	**Conditionnel**	**Subjonctif présent**	**Conditionnel passé**
je donnerai	je donnerais	que je donne	j'aurais donné
tu donneras	tu donnerais	que tu donnes	tu aurais donné
il donnera	il donnerait	qu'il donne	il aurait donné
nous donnerons	nous donnerions	que nous donnions	nous aurions donné
vous donnerez	vous donneriez	que vous donniez	vous auriez donné
ils donneront	ils donneraient	qu'ils donnent	ils auraient donné

With *donner*, as in all regular *"er"* verbs, the singular forms of the subjunctive present are identical to the indicative present.

AVOIR AND ÊTRE IN COMPOUND PAST TENSES

What Is an Auxiliary Verb?

It is a verb that loses its own meaning to help form a compound past tense for other verbs such as the *passé composé, plus-que-parfait, passé du subjonctif, conditionnel passé,* and *futur antérieur.* All verbs take either *avoir* or *être.* To make a sweeping generalization, **most verbs take *avoir*,** but verbs that indicate a **change of place** (*aller, venir, partir*) **or state** (*naître, mourir, devenir…*) **and all reflexive verbs** (*se laver, se lever…*) take *être.* Sound tricky? Just remember Dr. and Mrs. Vandertramp.

You're probably familiar with the *avoir* vs. *être* auxiliary verb divide from French class, but let's review just in case. When you are writing a sentence in *passé composé*, you must use either *avoir* or *être* as your helper verb before the past participle. Most of the time, the auxiliary verb that you'll use is *avoir* ("to have"), but sometimes it will be *être* ("to be"). To help you remember what verbs pair up with *être,* let me introduce you to my trusted friends, Dr. and Mrs. Vandertramp. Who are Dr. and Mrs. Vandertramp? They're a couple that every French student should know, even if doctors make you anxious. Memorize that pneumonic and it will help you recall a list of the verbs that use *être* as their auxiliary verb in *passé composé:*

Meet your new BFFs, Dr. and Mrs. Vandertramp!

Devenir	to become	**Venir**	to come
Revenir	to come back	**Aller**	to go
&		**Naître**	to be born
Monter	to climb	**Descendre**	to go down
Rester	to stay	**Entrer**	to enter
Sortir	to go out	**Rentrer**	to come back
		Tomber	to fall
		Retourner	to return
		Arriver	to arrive
		Mourir	to die
		Partir	to leave

What Is a Past Participle?

A past participle is the form of the verb that combines with "to have" (in English), or *être* or *avoir* (in French), in order to make the past tense.

Je mange mon petit déjeuner.
    I eat my breakfast. (present)

*J'ai **mangé** mon petit déjeuner.*
    I have eaten my breakfast. (past)

You'll most likely be given the choice of four different forms of the past participle—masculine singular, feminine singular, masculine plural, and feminine plural—with an occasional infinitive thrown in to confuse you. You must decide which is correct.

When Does the Past Participle Agree, and with What?

The past participle **agrees with the subject** of the sentence when:

> The past participle will agree with the *subject* if the verb takes ***être*** or is reflexive. It will agree with the *object* of the sentence if the verb takes ***avoir*** and the direct object is before the verb.

- The verb takes *être* as its auxiliary verb and there is **no direct object placed after the verb.**

Pauline et Chantal sont parties hier pour l'Afrique.
Pauline and Chantal left for Africa yesterday.

- The verb is **reflexive** and therefore takes *être,* and there is **no direct object.**

Elle s'est évanouie quand elle a entendu la nouvelle.
    She fainted when she heard the news.

The past participle **agrees with the direct object** of the sentence when:

- The **reflexive** verb has a **direct object placed before the verb**.

La jambe qu'elle s'est cassée en skiant lui fait toujours mal.
    The leg she broke skiing is still painful.

- The verb takes *avoir* and has a **direct object placed before the verb**.

La fille que nous avons vue au café est ma meilleure amie.
    The girl we saw in the café is my best friend.

When Is There No Agreement?

- The **reflexive** verb has a **direct object** (usually a body part) **placed after the verb**.

Elle s'est piqué le doigt en cousant.
    She pricked her finger while sewing.

Elle s'est lavé les cheveux ce matin.
    She washed her hair this morning.

- The verb takes *avoir* and has a **direct object placed after the verb**.

J'ai vu ma meilleure amie au café aujourd'hui.
    I saw my best girlfriend in the café today.

Since questions in Part C often contain several sentences, information about the gender and number may come earlier than the sentence in which the blank appears.

Try this:

Les deux sœurs ont très bien ------- à l'université.

(A) réussi
(B) réussie
(C) réussis
(D) réussies

Here's How to Crack It

The verb *réussir* (to succeed, to be successful) uses the auxiliary verb *avoir*. Is there a direct object that precedes the verb? No. There is no direct object in this sentence. The correct answer is (A).

La fille à côté de moi m'a donné les renseignements dont
j'avais besoin. Je l'ai ------.

(A) remercié
(B) remerciée
(C) remerciées
(D) remercier

Here's How to Crack It

The verb *remercier* (to thank) also takes *avoir* as its helper verb. Is there a direct object before
the verb? Yes, "*l*" refers to *la fille*. The correct answer is (B).

Oddball Verb Forms: Other Participles

There is a small chance that you will have a question or two on other participles: the present
participle, the gerund, or the perfect participle. You don't need to know these terms—just be
able to recognize how they work in a sentence. This type of question is most likely to appear on
Part C, where you choose the appropriate form of the verb based on the sequence of tenses in
the paragraph.

The Present Participle

The present participle is a verb form that ends in "-ing" in English. It shows that one action is
happening at the same time as another.

>*J'ai vu les enfants courant sur la pelouse.*
>>I saw the children running on the lawn.

The present participle "running" is also acting as an adjective, describing something about the
children. The present participle of *avoir* is *ayant*, and the present participle of *être* is *étant*.

The Gerund

The gerund is also like an "-ing" verb form in English, but in this case, it is acting as a noun
rather than an adjective. In French, it is always accompanied by the preposition *en*. It can show:

- **That one action is happening at the same time as another**

>*Elle montait l'escalier en chantant.*
>>She climbed the stairs while singing.

- **That one action is part of a process**

  En lisant, nous découvrons de nouveaux mondes.
  In reading, we discover new worlds.

- **That one action is part of a cause and effect**

  Eric apprend à danser en regardant des vidéos.
  Eric learns how to dance by watching videos.

The Perfect Participle

The perfect participle (made up of *ayant* or *étant* + the past participle) is the past tense of the present participle. An example in English would be "Having won the war, the army celebrated." This form is used to show that one action was completed before another began.

> ***Ayant fini*** *le repas, nous avons débarrassé la table.*
> Having finished the meal, we cleared the table.

If the verb takes *être*, you will see *étant* instead of *ayant*:

> ***Étant montée***, *elle ne pouvait plus entendre la discussion.*
> Having gone upstairs, she could no longer hear the discussion.

Since you're an expert by now, let's try tackling a full paragraph:

Hier, j'étais en train de ___(1)___ la maison quand j'ai vu à travers la fenêtre un lapin sur la pelouse. Son corps ___(2)___ brun, mais il avait de grandes oreilles blanches. Je l' ___(3)___ regardé pendant quelques instants, puis en entendant un bruit il a ___(4)___ et en un clin d'œil il a disparu.

1. (A) rouler
   (B) ranger
   (C) nager
   (D) hausser

2. (A) est
   (B) a été
   (C) serais
   (D) était

3. (A) aie
   (B) ai
   (C) aura
   (D) aurais

4. (A) choisi
   (B) établi
   (C) bondi
   (D) dormi

Here's How to Crack It

1. Which verb describes something that can be done in a house (*maison*)? *Rouler* means to roll, *ranger* means to tidy up, *nager* means to swim, and *hausser* means to raise. Only (B) makes sense in this context.

2. Which form of the verb *être* is correct here? Since the entire paragraph takes place in the past, we can eliminate both the present tense in (A), *est*, and the conditional in (C), *serais*. Now we have to choose between the *passé composé* in (B) or the imperfect in (D). Because the sentence is describing specific characteristics of the rabbit (*lapin*), we need to use the imperfect, which is used to describe states of being that are ongoing. The fact that the other verb in the sentence is also imperfect (*avait*) is another hint that (D), *était*, is the right answer.

3. Which form of the verb *avoir* is correct here? Again, all action is taking place in the past, and the other verbs in the sentence both appear to use the *passé composé*. Eliminate the future, (C), and the conditional, (D). In (A) we have the subjunctive form, but since there isn't any uncertainty or emotion here, it's incorrect, which leaves (B) as the correct answer.

4. Which past participle has the correct meaning for the sentence? Translating the second half of the sentence, we learn that upon hearing a noise (*en entendant un bruit*), it (the rabbit) does something and in the blink of an eye, it disappears (*en un clin d'œil il a disparu*). Choice (A) means the rabbit chose something, which doesn't fit. Choice (B) doesn't work either, as the rabbit didn't establish anything. Choice (C) is the past participle of *bondir*, which means to leap; this would be a logical thing for the rabbit to do. Choice (D) suggests the rabbit slept, which isn't correct. Choice (C) is the right answer.

DRILL 2: VERB QUESTIONS

Answers can be found in Part IV.

1. Si -------, je préparerais le dîner.

   (A) vous en avez envie
   (B) on me le demande
   (C) j'avais le temps
   (D) tu seras d'accord

2. Paul regrette que nous ------- pas réussi.

   (A) n'avons
   (B) n'avions
   (C) n'ayons
   (D) n'aurons

3. ------- une lettre quand on a sonné à la porte.

   (A) J'écris
   (B) J'écrirais
   (C) J'écrive
   (D) J'écrivais

4. Elle n'a jamais oublié ce que nous -------
   au moment de son départ.

   (A) disons
   (B) ayons dit
   (C) avons dit
   (D) aurions dit

5. Est-ce que vous ------- contents si je n'avais pas accepté
   l'invitation?

   (A) êtes
   (B) soyez
   (C) étiez
   (D) auriez été

6. Nous doutons ------- leur rendre visite chez eux.

   (A) qu'il ait le temps de
   (B) qu'il voudrait
   (C) qu'il peut
   (D) qu'elle avait envie de

7. -------, elle est partie pour le long trajet chez elle.

   (A) Disait au revoir
   (B) Dire au revoir
   (C) Ayant dit au revoir
   (D) Avoir dit au revoir

8. Tu pourras regarder la télé une fois que tu ---------
   ton travail.

   (A) aurais fini
   (B) finissais
   (C) auras fini
   (D) finisses

9. Quand j'avais quatre ans, --------- un enfant très difficile.

   (A) j'étais
   (B) je suis
   (C) j'ai été
   (D) je suis été

10. Il aimerait aller avec toi au musée, mais il --------- travailler.

   (A) doive
   (B) devra
   (C) devais
   (D) doit

PREPOSITIONS

Below is a list of the most important prepositions for you to know.

Common Prepositions	
à	= to
de	= from, of
sur	= on
sous	= under
pour	= for
avant (+ nom)	= before
avant de (+ verbe)	= before
après	= after
chez	= at, to (location)
en	= of, in, from, to
dans	= in, into
entre	= between
pendant	= during
vers	= toward
sans	= without
sauf	= except, unless
selon	= according to
durant	= during
malgré, en dépit de	= in spite of
afin de	= in order to

Just as in English, certain verbs or expressions in French require prepositions while others require none. Memorization is the key here.

These questions will ask you for the preposition required. Some verbs can take more than one preposition depending on the meaning. In some questions, you will have the option of no preposition, denoted by dashes in the answer choice (---).

Il a refusé ------- faire son lit.

(A) ---
(B) à
(C) de
(D) sur

Out of context, *refuser* could take the preposition *à* or *de*, or no preposition at all. Each has a different meaning.

refuser quelque chose—to refuse something

> *Il a refusé l'offre.*
> He refused the offer.

refuser quelque chose à quelqu'un—to deny something to someone

> *Le juge a refusé les droits de visite à la mère.*
> The judge denied visitation rights to the mother.

refuser de faire quelque chose—to refuse to do something

> *L'enfant a refusé de manger ses carottes.*
> The child refused to eat her carrots.

Which is appropriate for this question? Because someone is refusing to do something in this sentence, the correct answer is *de*, (C).

> Prepositions are tested on Parts A and B of your SAT Subject Test in French. As parts of grammar, prepositions join words and have specific meanings, and certain verbs can be used only with certain prepositions (also known as "idioms").

Back to Pronouns

Keep in mind that the verb's appropriate preposition may determine your choice of pronoun. If a verb requires a preposition in a given circumstance, for example, then you know that it takes an indirect and not a direct object. Or, if a given verb requires *de*, the relative pronoun used with it will reflect that.

C'est la robe ------- j'ai envie.

(A) que
(B) qui
(C) dont
(D) à qui

Here's How to Crack It

The verb *avoir envie* takes the preposition *de*. Choice (A) can be eliminated because *que* is never used with a preposition. Choice (B) can also be eliminated because *qui* cannot be a subject here (*j'* is the subject). *Avoir envie* takes *de*, so (D), which is used with *à*, cannot be right. Choice (C) *dont* is correct because *dont* in a sense means *de* + *que*.

> Your knowledge of prepositions will affect your choice of pronouns. For example, *dont* will be a correct choice only if the verb takes *de* as a preposition.

Your experience studying French will probably provide you with a good sense of which verb takes which preposition, if you take the time to think about it. To refresh your memory, here is a partial list of verbs. Some never take a preposition, others sometimes take a preposition, and still others always take a preposition.

Verbs That Don't Take a Preposition

Verbs that don't take prepositions will be used with either the infinitive (the "to" form of a verb).

pouvoir + infinitive — *Je peux faire n'importe quoi.*
I can do anything I want.

espérer + infinitive — *J'espère venir demain.*
I hope to come tomorrow.

vouloir + infinitive — *Je veux chanter.*
I want to sing.

devoir + infinitive — *Je dois travailler.*
I have to work.

désirer + infinitive — *Je désire partir en vacances.*
I wish to leave on vacation.

souhaiter + infinitive — *Je souhaite travailler moins.*
I wish to work less.

adorer + infinitive — *J'adore parler français.*
I love to speak French.

Verbs That Sometimes Take Prepositions and Sometimes Don't

aller + **infinitive**   *Je vais chercher ma sœur à l'école.*
                                     I am going to get my sister at school.

aller à   *Je vais aux États-Unis.*
                                     I am going to the United States.

refuser + **object**   *Je refuse l'offre.*
                                     I refuse the offer.

refuser de   *Je refuse de faire mes devoirs.*
                                     I refuse to do my homework.

oublier + **noun**   *J'ai oublié mon stylo.*
                                     I forgot my pen.

oublier de   *J'ai oublié de dire au revoir.*
                                     I forgot to say good-bye.

accepter + **object**   *J'accepte votre invitation.*
                                     I accept your invitation.

accepter de   *J'accepte de nettoyer la cuisine.*
                                     I agree to clean the kitchen.

compter + **object**   *Je compte ma monnaie.*
                                     I am counting my change.

compter sur   *Nous comptons sur vous pour nous aider.*
                                     We count on you to help us.

> A good resource to have on hand is a verb book. A good verb book will tell you how to conjugate a given verb and which prepositions are used with that verb.

Verbs That Always Take Prepositions

réfléchir à   *Je réfléchis à mon avenir.*
                                     I am thinking of my future.

penser à   *Je pense à ma mère.*
                                     I am thinking of my mother.

penser de   *Que pensez-vous du nouveau président?*
                                     What do you think of (about) the new president?

participer à	*Je participe aux Jeux Olympiques.* I am in the Olympic games.
assister à	*Est-ce que vous allez assister au concert?* Are you going to attend the concert?
faire attention à	*Faites attention aux assiettes en porcelaine!* Be careful with the porcelain plates!
répondre à	*Les élèves répondent aux questions du professeur.* The students answer the teacher's questions.
obéir à	*Le soldat obéit aux ordres.* The soldier obeys the orders.
parler de	*De quoi parlez-vous? Du chat?* What are you talking about? About the cat?
avoir peur de	*J'ai peur des araignées.* I am afraid of spiders.
risquer de	*Il risque de tomber.* He may fall.
venir de	*Je viens du supermarché.* I come from the supermarket.
avoir envie de	*J'ai envie d'un café.* I feel like having a coffee.
avoir besoin de	*J'ai besoin d'un crayon pour écrire.* I need a pencil to write.
s'intéresser à	*Je m'intéresse aux oiseaux.* I am interested in birds.

Set Expressions

Certain rules govern the use of some prepositions.

When Discussing Going to a Country:

Je passe mes vacances . . .

Use *en* for feminine, singular countries, and countries beginning with a vowel.

> *en France*
> *en Italie*
> *en Iran*

Use *au* (*à + le*) for masculine, singular countries.

> *au Canada*
> *au Brésil*

Use *aux* (*à + les*) for multi-state countries, whether feminine or masculine.

> *aux États-Unis*
> *aux Bermudes*

When Discussing Being in or Going to a Town or City:

> *Je reste . . .*
> *Je vais . . .*

Use *à*:

> *à Paris*
> *à New York*
> *à Londres*

| You always use the preposition *à* when referring to being in or going to a city. |

When Discussing Coming from a Country or Town:

> *Il est venu . . .*

Use *de* or *des* for feminine countries.

> *de Russie*
> *d'Allemagne*
> *des Bermudes*

Use *du* or *des* for masculine countries.

> *du Japon*
> *des États-Unis*

Use *de* for all towns.

> *de Paris*
> *de Lyon*

| When discussing being in or going to the mountains or many American states, use *dans* + the definite article:
• *dans les Alpes*
• *dans les Rocheuses*
• *dans le Vermont*
• *dans le Mississippi* |

List of Some Countries with Their Genders		
Feminine	**Masculine**	**Multi-State**
la Russie	*le Canada*	*les États-Unis (masc.)*
la France	*le Japon*	*les Pays-Bas (masc.)*
l'Italie	*le Brésil*	*les Bermudes (fem.)*
l'Autriche	*le Maroc*	*les Bahamas (fem.)*
l'Allemagne	*le Pérou*	*les Philippines (fem.)*
la Belgique	*le Viêt-Nam*	
la Grèce	*le Luxembourg*	
la Roumanie	*le Mexique*	
l'Espagne	*le Chili*	
l'Angleterre	*le Liban*	
l'Algérie	*le Sénégal*	

Use of *en* and *de* + Name of Materials

To describe the material an object is made of, use either ***de*** or ***en*** + the name of the material.

un sac en cuir	a leather purse
un pot de terre	an earthenware pot
un mur de pierre	a stone wall
un pantalon en velours côtelé	corduroy pants
un collier de diamants	a diamond necklace
un bracelet en argent	a silver bracelet
une maison en brique	a brick house
une chaise en bois	a wooden chair
un fil de fer	a wire

Adverbs

You will want to be able to recognize French adverbs and not get confused by their various forms.

In English, most adverbs are formed with an adjective + the suffix **–ly**.

In French, most adverbs are formed with the feminine form of the adjective and the suffix –***ment***.

active	→	*activement*
ponctuelle	→	*ponctuellement*
calme	→	*calmement*

When the adjectives end with *–i, –ai, –u,* and *–é,* the adverbs are formed with the masculine form of the adjective.

vrai	→	*vraiment*
assidu	→	*assidûment*
poli	→	*poliment*

When the adjectives end with *–ant* or *–ent,* the endings of the adverbs change to *–mment.*

prudent	→	*prudemment*
négligent	→	*négligemment*
savant	→	*savamment*

Also remember that some irregular adverbs are different from the adjectives:

bon	→	*bien*
rapide	→	*vite*
meilleur	→	*mieux*
mauvais	→	*mal*

Be aware of certain adverbs placed as attributive adjectives. They do not agree with the nouns, of course, but you might mistakenly think they need to be eliminated because of their position in the sentence. Take a look at a few examples:

*Il y a encore des places **debout** dans la salle de spectacle.*
*Les roues **avant** sont à changer.*

DRILL 3: PREPOSITION QUESTIONS

Answers can be found in Part IV.

1. Marie ------- les résultats de ses examens.

    (A) pense
    (B) attend
    (C) compte
    (D) a envie

2. Je ------- de leur écrire.

    (A) suis obligé
    (B) espère
    (C) veux
    (D) réfléchis

3. Je n'ai jamais eu l'occasion ------- voir ce film.

    (A) ---
    (B) à
    (C) de
    (D) sur

4. ------- le concert, elles bavardaient sans cesse.

(A) Pendant
(B) Dans
(C) Avec
(D) En

5. Je la vois souvent à -------.

(A) France
(B) ville
(C) la boulangerie
(D) loin

6. Elle n'a pas réfléchi ------- de refuser l'offre.

(A) ---
(B) avant
(C) après
(D) à

7. Nous pensons toujours ------- leurs parents.

(A) les
(B) de
(C) à
(D) aux

8. Ils viennent ------- l'aéroport.

(A) pendant
(B) de
(C) à
(D) après

9. Elle a assisté au concert ------- les objections de ses parents.

(A) sauf
(B) malgré
(C) selon
(D) pendant

10. Passez-vous vos vacances ------- Canada?

(A) au
(B) à
(C) en
(D) de

ODDS AND ENDS

At most, these topics will come up once or twice on the test.

Odds and ends are just that: small, picky questions that show up from time to time but don't appear on every test.

Adjective Versus Adverb

Adjectives modify nouns. Adverbs modify verbs, adjectives, and other adverbs. In French, adverbs often end in -*ment*.

> Elle a remplacé le vase -------.
>
> (A) doux
> (B) brusquement
> (C) difficile
> (D) ennuyeuse

Choices (A), (C), and (D) are all adjectives. Choice (B) is the right answer.

When modifying an adjective, use the adverbs *trop*, *plus*, *très*, *si*, or *moins*.

Mieux, like *pire*, cannot be used to modify an adjective.

> Ce cassoulet est ------- bon.
>
> (A) mieux
> (B) sans
> (C) si
> (D) pas

Bon is an adjective. The word in the blank must be an adverb. Only *si* is an adverb that can be used to modify an adjective. Choice (C) is the right answer.

Active Versus Passive

If you use *être* with the past participle of a verb that normally takes *avoir*, you are forming the passive tense of the verb.

Active (present)	Passive (present)
Le facteur distribue le courrier.	*Le courrier est distribué par le facteur.*
The postman delivers the mail.	The mail is delivered by the postman.

Possessive Adjectives

Possessive adjectives (not pronouns) show that a given noun belongs to a given person. But, unlike in English, French possessive adjectives agree with the gender and number of what is owned, not who owns it. The form of the adjective also changes depending on whether the noun begins with a vowel or a silent "h."

Son is the masculine singular and *sa* is the feminine singular. However, if a feminine noun begins with a vowel or a silent "h," the possessive adjective that goes with it will be *son*. *Sa* does not shorten to *s'*.

Elle avait de la soupe dans ------- assiette.

(A) son
(B) sa
(C) s'
(D) ses

Is *assiette* masculine or feminine? Singular or plural?

Assiette is feminine, but the word begins with a vowel; you can't say *sa assiette*, so eliminate (B). Possessive adjectives don't contract, so eliminate (C). *Assiette* is singular; cancel (D), which is plural. Choice (A) is the right answer.

Even though *amie* is feminine, you <u>can't</u> say *sa amie* or *s'amie*. When you have a feminine noun that begins with a vowel, it will take the masculine version of the possessive adjective—in this case, *son amie*. The College Board loves to ask this kind of question.

	Only one object		More than one object
	masculin	*féminin*	*masculin et féminin*
One owner	mon livre	ma cravate	mes sœurs
	ton frère	ta santé	tes vacances
	son amie	sa voiture	ses cheveux
	masculin et féminin		*masculin et féminin*
More than one owner	notre professeur		nos vœux
	votre chemise		vos souhaits
	leur voiture		leurs cahiers

SPECIAL POINTS FOR PART C

1. Is It Vocabulary or Grammar?

How can you tell? **A vocabulary question** will have **four words with clearly different meanings**. **A grammar question** will usually have **one word in four different forms** (for example, the same verb in four different tenses or with four different prepositions). When you see practice examples, the difference will be obvious.

2. Think of the Paragraph as a Whole

The paragraph is telling a story, so all sentences are connected. The key to this section is realizing that the correct answer can be based on both the sentence with the blank and on the sentences that precede it. You may even need to read past the blank sometimes in order to get a better understanding of what's going on. **Don't think of each sentence as a separate question.**

3. Special Grammar Points

Some grammatical points are tested more frequently in Part C than in Part B. All of the following points are thoroughly discussed earlier in this chapter.

Verb Sequence

The action described in the paragraph must unfold **in a logical sequence**. **Make sure all the verbs** that you choose as answers **match the tense of the story.** Pay special attention to the rules for use of the imperfect and the conditional.

Agreement of the Past Participle

As we discussed earlier in this chapter, a past participle will agree with the *subject* if the verb takes *être*. If the verb takes *avoir* and the direct object comes before the verb, it will agree with the *object* of the sentence. In some cases, whether the direct object is masculine or feminine is revealed in a previous sentence.

Comprehensive Drill

Answers can be found in Part IV.

Part B

Directions: Each of the following sentences contains a blank. From the four choices given, select the one that can be inserted in the blank to form a grammatically correct sentence. Choice (A) may consist of dashes that indicate that no insertion is required to form a grammatically correct sentence.

1. Marie a ------- à m'offrir.

    (A) quelque chose
    (B) rien
    (C) plusieurs
    (D) quelques

2. Claude ------- de faire les courses.

    (A) a rejeté
    (B) a aimé
    (C) est obligé
    (D) a voulu

3. C'est grâce à son ------- qu'il a réussi.

    (A) talents
    (B) amie
    (C) gentillesse
    (D) oncles

4. Je ferai la vaisselle -------.

    (A) avant de partir
    (B) à tout à l'heure
    (C) hier
    (D) jamais

5. C'est ------- qui a gagné!

    (A) personne
    (B) je
    (C) leur
    (D) elle

6. Nos voisins ------- aller à la piscine.

    (A) préfèrent
    (B) rêvent
    (C) plaisent
    (D) insistent

7. Je ------- demande s'il est temps de partir.

    (A) elle
    (B) moi
    (C) se
    (D) vous

8. Les dames sont arrivées avec -------.

    (A) leur
    (B) il
    (C) eux
    (D) les

9. La voiture verte est -------.

    (A) les leurs
    (B) la vôtre
    (C) à aucun
    (D) ma

10. L'année dernière j'ai voyagé en -------.

    (A) Russie
    (B) États-Unis
    (C) New York
    (D) Canada

11. La réussite de ce projet est -------.

   (A) certainement
   (B) peu
   (C) probable
   (D) malgré

12. ------- ce soit fini.

   (A) Nous savons que
   (B) Il regrette que
   (C) Elle a oublié que
   (D) C'est lui qui a décidé que

13. C'est le collègue ------- j'ai beaucoup parlé.

   (A) dont
   (B) de quoi
   (C) sauf qui
   (D) avant que

14. ------- est le metteur en scène de ce film?

   (A) Quelle
   (B) Qu'est-ce qui
   (C) Où
   (D) Quoi

15. ------- avez-vous envie?

   (A) Quel
   (B) Y
   (C) Dont
   (D) De quoi

16. Le gouvernement ------- de négocier un accord.

   (A) va
   (B) espère
   (C) essaie
   (D) peut

17. ------- qu'il sache les nouvelles d'hier.

   (A) Sans doute
   (B) Je sais
   (C) Je crains
   (D) C'est à cause de Michel

18. Jean a réussi à trouver du travail ------- la grève.

   (A) afin de
   (B) lorsque
   (C) en dépit de
   (D) à moins de

19. -------, nous partirions.

   (A) Si elle en avait envie
   (B) Si tu peux
   (C) S'ils voudront
   (D) Si vous l'aviez permis

20. C'est le gâteau le plus délicieux -------.

   (A) que vous avez jamais mangé
   (B) qu'elle a jamais acheté
   (C) que nous avons jamais fait
   (D) que tu puisses jamais imaginer

Part C

Directions: The paragraphs below contain blank spaces indicating omissions in the text. For some blanks it is necessary to choose the completion that is most appropriate to the meaning of the passage; for other blanks, to choose the one completion that forms a grammatically correct sentence. In some instances, choice (A) may consist of dashes that indicate that no insertion is required to form a grammatically correct sentence. In each case, indicate your answer by filling in the corresponding circle on the answer sheet. Be sure to read each paragraph completely before answering the questions related to it.

Si j'avais su, ___(21)___ aller avec Marie et Christine. Trop tard, j'ai essayé de ___(22)___ téléphoner chez ___(23)___ mais ___(24)___ n'était là. ___(25)___ , j'ai tenté de les retrouver au café. Quand ___(26)___ suis arrivé, je les ai ___(27)___ entrer ___(28)___ cinéma.

21. (A) je pouvais
    (B) j'avais pu
    (C) je peux
    (D) j'aurais pu

22. (A) elles
    (B) leur
    (C) eux
    (D) la

23. (A) elles
    (B) tu
    (C) leur
    (D) ils

24. (A) personne
    (B) une personne
    (C) rien
    (D) nulle

25. (A) Finalement
    (B) Terminé
    (C) Maintenant
    (D) Afin de

26. (A) j'en
    (B) j'y
    (C) je le
    (D) je me

27. (A) vu
    (B) vue
    (C) vus
    (D) vues

28. (A) à la
    (B) au
    (C) par la
    (D) par le

Avant __(29)__ partir en vacances, Jean et Camille ont __(30)__ à l'aéroport __(31)__ demander __(32)__ l'avion partait __(33)__.

29. (A) ---
    (B) à
    (C) de
    (D) que

30. (A) téléphoné
    (B) téléphonée
    (C) téléphonés
    (D) téléphonées

31. (A) ---
    (B) à
    (C) de
    (D) pour

32. (A) si
    (B) quand
    (C) quel
    (D) qui

33. (A) en temps
    (B) chaque heure
    (C) à l'heure
    (D) de temps en temps

Summary

Questions in Parts B and C of the SAT Subject Test in French evaluate your ability to choose correct words or expressions based on your understanding of French grammar. Here are the main grammar points you should review before the test:

- **Pronouns**
  Check which pronoun should be used in the sentence. Is it subject, direct object, reflexive, indirect object, or stressed? How about demonstrative, interrogative, relative, indefinite, or even another type of pronoun?
  - Check its gender and number if needed (masculine, feminine, plural).
  - Check whether it is also replacing a preposition.
  - Check where it is placed in the sentence relative to the verb.

- **Verbs**
  Can you figure out the tense or mode, the use of the auxiliary verb, the agreement with the past participle, the tense sequence, or the specific use of certain verbs?
  - Check the subject of the sentence.
  - Check the tense sequence by looking at the meaning of the main clause.
  - Check whether the verb takes *être* or *avoir* in compound past tense.
  - Look at prepositions and conjunctions to help you decide what verb form or mode you should use.

- **Prepositions**
  Can you specify which one to use with which verb? What is the meaning when the preposition is combined with certain verbs and other words? How could it be replaced by a pronoun in a sentence?
  - Check whether the verb takes *de* or *à*.
  - Check whether the general meaning of the sentence indicates a place, a time, a cause, or something else.
  - Check if the preposition is included in a pronoun form or if it should be transformed (*dont, auquel, duquel*, etc.).

- **Adverbs**
  Can you see the difference between adjectives and adverbs?
  - Check the word's position in the sentence.
  - Check the ending of the word and memorize the irregular adverb forms so you don't get tricked.

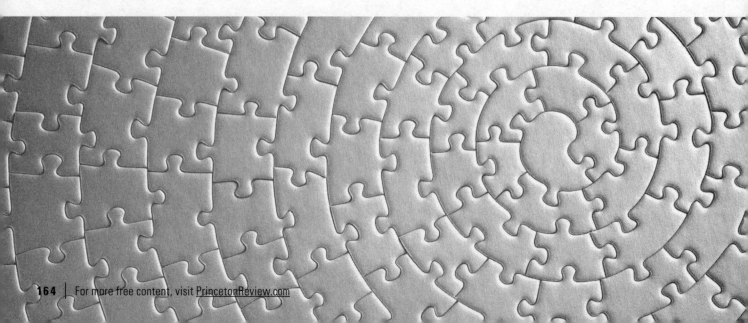

Chapter 6
Reading
Comprehension

For Reading Comprehension, Part D of the SAT Subject Test in French, you will have to read passages in French and answer critical questions. You will have anywhere from 4 to 6 literary or journalistic passages, each about 20 to 30 lines. In addition, you may see 1 to 3 ticket/schedule/advertisement-type texts; these may or may not be accompanied by pictures.

It is best to preview the questions first so you have a better sense of what to look for as you read the passages. The passages are generally quite short. Read them through at a moderate pace to get the general idea of what the passage is about. Do not become obsessed if you don't understand every word or sentence; however, keep an eye out for trap answers.

Get acquainted with the format of the test. Follow the suggestions we give you and then try the practice section at the end of this chapter.

PART D: READING COMPREHENSION

Pace Yourself

Do not be anxious about this section. There is no clear order of difficulty, so just go to the next question if you find something too difficult and then go back if you have time. Hard questions and easy questions give you the same number of points for each correct answer, so get points where you can without wasting too much time on hard questions. The short passages are not necessarily easier than the long ones, so make sure you choose wisely.

> The questions on reading comprehension go in order of the text. The early questions relate to information early in the passage. Later questions refer to information that appears later in the passage.

The Questions Are in Order

Reading the questions first will give you an idea of what you are about to read and what to look for. Use the fact that the questions are in roughly chronological order to help you find the answers in the passage.

Go Back

Once you have an idea of what the answer is, go back to the passage and make sure you are not falling for a trap answer. Reread the entire sentence or group of sentences that relate to the question to make sure you have evidence for your answer. A best practice is to underline the evidence you find in the passage. This will ensure you fall for fewer trap answers.

The Answer Is in There

Remember that reading comprehension multiple-choice questions are always asking you about the specifics of the text, not your opinions or interpretations. The correct answer is ALWAYS supported by evidence in the text.

Use Process of Elimination: POE

Common Sense

You can eliminate answers that don't make sense in the context of the passage.

Familiar Words—Wrong Context

Sometimes the words in an answer choice will be strongly reminiscent of the words used in the passage. If a word or phrase is directly lifted from the passage, be careful—you may be falling into a trap.

Misleading Look-Alikes

Sometimes, instead of repeating words verbatim, the College Board will take a word and twist it subtly. For example, if the word *errer* appears, they might have a trap answer choice containing the word *erreur*.

What Is This Weird Tense?

In formal French, literary writing uses a tense called the *passé simple* (or past historic) instead of the *passé composé*. You don't need to know how to conjugate it or when to use it. You simply need to recognize which verb is being used.

Infinitive	Present	Past Participle	Passé Simple
donner	*il donne*	*donné*	*il donna*
croire	*il croit*	*cru*	*il crut*
mettre	*il met*	*mis*	*il mit*
faire	*il fait*	*fait*	*il fit*
venir	*il vient*	*venu*	*il vint*
être	*il est*	*été*	*il fut*
avoir	*il a*	*eu*	*il eut*

You will usually recognize the verb in the *passé simple* since it is usually (except in the case of irregular verbs) formed by taking off the last two letters of the infinitive and adding the appropriate endings.

Try the following passage, looking for the types of trap answers mentioned above.

> You should be able to recognize the *passé simple* forms of some commonly used French verbs, such as *aller, avoir, dire, être, faire, lire, mettre, pouvoir, prendre, savoir, venir,* and *vouloir*.

Part D

Directions: Read the following selections carefully for comprehension. Each selection is followed by a number of questions or incomplete statements. Select the completion or answer that is BEST according to the selection and fill in the corresponding circle on the answer sheet.

La cité elle-même, on doit l'avouer, est laide. D'aspect
Ligne tranquille, il faut quelque temps pour apercevoir ce qui la
rend différente de tant d'autres villes commerçantes, sous
toutes les latitudes. Comment faire imaginer, par exemple,
5 une ville sans pigeons, sans arbres et sans jardins, où l'on
ne rencontre ni battements d'ailes ni froissements de feuilles,
un lieu neutre pour tout dire? Le changement des saisons ne
s'y lit que dans le ciel. Le printemps s'annonce seulement
par la qualité de l'air ou par les corbeilles de fleurs que des
10 petits vendeurs ramènent des banlieues; c'est un printemps
qu'on vend sur les marchés. Pendant l'été, le soleil incendie
les maisons trop sèches et couvre les murs d'une cendre grise;
on ne peut plus vivre alors que dans l'ombre des volets clos.
En automne, c'est, au contraire, un déluge de boue. Les beaux
15 jours viennent seulement en hiver.
(Camus, *La Peste*, Folio)

> The best way to get the right answer is to take the time to go back and carefully reread the sentence or sentences that relate to the question.

1. Ce passage nous décrit

   (A) une ville idéale
   (B) un marché en ville
   (C) le changement des saisons
   (D) les attributs principaux d'une cité

2. Qu'est-ce qui rend la cité différente des autres villes?

   (A) la présence des pigeons
   (B) la latitude
   (C) le manque de verdure et d'oiseaux
   (D) la couleur du ciel

3. Aux lignes 10–11, "c'est un printemps qu'on vend sur les marchés" veut dire

   (A) qu'on peut tout acheter au marché
   (B) qu'on sait que le printemps est arrivé quand on peut acheter des fleurs
   (C) qu'on voit mieux le printemps dans les banlieues
   (D) que le printemps est comme un marché

4. Comment réagissent les habitants de la ville à l'arrivée de l'été?

   (A) Ils font des feux.
   (B) Ils se plaignent.
   (C) Ils restent à l'intérieur.
   (D) Ils deviennent des voleurs.

> Don't be afraid to eliminate answer choices that don't make sense.

Here's How to Crack It

1. Ce passage nous décrit

   (A) une ville idéale
   (B) un marché en ville
   (C) le changement des saisons
   (D) les attributs principaux d'une cité

You are asked to choose what the passage describes:

(A) "an ideal town" is a misunderstanding of the first sentence. The first sentence tells us that the city is ugly, and the passage goes on to list primarily negative qualities. Eliminate this choice.

(B) "a marketplace in town" is an example of familiar words / wrong context. The word *marché* appears, as does the word *vendeurs*; however, the passage as a whole is not about the market. This choice is too specific. Eliminate it.

(C) "the changing of the seasons" is another example of familiar words—wrong context. The change of seasons is discussed, but again, it is too specific for this question.

(D) "the principal attributes of a town" is the correct answer. The passage discusses several distinctive features of a city.

2. Qu'est-ce qui rend la cité différente des autres villes?

    (A) la présence des pigeons
    (B) la latitude
    (C) le manque de verdure et d'oiseaux
    (D) la couleur du ciel

You are asked to choose what makes the city different from other cities. The answer is in the section that starts with the second sentence of the passage.

(A) "the presence of pigeons" is an example of familiar words—wrong context. Pigeons are mentioned, but what is significant is their absence.

(B) "the latitude" is another example of familiar words—wrong context. The word "latitude" appears in the second sentence, but it is used to describe the location of other cities, in any latitude.

(C) "the lack of greenery and birds" is the correct answer. Notice that it paraphrases part of the third sentence: *sans pigeons, sans arbres et sans jardins.*

(D) "the color of the sky" takes the word *ciel* out of context. It is a misunderstanding of the sentence: *Le changement des saisons ne s'y lit que dans le ciel.*

> Watch out for answers that use familiar words from the passage out of context.

3. Aux lignes 10–11, "c'est un printemps qu'on vend sur les marchés" veut dire

    (A) qu'on peut tout acheter au marché
    (B) qu'on sait que le printemps est arrivé quand on peut acheter des fleurs
    (C) qu'on voit mieux le printemps dans les banlieues
    (D) que le printemps est comme un marché

You are asked to interpret the sentence "it is a spring that is sold in the marketplace" within the context of the passage.

(A) "that one can buy everything at the market" is too literal and does not relate to the passage.

(B) "that one knows spring has arrived when one can buy flowers" is the correct answer. It corroborates the meaning, connecting it to the previous sentence about how few signs there are of the change of seasons.

(C) "that it is easier to see the spring in the suburbs" takes the word *banlieues* out of context.

(D) "that spring is like a marketplace" is a literal interpretation.

4. Comment réagissent les habitants de la ville à l'arrivée de l'été?

    (A) Ils font des feux.
    (B) Ils se plaignent.
    (C) Ils restent à l'intérieur.
    (D) Ils deviennent des voleurs.

"How do the inhabitants of the town react to the arrival of summer?" This topic is discussed in the third-to-last sentence of the passage.

(A) "They make fires" misinterprets the phrase *"le soleil incendie les maisons."*

(B) "They complain" comes out of the blue. Complaining is not discussed anywhere in the passage.

(C) "They stay indoors" is the correct answer. This is what the sentence *"on ne peut plus vivre alors que dans l'ombre des volets clos,"* implies—"then one can only live in the shade of closed shutters."

(D) "They become thieves" is an example of a misleading look-alike. Here the word *volets* (shutters) has been twisted into the word *voleurs*.

TICKETS/SCHEDULES/ADVERTISEMENTS

These graphical passages can be a blessing because you have less to read and because common sense works so well. Pay special attention to the small print.

- Read through the schedule or advertisement.
- Get a sense of the layout. Read all sizes of print.
- Use your common sense.
- Eliminate misleading look-alike words.

> **The Small Print**
> On ticket/schedule/advertisement-type questions, pay special attention to the small print and the titles!

les jeunes aiment l'argent

Ils aiment l'argent signé Ravinet d'Enfert
Ravinet d'Enfert a créé, en métal argenté, une collection contemporaine de qualité.
Héritier d'une longue tradition, éditeur d'une collection classique très réputée,
Ravinet d'Enfert propose des créations de notre temps comme
les services "Président" et "Brantôme." Ravinet d'Enfert les présente
avec des couverts, des plats, des luminaires et des accessoires de table
dans son catalogue "lignes actuelles."
Demandez-le dans les magasins ou à l'aide du bon à découper qui
se trouve à droite.

RAVINET D'ENFERT
83, RUE DU TEMPLE—PARIS—3e

Veuillez
m'adresser
gratuitement
vos catalogues
○ tradition
○ lignes actuelles

Nom _____
Prénom _____
Adresse _____

1. Selon la publicité, les services "Président" et "Brantôme"

   (A) sont d'une collection classique
   (B) coûtent beaucoup d'argent
   (C) sont très réputés
   (D) sont d'un style contemporain

2. Le bon à découper vous offre

   (A) des produits gratuits
   (B) un choix de catalogues
   (C) des adresses
   (D) une description de nouvelles lignes

SAT Subject Test French Prep

Here's How to Crack It

1. Selon la publicité, les services "Président" et "Brantôme"

   (A) sont d'une collection classique
   (B) coûtent beaucoup d'argent
   (C) sont très réputés
   (D) sont d'un style contemporain

"According to the advertisement, the '*Président*' and '*Brantôme*' collections . . . "

(A) "are from a classic collection" takes a phrase out of context. The company produces a traditional line, but these styles, in contrast, are modern.

(B) "cost a lot of money" is also out of context. *Argent* is used here to mean "silver," not "money." This answer could be true, but there is no evidence of it in the ad.

(C) "have a good reputation" is also out of context. Again, the company is renowned, but we don't know about these specific lines.

(D) "are of a contemporary design" is the correct answer. Notice that it paraphrases the actual description *des créations de notre temps.*

2. Le bon à découper vous offre

   (A) des produits gratuits
   (B) un choix de catalogues
   (C) des adresses
   (D) une description de nouvelles lignes

"The coupon offers you . . . "

Le bon à découper vous offre refers to the coupon in the corner.

(A) "free products" is a familiar word, but it's in the wrong context. The catalog is free; the products are not.

(B) "a choice of catalogs" is the correct answer. The two boxes name two types of catalogs.

(C) "addresses" is a familiar word—wrong context. *Adresser* is part of a request to the company to send or address a catalog to the reader.

(D) "a description of new lines" is not terrible, but is not as good as (B). The coupon itself is not providing an actual description of the contemporary lines.

6. Reading Comprehension | 173

Comprehensive Drill

Answers can be found in Part IV.

Part D

Directions: Read the following selections carefully for comprehension. Each selection is followed by a number of questions or incomplete statements. Select the completion or answer that is best according to the text and fill in the corresponding circle on the answer sheet.

Chez Rasseneur, après avoir mangé une soupe, Etienne, remonté dans l'étroite chambre qu'il allait occuper sous le toit, en face du Voreux, était tombé sur son lit, tout vêtu, assommé de fatigue. En deux jours, il n'avait pas dormi *Ligne* quatre heures. Quand il s'éveilla, au crépuscule, il resta
5 étourdi un instant, sans reconnaître le lieu où il se trouvait; et il éprouvait un tel malaise, une telle pesanteur de tête, qu'il se mit péniblement debout, avec l'idée de prendre l'air, avant de dîner et de se coucher pour la nuit.
(Zola, *Germinal*, Garnier)

1. Etienne n'avait pas l'énergie de

   (A) dormir
   (B) se déshabiller
   (C) manger
   (D) mettre ses habits

2. Selon le passage, pour quelle raison Etienne est-il fatigué?

   (A) Il a trop mangé.
   (B) Il n'a pas dormi du tout depuis deux jours.
   (C) Il s'est couché à quatre heures du matin.
   (D) Il n'a dormi que quelques heures en 48 heures.

3. A quel moment de la journée s'est-il réveillé?

   (A) tôt le matin
   (B) à midi
   (C) tôt le soir
   (D) à minuit

4. Comment réagit-il au moment de se réveiller?

   (A) Il ne se souvient pas où il est.
   (B) Il ne trouve pas ses habits.
   (C) Il se sent en retard.
   (D) Il a faim.

5. Que voulait-il faire avant de dîner?

   (A) respirer
   (B) se promener
   (C) s'éveiller
   (D) courir

Chaque dimanche, avant la guerre, Morissot partait dès l'aurore, une canne en bambou d'une main, une boîte en fer-blanc sur le dos. Il prenait le chemin de fer d'Argenteuil, descendait à Colombes, puis gagnait à pied *Ligne* l'île Marante. A peine arrivé en ce lieu de ses rêves, il se
5 mettait à pêcher; il pêchait jusqu'à la nuit.

Chaque dimanche, il rencontrait là un petit homme replet et jovial, M. Sauvage, mercier, rue Notre-Dame-de-Lorette, un autre pêcheur fanatique. Ils passaient souvent
10 une demi-journée à côté, la ligne à la main et les pieds ballants au-dessus du courant; et ils s'étaient pris d'amitié l'un pour l'autre.

(Guy de Maupassant, *Deux Amis*, Le Livre de Poche)

6. Quand Morissot partait-il pour l'île?

   (A) après le coucher du soleil
   (B) au moment du coucher du soleil
   (C) au moment du lever du soleil
   (D) l'après-midi

7. Comment gagnait-il l'île?

   (A) en autobus et à pied
   (B) en bateau
   (C) en voiture et à pied
   (D) en train et à pied

8. A quel moment commençait-il à pêcher?

   (A) pratiquement au moment où il arrivait
   (B) au moment où il commençait à rêver
   (C) à la tombée de la nuit
   (D) quand son ami arrivait

9. Qu'est-ce qui se trouvait dans la rue Notre-Dame-de-Lorette?

   (A) l'île Marante
   (B) l'endroit où les deux amis se rencontraient
   (C) le magasin de M. Sauvage
   (D) la gare

Claire.—Tes parents t'interdisent-ils d'aller voir un film?

Ligne **Guillaume**.—Non, puisque je leur demande ce qu'ils en pensent. Quelquefois, ils me disent: "Il vaut mieux que
5 tu ailles voir un autre film."

Claire.—Moi, mes parents pensent qu'à mon âge, le cinéma n'est pas très bon, de toute façon.

Gilles.—Tu n'y vas jamais, alors?

Claire.—Si, mais en cachette.

10 **Guillaume**.—Ça alors, moi je ne le ferai jamais . . . Je ne peux pas mentir à mes parents. Je crois que je me sens libre parce que mes parents pensent que c'est un peu à moi de choisir, mais pas n'importe quoi.

(*Pour ou contre*, Hachette)

10. Les parents de Guillaume

    (A) lui conseillent de ne jamais aller au cinéma

    (B) ne sont pas concernés par ce qu'il fait

    (C) n'aiment pas le cinéma

    (D) lui donnent leur avis sur les films qu'il choisit

11. A la question de Gilles, Claire répond

    (A) qu'elle ne va jamais au cinéma

    (B) qu'elle va au cinéma si ses parents sont d'accord

    (C) qu'elle va au cinéma sans le dire à ses parents

    (D) qu'elle va souvent au cinéma

12. Quelle raison Guillaume donne-t-il pour ne pas mentir à ses parents?

    (A) Ses parents le laissent faire n'importe quoi.

    (B) Ses parents lui donnent la responsabilité de décider que faire.

    (C) Il vaut mieux ne pas le faire.

    (D) Ses parents n'aiment pas le cinéma.

Attention! Dans le 5e, le boulevard Saint-Michel et la place Saint-André-des-Arts ne sont plus fréquentables! *Ligne* Les petits bars sympathiques et les restaurants à petits prix ont disparu au profit d'établissements prétentieux où
5 un personnel pressé sert des bières à la chaîne. On débite des sandwiches sous cellophane, des frites et, signe des temps, McDonald et Wimpy se font face, à deux pas du Luxembourg. Cinémas et librairies semblent résister, pour l'instant, à cette invasion "made in U.S." Les jeunes se
10 pressent chez "Gibert" et dans les salles d'art et d'essai où passent les vieux films d'hier et ceux d'avant-garde. Pour se rencontrer, les jeunes préfèrent les petites rues plus anonymes, les petits restaurants à six ou sept tables, les bars sans faux clinquant que l'on trouve autour du
15 Panthéon.
(*Paris*, Hachette)

13. L'auteur réagit au changement sur le boulevard Saint-Michel et sur la place Saint-André-des-Arts avec

    (A) impatience
    (B) regret
    (C) indifférence
    (D) plaisir

14. Qu'est-ce qu'on trouve près du Luxembourg?

    (A) des petits restaurants anonymes
    (B) des cafés sympathiques
    (C) des librairies prétentieuses
    (D) des établissements américains

15. D'après le passage, on comprend que "Gibert" est

    (A) un film
    (B) un café
    (C) une librairie
    (D) un musée

16. Que font les jeunes au lieu d'aller au boulevard Saint-Michel?

    (A) Ils fréquentent la place Saint-André-des-Arts.
    (B) Ils sont pressés d'aller voir des films américains.
    (C) Ils cherchent des bars sympathiques dans un autre endroit.
    (D) Ils résistent à l'envie d'aller dans les librairies.

Je n'ai rien à cacher. J'étais orpheline et pauvre, j'élevais mon frère cadet. Un vieil ami de mon père m'a demandé
Ligne ma main. Il était riche et bon, j'ai accepté. Qu'auriez-vous fait à ma place? Mon frère était malade et sa santé
5 réclamait les plus grands soins. J'ai vécu six ans avec mon mari sans un nuage. Il y a deux ans, j'ai rencontré celui que je devais aimer. Nous nous sommes reconnus tout de suite, il voulait que je parte avec lui et j'ai refusé. (Sartre, *Huis-clos*, Folio)

17. La narratrice donne à entendre qu'elle

   (A) travaillait beaucoup
   (B) était invalide
   (C) avait beaucoup de soucis
   (D) s'était mariée avec l'ami de son père

18. Le frère de la narratrice

   (A) a vécu avec elle pendant six ans
   (B) était plus jeune qu'elle
   (C) était soldat
   (D) n'aimait pas son mari

19. Le passage nous donne l'impression

   (A) qu'elle voulait défendre ses actions
   (B) que son mari lui manquait
   (C) que son frère était guéri
   (D) qu'elle aimait le beau temps

20. Après six ans, qu'est-ce qui s'est passé?

   (A) Le mari de la narratrice est parti.
   (B) Le beau temps a changé.
   (C) La narratrice a décidé de partir.
   (D) La narratrice a trouvé un amant.

Antoine Lemurier, qui avait manqué mourir, sortit heureusement de maladie, reprit son service au bureau, et, tant bien que mal, pansa ses plaies d'argent. Durant cette épreuve, les voisins s'étaient réjouis en pensant que le mari allait crever, le mobilier être vendu, la femme à la rue. Tous étaient d'ailleurs d'excellentes gens, des cœurs d'or, comme tout le monde, et n'en voulaient nullement au ménage Lemurier, mais voyant se jouer auprès d'eux une sombre tragédie avec rebonds, péripéties, beuglements de proprio, huissier et fièvre montante, ils vivaient anxieusement dans l'attente d'un dénouement qui fût digne de la pièce.
(Marcel Aymé, *Les Sabines*, Folio)

Ligne markers: Ligne (left margin), 5, 10

21. On comprend qu'Antoine Lemurier

    (A) est mort
    (B) a raté le train
    (C) a quitté son bureau
    (D) a failli succomber à une maladie

22. Qu'est-ce que les voisins pensaient de la maladie de Lemurier?

    (A) Ils attendaient une fin intéressante à la tragédie.
    (B) Ils étaient tristes.
    (C) Ils étaient fâchés contre Lemurier.
    (D) Ils tombaient malades.

23. Selon les voisins, qu'est-ce qui serait "un dénouement . . . digne" de la situation?

    (A) M. Lemurier perd son travail.
    (B) M. Lemurier récupère complètement.
    (C) Mme Lemurier est sans abri.
    (D) Mme Lemurier vend la maison.

Summary

For Part D, Reading Comprehension, practice is the best way to improve your score. Make sure you do the following:

- o   Memorize the instructions to save time on test day.

- o   Read the questions first so you know what to look for in the passage.

- o   Read and eliminate wrong answer choices.

- o   Do not get stuck on difficult passages or questions. Move on and come back later if you have the time.

Chapter 7
French Listening

The SAT Subject Test in French with Listening evaluates your reading and listening skills of spoken French. It is an hour long: 20 minutes for listening and 40 minutes for reading questions.

The test is only administered once a year at designated test centers. You will need to fill out a special registration form and find the testing center nearest to you. **On test day, you must take an appropriate CD player with earphones.**

In this chapter, we explore the overall structure and describe each part of the listening test.

OVERALL STRUCTURE OF THE LISTENING TEST

The SAT Subject Test in French with Listening consists of **40 minutes of reading (written questions)** and **20 minutes of listening (oral questions)**, with 85 to 90 questions in all. This means that about two-thirds of the French with Listening Subject Test consists of question types we've already discussed. You will have 40 minutes to work on those. There are, however, fewer of each type.

- Part A—Vocabulary Completions: 12–16 questions
- Part B—Grammar Blanks: 12–16 questions
- Part C—Paragraph Blanks: 15–17 questions
- Part D—Reading Comprehension: 20–25 questions

In addition to those regular questions, you will have 20 minutes to work on the listening part of the test. There will be three parts with a total of about 40 questions covering pictures (8–12 questions), short dialogues (6–12 questions), and long dialogues (10–15 questions).

- Listening—Part A: Pictures
- Listening—Part B: Short Dialogues
- Listening—Part C: Longer Dialogues

Samples of each type of question are available on the College Board's website, www.collegeboard.org.

Should You Sign Up for the French Subject Test with Listening?

The results of your test will give colleges a more complete picture of your French language proficiency. Your aim should be to give them the best picture of your abilities for the purpose of class placement.

You do not have to speak French on either of the SAT Subject Tests in French. Therefore, do not feel anxious about the listening portion of the test. Many students tend to do better on this section than they do on the written portion. There are fewer grammar and reading questions, which will benefit students who are better at spoken French than at grammar or reading comprehension. To prepare for the listening test, you may want to visit www.laguinguette.com. You'll also find it helpful to watch and listen to French TV news and as many French movies as you can get your hands on.

> **Don't Forget!**
> Test your CD player before you enter the exam room to make sure it functions properly. Also, don't forget extra batteries!

If you decide to take the French Subject Test with Listening, you must provide your own portable CD player and headphones. This CD player must be portable and battery powered. CD players that plug in or that have a radio function are not permitted. **Any student who arrives at the test without an appropriate listening device will be asked to leave the test.** You will not be permitted to sit any portion of the French test, even though listening is only 20 minutes long.

LISTENING—PART A: PICTURES

The first part of the Listening Test consists of choosing which spoken phrase best matches the provided picture. Each sentence will be designated (A), (B), (C), or (D).

> **Directions:** For each item in this part, you will hear four sentences designated (A), (B), (C), and (D). They will not be printed in your test booklet. As you listen, look at the picture in your test booklet and select the choice that best reflects what you see in the picture or what someone in the picture might say. Then fill in the corresponding circle on the answer sheet. You will hear the choices only once. Now look at the following example.

Look at the picture before the answer choices are played. Get a general idea of what is going on.

Make a Decision as You Hear Each Choice

As each answer choice is read to you, decide if that choice is at all appropriate. If it is not, cross out that choice on your answer sheet. You may not be allowed to write in your book. If the choice is good or possible, make a small mark inside the bubble. Probably only one will make any sense. If not, guess. **Don't wait to hear all the choices before deciding about each of them.** Decide "yes" or "no" as you go, for you will hear each choice only one time, so you must think quickly. Erase all stray marks once you select an answer.

> Don't forget: if you're taking the Listening Test you MUST bring your own CD player and headphones or you will not be allowed into the testing room.

LISTENING—PART B: SHORT DIALOGUES

On this section you will hear either a dialogue between two people or a monologue. It will be followed by three answer choices labeled (A), (B), or (C). The answer choices will be played only once. Again, listen closely because nothing is repeated.

Directions: In this part of the test you will hear several short selections. A tone will announce each new selection. The selections will not be printed in your test booklet, and will be heard only <u>once</u>. At the end of each selection, you will be asked one or two questions about what was said, each followed by three possible answers, (A), (B), and (C). The answers are not printed in your test booklet. You will hear them only once. Select the **BEST** answer and fill in the corresponding circle on the answer sheet. Now listen to the following example, but do not mark the answer on your answer sheet.

Make a Decision as You Hear Each Choice

As you hear each answer choice, decide if it is appropriate or not. Eliminate it or keep it on your answer sheet. Once you've selected an answer, erase all stray marks. Do not mark (D) or (E) as choices.

LISTENING—PART C: LONG PASSAGES

This section consists of longer monologues or dialogues that will be heard only once. In this section, the questions and the four answer choices will be in the test booklet.

Hear Ye, Hear Ye
On Part C of the listening part of the test, answer the questions as you hear the information being presented. Don't wait to hear the whole thing!

Directions: You will now hear some extended dialogues or monologues. You will hear each only once. After each dialogue or monologue, you will be asked several questions about what you have just heard. These questions are also printed in your test booklet. Select the best answer to each question from among the four choices printed in your test booklet and fill in the corresponding circle on the answer sheet. There is no sample question for this part.

Forewarned, Forearmed

The great thing about this question type in Part C is that the questions and answer choices are printed in your booklet. As the instructions are being read (familiarize yourself with them now so that you don't waste time on test day) and before the passage is read, read the questions and their answers to get a sense of the topic.

As in Reading Comprehension, the questions are in chronological order. Don't wait for the entire passage to be read before answering the questions. (It would be hard for even a native speaker to remember all those details for very long.) As the passage is being read, look at each question and mark the correct answer as soon as you hear it. The questions will either ask you to repeat specific details or paraphrase them. You are not required to interpret or infer.

Summary

Practice is the number one way to improve your score on the SAT French Listening Test. In order to get your best score, make sure you do the following:

- o Memorize the instructions to save time on test day.

- o **Bring the required CD player and fresh batteries.**

- o Go to the test rested and well fed.

- o Follow the pace of the recording.

- o Make your decision as you hear the choices because you might not remember them if you wait.

- o If there is a picture, look at all the details.

- o On the Long Passages section, do not wait for the entire passage to be read. Answer as soon as you figure out the right choice.

Don't forget! After the November 2020 exam date, the French with Listening Subject Test will only be offered in May (starting with May 2021).

Part IV
Drill Answers and Explanations

CHAPTER 3 DRILL ANSWERS AND EXPLANATIONS

Drill 1

une usine	a factory
la honte	the shame
l'œuvre	the work
en vouloir à	to be angry at, to have a grudge against
mou	soft, limp, looseness
taquiner	to tease
la foule	the crowd
ramasser	to gather, to pick up
soutenir	to support, to sustain
repasser	to come back, to cross again, to iron
se méfier de	to distrust, to be suspicious
se débarrasser de	to get rid of

Drill 2

évaluer	to evaluate
sacré	sacred
retarder	to delay, to slow down
fréquenter	to go somewhere frequently, to see someone on a regular basis
nombre	number
assurer	to assure
raison	reason
plante	plant
attraper	to catch, to trap
servir	to serve
content	content or happy
accord	accord or harmony
cru	crude or raw

Drill 3

Question	Answer	Explanation
1. xxxxx xxxxxxxx *légumes* xxxx xxxxx . . . vegetables	B	(A) *cheminée* chimney **(B) *jardin*** **garden** (C) *gazon* lawn (D) *quartier* quarter or neighborhood
2. xxxx xxxxxxx x *tombée* xxx xxxx . . . fallen	C	(A) *envolée* taken flight (B) *échappée* escaped **(C) *cassée*** **broken** (D) *attrapée* caught
3. xx x xxx xxxxx *chaises* xxxx . . . xxxx xx xxxxx. chairs	B	(A) *assommer* to knock out **(B) *s'asseoir*** **to sit down** (C) *assurer* to assure (D) *associer* to associate
4. xxx xxxx *ne se sent pas bien* xxxxx xxx . . . doesn't feel well	A	**(A) *une fièvre*** **a fever** (B) *une armoire* a wardrobe (C) *un verger* an orchard (D) *une annonce* an announcement

Question	Answer	Explanation

5. xxxxx xxxx xxxxxxxxx xxxxx *mangé* xxx xxx . . . eaten	C	(A) *soutenir*
		    to support
		(B) *emporter*
		    to take or carry away
		(C) *avaler*
		    to swallow
		(D) *évaluer*
		    to evaluate

Comprehensive Drill

Part A

Question		Answer	Key Word or Phrase	Fill In
1	It's cold outside. Are all the . . . closed?	C	*fait froid*	windows
2	Don't make any noise; the children are . . .	B	*bruit, enfants*	asleep
3	Are these flowers from your . . . ?	C	*fleurs*	garden
4	This coat lacks . . . where I can put my wallet.	C	*manteau, porte-monnaie*	pockets
5	Jeanne woke up . . . in order to see the sunrise.	D	*lever du soleil*	early
6	The train left the . . . at noon.	D	*train*	station
7	For Sunday's meal, we eat a . . . with potatoes.	A	*repas*	a roast
8	The tarts that are sold in this . . . are delicious.	A	*tartes*	pastry shop
9	You can wash yourself now. The bathroom is . . .	B	*salle de bains*	open, empty
10	My . . . for class is to translate a poem of Rimbaud's.	D	*classe*	homework, assignment
11	The noise in a club can be so loud that it hurts one's . . .	A	*bruit*	ears
12	The moon is so . . . that I cannot imagine that man has gone there.	C	*lune*	far away

Question		Answer	Key Word or Phrase	Fill In
13	It's not necessary to take out the garbage; Jean did it . . .	C	*l'a . . . fait*	already
14	We are spending Christmas with my grandparents this . . .	C	*Noël*	winter
15	You've already done your homework? That . . .	D	*déjà*	surprises me, pleases me
16	Aren't you . . . of doing that stupid thing?	D	*bêtise*	ashamed, embarrassed
17	This fabric is . . . like the skin of a baby.	C	*peau d'un bébé*	soft
18	The fox . . . the hunters.	C	*renard, chasseurs*	escaped from
19	The film starts at exactly 8 o'clock; be . . .	A	*commence*	on time, early
20	There are too many people here; I prefer cafés that are less . . .	D	*trop de monde*	crowded
21	There is not enough evidence . . . this man.	D	*pas assez de preuves*	to convict, charge, indict
22	My brother is . . . ; he never wants to help me clean the kitchen.	B	*il ne veut jamais m'aider*	lazy, selfish
23	The vase that I dropped . . .	D	*laissé tomber*	broke, shattered
24	You can find your grandmother's wedding dress if you look in . . .	B	*la robe de mariée de votre grand-mère*	the attic
25	She got rid of her . . . clothing.	C	*s'est débarrassée*	unwanted, messed up
26	Diane cut her . . . so she would be more fashionable.	C	*s'est coupé*	hair
27	To establish the validity of his theory, the scientist conducted . . .	B	*établir la validité*	an experiment, study

CHAPTER 5 DRILL ANSWERS AND EXPLANATIONS

Drill 1: Pronoun Questions

Question		Answer	Explanation
1	------- *est arrivé à Paul hier?* What happened to Paul yesterday?	D	(A) *Quel* *Quel* means "which" and is used to modify a noun (*Quelle voiture est la vôtre?*). We need something that means "what." (B) *Quoi* In questions, *quoi* is used only with a preposition (*À quoi sert cet exercice?*). (C) *Qu'* *Qu'* is a shortened form of *que*. Since the "what" of the question is the subject (what happened), it cannot be *que*. **(D) *Qu'est-ce qui* is correct. You cannot use *qui* alone because that would mean "who happened to Paul yesterday?" And you need *qui* here because it is directly followed by a verb.**
2	*C'est* -------. It is he.	C	With *c'est* or *ce sont* you use either a noun or a stressed pronoun. (A) *eux* *Eux* is a stressed pronoun, which is proper, but since it is plural, the correct sentence would be *Ce sont eux*. (B) *il* *Il* is a subject pronoun. No good here. **(C) *lui*** ***Lui* can be a singular stressed pronoun. This is the correct answer.** (D) *le* *Le* is a direct object pronoun. Cancel it.

Question		Answer	Explanation
3	*C'est grâce à ------- que nous avons pu venir.* It is thanks to them that we could come.	A	Because the pronoun is being used with a preposition (but not as an indirect object), we want a stressed pronoun. **(A) *eux*** ***Eux* is a stressed pronoun, so this is the correct choice.** (B) *les* *Les* is the direct object pronoun. (C) *leur* *Leur* is the indirect object pronoun. (D) *ils* *Ils* is the subject pronoun.
4	*La chose la plus difficile est de ------- réveiller le matin.* The most difficult thing is to wake him up in the morning.	C	The verb in this sentence is *réveiller*, a verb that takes a direct object. The correct answer must serve as a direct object pronoun. (A) *lui* *Lui* can be an indirect object pronoun or a stressed pronoun. (B) *il* *Il* is the subject pronoun. **(C) *le*** ***Le* is the direct object pronoun, so this is the correct answer.** (D) *moi* *Moi* is the stressed pronoun.
5	*------- a sorti la poubelle.* No one took out the garbage.	B	(A) *Il n'* This choice does not work because the sentence lacks the *pas* that must be used with *ne* (*n'*) to make a negative. **(B) *Personne n'*** **This is the correct answer. *Personne* must be used with *ne* and does not need the *pas*.** (C) *Aucun* Like *personne*, *aucun* must be used with *ne*. (D) *Qui* *Qui* can begin the sentence in a question, but not in a statement.

Question		Answer	Explanation
6	*Le livre ------- je suis l'auteur est une histoire d'Amérique pendant le 19ème siècle.* The book of which I am the author is a history of America during the 19th century.	B	(A) *lequel* Is an interrogative pronoun meaning "which one" **(B) *dont*** **Use *dont* if the verb takes an object introduced by *de* or *d'*.** (C) *que* Is never used when the object takes a preposition (D) *qui* Is used when there is no subject—*qui* replaces the subject.
7	*La femme ------- Isabelle est assise est le chef de la compagnie.* The woman next to whom Isabelle is sitting is the head of the company.	A	**(A) *à côté de laquelle*** **Use *de* + *lequel / laquelle / lesquels / lesquelles* when the preposition takes *de*.** (B) *à côté auquel* Use *a* + *lequel / laquelle / lesquels / lesquelles* when the preposition takes *à*. (C) *côté qui* The expression requires the *a* in front of *cote* and the *de* following it. (D) *à côté* The expression requires the *de* following it.
8	*J'ai interviewé beaucoup de célébri-tés, mais ------- ne me fait cet effet.* I've interviewed a lot of celebrities, but none has (had) this effect on me.	D	(A) *personne* A subtle difference in context, but personne refers to no one, as opposed to not a single one, as in not one of those celebrities had an effect on me, rather than no one (celebrities or others) had an effect. (B) *jamais* Never (does not make sense in context) (C) *quelque chose* Something (does not make sense in context). Does not take "ne" before it. **(D) *aucun*** **Use *aucun* (the negative of chacun) to mean "none" or "not one."**

Question		Answer	Explanation
9	------- *d'extraordinaire est arrivé aujourd'hui. J'ai reçu mon doctorat.* Something extraordinary happened today. I received my doctorate.	C	(A) *Quelqu'un* *Quelqu'un* is used to refer to a person. (B) *Quelques fois* *Quelque fois* is used to refer to a point in time. **(C) *Quelque chose*** **Used in the affirmative or interrogative to refer to a thing, while *quelqu'un* is used to refer to a person.** (D) *Aucun* "Not one"; requires a "ne" in any construction.
10	*On comprend très bien ------- les citoyens avaient peur pendant la premiere guerre mondiale.* One easily understands what citizens feared during the first world war.	D	(A) *quoi* *Quoi* needs to follow a preposition, and here it does not, so eliminate. (B) *d'où* This means "from where," which doesn't make sense with the verb phrase *avaient peur*. (C) *qui* Use *qui* when the subordinate (dependent) clause has no other subject. But the subject of *avaient peur* (i.e., the ones who were afraid) is *les citoyens*. **(D) *ce dont*** **Use *ce dont* when the subordinate clause needs an object with *de*.**

Drill 2: Verb Questions

Question		Answer	Explanation
1	*Si -------, je préparerais le dîner.* If I had time, I would make dinner.	C	Since the conditional tense is used in the portion of the sentence following the blank, the verb that precedes it must be in the **imperfect**. Only (C) has a verb in the imperfect. (A) *vous en avez envie*—present (B) *on me le demande*—present **(C) *j'avais le temps*—imperfect** (D) *tu seras d'accord*—future

Question	Answer	Explanation
2	*Paul regrette que nous ------- pas réussi.* Paul regrets that we have not succeeded.	C	What mode is used with verbs like *regretter que*? The subjunctive. Only (C) has the subjunctive. (A) *n'avons*—present (B) *n'avions*—imperfect **(C) *n'ayons*—subjunctive (present)** (D) *n'aurons*—future
3	*------ une lettre quand on a sonné à la porte.* I was writing a letter when the doorbell rang.	D	The use of the *passé composé* indicates that the sentence takes place in the past, so you can eliminate (A), (B), and (C). The answer is (D). The use of the imperfect indicates that the action of letter writing was ongoing when the doorbell rang. (A) *J'écris*—present (B) *J'écrirais*—conditional (C) *J'écrive*—subjunctive (present) **(D) *J'écrivais*—imperfect**
4	*Elle n'a jamais oublié ce que nous ------- au moment de son départ.* She never forgot what we said at the moment of her departure.	C	Does the expression *ce que* take the subjunctive? No. Eliminate (B). The use of the *passé composé* in the first part of the sentence indicates that the sentence takes place in the past and the verb does not need to be in the subjective or conditional mood. Eliminate (A) and (D). The correct answer is (C). (A) *disons*—present (B) *ayons dit*—past of the subjunctive **(C) *avons dit*—passé composé** (D) *aurions dit*—past of the conditional
5	*Est-ce que vous ------- contents si je n'avais pas accepté l'invitation?* Would you have been happy if I had not accepted the invitation?	D	Since a form of the imperfect is being used with *si*, the other verb must be in the conditional. Choice (D) is the only verb in the conditional. Since one part of the sentence has the past form of the imperfect (the *plus-que-parfait*), it makes sense that the conditional verb would also be in a past form. (A) *êtes*—present (B) *soyez*—subjunctive (C) *étiez*—imperfect **(D) *auriez été*—past of the conditional**

Question	Answer	Explanation
6	*Nous doutons ------- leur rendre visite chez eux.* We doubt that he has time to visit them.	A	Does the verb *douter que* take the subjunctive? Yes, so (B), (C), and (D) must be wrong. Choice (A) is the correct answer because the subjunctive is used. **(A)** ***qu'il ait le temps de*—subjunctive** (B) *qu'il voudrait*—conditional (C) *qu'il peut*—present (D) *qu'elle avait envie de*—imperfect
7	*------- , elle est partie pour le long trajet chez elle.* Having said goodbye, she left for the long journey home.	C	We need a verb form that shows when she said goodbye (the verb is in all the answer choices). We can eliminate (B), since it is the infinitive and the sentence is in the past. To show that she said goodbye either before or as she left, we need either the perfect or the present participle. The only participle here is (C), the perfect participle, "having said goodbye." This is our answer. Choices (A) and (D), cannot be used by themselves in a phrase. (A) *Disait au revoir*—imperfect (B) *Dire au revoir*—infinitive **(C)** ***Ayant dit au revoir*—perfect participle** (D) *Avoir dit au revoir*—past infinitive
8	*Tu pourras regarder la télé une fois que tu --------- ton travail.* You will be allowed to watch TV once you have finished your homework.	C	Does the conjunction *une fois que* take the subjunctive? No. Eliminate (D). We need a verb form that shows that your homework must be finished in the future before you may watch TV. Choice (B) is the imperfect so it does not work. Choice (A) is the past form of the conditional, so it does not work either. The correct answer is (C), *futur antérieur*, future perfect tense. (A) *aurais fini*—past conditional (B) *finissais*—imperfect **(C)** ***auras fini*—future perfect** (D) *finisses*—subjunctive
9	*Quand j'avais quatre ans, --------- un enfant très difficile.* When I was four years old, I was a very difficult child.	A	**(A)** ***j'étais*—use the imperfect when the action started in the past and continues in the past.** (B) *je suis*—present tense (C) *j'ai été*—passe compose (D) *je suis été*—incorrect form of passe compose

Question		Answer	Explanation
10	*Il aimerait aller avec toi au musée, mais il --------- travailler.* He would like to go to the museum with you, but he has to work.	D	(A) *doive*—subjunctive form (there is no wish or mood or indefinite stance). (B) *devra*—future tense (does not work with the conditional as it states something definite). (C) *devais*—imperfect tense (not appropriate following a wish in the conditional form). **(D) *doit*—use the present tense following "aimer" in the conditional form, which indicates a wish.**

Drill 3: Preposition Questions

Question		Answer	Explanation
1	*Marie ------- les résultats de ses examens.* Marie is waiting for the results of her exams.	B	(A) *pense* Penser requires the preposition *à* or *de*. **(B) *attend*** ***Attendre* requires no preposition. This is the correct answer.** (C) *compte* *Compter* requires the preposition *sur*. Without a preposition, it means "to count" and makes no sense here. (D) *a envie* *Avoir envie* requires the preposition *de*.
2	*Je ------- de leur écrire.* I am compelled to write them.	A	**(A) *suis obligé*** **This is the correct answer. *Être obligé* requires the preposition *de*.** (B) *espère* *Espérer* takes no preposition in French. (C) *veux* *Vouloir* takes no preposition. It cannot be used with *de*. (D) *réfléchis* *Réfléchir* takes the preposition *à*. It cannot be used with *de*.

Question	Answer	Explanation
3	*Je n'ai jamais eu l'occasion ------- voir ce film.* I have never had the opportunity to see this film.	C	The expression *avoir l'occasion* takes the preposition *de*. **(C) is the correct answer.**
4	*------- le concert, elles bavardaient sans cesse.* During the concert, they chattered endlessly.	A	**(A) Pendant** **Pendant means "during." This is the correct answer.** (B) *Dans* *Dans* means "in." You cannot say *dans le concert*. (C) *Avec* *Avec* means "with." You might find a context in which *avec* works with *le concert*, but in this context, it does not. (D) *En* There might be a context in which *en concert* is acceptable, but *en le concert* is never correct.
5	*Je la vois souvent à -------.* I see her often at the bakery.	C	(A) *France* The correct expression would be *en France*. (B) *ville* You can say either *à la ville* or *en ville*. **(C) la boulangerie** **This is the correct answer. You can say *à la boulangerie*.** (D) *loin* *Loin* is never used with *à*.
6	*Elle n'a pas réfléchi ------- de refuser l'offre.* She did not think before refusing the offer.	B	(A) --- *Réfléchir* must be used with a preposition. **(B) avant** **This is the correct answer.** (C) *après* You cannot say *après de*. *Après* is used with the infinitive (e.g., *après avoir réfléchi*). (D) *à* You cannot have these two prepositions, *à* and *de*, following each other.

Question	Answer	Explanation
7 *Nous pensons toujours ------- leurs parents.* We always think of their parents.	C	(A) *les* The idiomatic expression is *penser à quelqu'un,* so the definite article is not appropriate. (B) *de* *De* is the wrong preposition in this expression. **(C) *à*** **Penser takes the preposition "à" when one is thinking of someone else.** (D) *aux* *Aux (a + les)* is not appropriate since we do not need a definite article thanks to the pronoun *leurs.*
8 *Ils viennent ------- l'aéroport.* They're coming from the airport.	B	(A) *pendant* Wrong preposition that makes no sense in context. **(B) *de*** ***Venir* takes the preposition "de" when one is coming from somewhere** (C) *à* Wrong preposition for this expression—it would imply you are coming to a place. (D) *après* Wrong preposition—changes the meaning by implying they are coming after the airport.
9 *Elle a assisté au concert ------- les objections de ses parents.* She attended the concert despite the objections of her parents.	B	(A) *sauf* Means without, and is the wrong preposition. **(B) *malgré*** ***Malgré* means despite and is the most appropriate preposition for this sentence.** (C) *selon* Means according to, and is also the wrong preposition. (D) *pendant* Means during, and is also the wrong preposition.

Question		Answer	Explanation
10	*Passez-vous vos vacances -------* *Canada?* Are you spending your vacation in Canada?	A	**(A) *au*** **Masculine, singular countries take *au* when you are referring to that country.** (B) *à* Used for cities or towns. (C) *en* Used for feminine, singular countries. (D) *de* Refers to coming from a country.

Comprehensive Drill

Part B

Question	Category	Answer	Explanation
1	Odds and Ends	A	**(A) *quelque chose* is correct** (B) *rien* must be used with *ne*—*n'a rien* (C) *plusieurs* must modify a noun (D) *quelques* must modify a noun
2	Prepositions	C	(A) *rejeter* cannot be followed by a verb (B) *aimer* takes the infinitive **(C) *être obligé* takes *de*, so it is correct** (D) *avoir voulu* takes the infinitive
3	Odds and Ends	B	(A) plural **(B) *amie* is feminine, but it's correct because *amie* begins with a vowel** (C) feminine (D) plural
4	Odds and Ends	A	**(A) *avant de partir* works with the future tense** (B) *tout à l'heure* is okay, but not with *à* (C) *hier* does not work with the future (D) *jamais* must be used with *ne*
5	Pronouns	D	(A) *personne* requires *ne* (B) subject pronoun (C) indirect object **(D) stressed pronoun is correct with *c'est***

Question	Category	Answer	Explanation
6	Prepositions	A	**(A) *préférer* takes the infinitive—correct** (B) *rêver* takes *de* and then the infinitive (C) *plaire* takes no direct object (D) *insister* takes *pour* and the infinitive
7	Pronouns	D	(A) subject or stressed pronoun (B) stressed pronoun (C) reflexive, but wrong person **(D) *demander quelque chose à quelqu'un*—indirect object is correct**
8	Pronouns	C	(A) indirect object pronoun (B) subject pronoun **(C) stressed pronoun is correct with *avec*** (D) direct object pronoun
9	Pronouns	B	(A) plural **(B) singular and feminine possessive pronoun—correct** (C) *aucun* requires *ne* (D) possessive adjective
10	Prepositions	A	**(A) *Russie* is feminine—correct with *en*** (B) *États-Unis* is plural (*aux*) (C) New York takes *à* (D) Canada is masculine (*au*)
11	Odds and Ends	C	(A) adverb (B) adverb **(C) adjective—correct** (D) preposition
12	Verbs	B	(A) *savoir que* doesn't take the subjunctive **(B) *regretter que* takes the subjunctive—correct** (C) *oublier que* doesn't take the subjunctive (D) nothing hypothetical, so no subjunctive
13	Pronouns/Prepositions	A	**(A) *parler* takes *de*—therefore *dont* is correct** (B) *quoi* is used with things (C) *parler* cannot work with *sauf* (D) *avant que* is a conjunction, not a pronoun

Question	Category	Answer	Explanation
14	Pronouns	C	(A) *quelle* is feminine (B) *qu'est-ce qui* is used to refer to things **(C) *où* means "where"—correct** (D) *quoi* is used with things
15	Pronouns	D	(A) *quel* must modify something (B) *y* refers to place or location (C) *dont* cannot be used to begin a question **(D) *avoir envie* takes *de*—correct**
16	Prepositions	C	(A) *aller* does not take *de* (B) *espérer* takes either the infinitive or *que* **(C) *essayer* takes *de*—correct** (D) *pouvoir* does not take *de*
17	Verbs	C	(A) *sans doute* means "probably" (B) certain, so no subjunctive **(C) *Je crains* means "I fear." This expression takes the subjunctive—correct** (D) no doubt or uncertainty, so no subjunctive
18	Prepositions	C	(A) in order to (B) when **(C) in spite of—correct** (D) unless
19	Verbs	A	**(A) imperfect followed by conditional—correct** (B) present, so following clause can't be conditional (C) future cannot follow *si* (D) past imperfect would take past conditional
20	Verbs	D	(A) *passé composé* (B) *passé composé* (C) *passé composé* **(D) subjunctive is used with superlatives—correct**

Part C

Question	Category	Answer	Explanation
21	Verbs	D	(A) imperfect (B) past imperfect (C) present **(D) past conditional follows a clause with *si* and the past imperfect—correct**
22	Pronouns	B	(A) subject or stressed pronoun **(B) indirect object—correct** (C) stressed pronoun and masculine (D) direct object and singular
23	Pronouns	A	**(A) stressed pronoun with *chez*—correct** (B) subject (C) indirect object (D) subject and masculine
24	Vocabulary	A	**(A) no one—correct** (B) a person (C) nothing (D) *nulle* is an adjective
25	Vocabulary	A	**(A) Finally—correct** (B) *Terminé* is not an adverb, but a past participle (C) Now (D) In order to
26	Pronouns	B	(A) *arriver de* makes no sense in this context **(B) *y* indicates place: in this case, the café—correct** (C) *le* is a direct object pronoun (D) *arriver* cannot be reflexive
27	Verbs	D	(A) no agreement or masculine singular (B) feminine singular (C) masculine plural **(D) feminine plural: requires agreement because direct object precedes verb—correct**
28	Prepositions	B	(A) *cinéma* is masculine **(B) *au* is correct because *cinéma* is masculine** (C) *entrer par* doesn't make sense in this context and *cinéma* is masculine (D) *entrer par* doesn't make sense in this context

Question	Category	Answer	Explanation
29	Prepositions	C	(A) you cannot use *avant* and a verb without a preposition (B) *avant à* does not exist **(C) the correct expression is *avant de*** (D) *avant que* would have to be followed by a clause using the subjunctive
30	Verbs	A	**(A) no agreement required—correct** (B) feminine (C) masculine plural (D) feminine plural
31	Prepositions	D	(A) needs a preposition to make sense (B) *à demander* makes no sense (C) *de demander* makes no sense **(D) *pour demander*: in order to ask—correct**
32	Conjunctions	A	**(A) *si*—if or whether—correct** (B) when (C) which (D) who
33	Vocabulary	C	(A) *en temps* does not exist; *à temps* (on time) would be correct (B) every hour **(C) on time—correct** (D) from time to time

CHAPTER 6 DRILL ANSWERS AND EXPLANATIONS

Comprehensive Drill

Part D

Question		Answer	Explanation
1	Etienne lacked the energy to	B	(A) "sleep": familiar word—wrong context **(B) "undress": see phrase *tout vêtu* (fully dressed)** (C) "eat" (D) "put on his clothes"
2	According to the passage, why is Etienne tired?	D	(A) "He ate too much." familiar words—wrong context (B) "He did not sleep at all in two days." Too extreme; he did get some sleep. (C) "He went to sleep at four in the morning." familiar words—wrong context **(D) "He has slept only for a few hours in 48 hours": see *En deux jours, il n'avait pas dormi quatre heures.***
3	At what time of day did he get up?	C	(A) "early in the morning" (B) "noon" **(C) "early in the evening": see *au crépuscule, avant de . . . se coucher pour la nuit*** (D) "midnight"
4	How does he react at the moment he wakes up?	A	**(A) "He doesn't remember where he is": see *sans reconnaître le lieu où il se trouvait*** (B) "He can't find his clothes." (C) "He feels that he is late." (D) "He is hungry."
5	What did he want to do before eating dinner?	B	(A) "breathe" **(B) "go for a walk": see *prendre l'air*** (C) "wake up": familiar words—wrong context (D) "run"
6	When did Morissot leave to reach the island?	C	(A) "after sunset" (B) "at sunset" **(C) "at sunrise": see *dès l'aurore*** (D) "in the afternoon"

Question		Answer	Explanation
7	How did he reach the island?	D	(A) "by bus and on foot" (B) "by boat" (C) "by car and on foot" **(D) "by train and on foot": see *chemin de fer* (railway), *à pied***
8	At what point did he start fishing?	A	**(A) "at almost the moment he arrived": see *à peine arrivé*** (B) "at the moment he started to dream" (C) "at nightfall" (D) "when his friend arrived"
9	What is located on Notre-Dame-de-Lorette Street?	C	(A) "the island": makes no sense (B) "the place the two friends would meet" **(C) "Mr. Savage's shop": see *mercier* (dealer in sewing wares)** (D) "the train station"
10	The parents of Guillaume	D	(A) "advise him never to go to the movies" (B) "don't concern themselves with what he does" (C) "don't like the movies" **(D) "give their opinion about the films he chooses": see *je leur demande ce qu'ils en pensent***
11	To Gilles's question, Claire replies	C	(A) "that she never goes to the movies" (B) "that she goes to the movies if her parents agree" **(C) "that she goes to the movies without telling her parents": see *en cachette* (secretly)** (D) "that she goes to the movies often"
12	What reason does Guillaume give for not lying to his parents?	B	(A) "His parents let him do anything.": familiar words—wrong context **(B) "His parents let him decide what to do.": see *Je crois que je me sens libre*** (C) "It is better not to do it." (D) "His parents don't like the movies."
13	The author reacts to the change in Boulevard St. Michel and Place Saint-André-des-Arts with	B	(A) "impatience" **(B) "regret"** (C) "indifference" (D) "pleasure": makes no sense

Question		Answer	Explanation
14	What does one find near Luxembourg?	D	(A) "small, anonymous restaurants": familiar words—wrong context (B) "pleasant cafés": familiar words—wrong context (C) "pretentious bookstores" **(D) "American establishments":** *McDonald's*
15	According to the passage, "Gibert" is	C	(A) "a film" (B) "a café" **(C) "a bookstore": see** *cinémas et librairies semblent résister* (D) "a museum"
16	What do young people do instead of going to Boulevard St. Michel?	C	(A) "They go to Place Saint-André-des-Arts." (B) "They are in a rush to see American films." **(C) "They look for cool bars in another area.": see** *autour du Panthéon* (D) "They resist going to bookstores."
17	The narrator lets it be understood that she	D	(A) "worked a lot" (B) "was an invalid" (C) "had many worries" **(D) "married her father's friend": see** *Un vieil ami de mon père m'a demandé ma main.*
18	The brother of the narrator	B	(A) "lived with her for six years": familiar words—wrong context **(B) "was younger than she":** *cadet* (C) "was a soldier" (D) "didn't like her husband"
19	The passage gives us the impression	A	**(A) "that she wanted to defend her actions": see** *Qu'auriez-vous fait à ma place?* (B) "that she missed her husband" (C) "that her brother was cured" (D) "that she liked good weather": misunderstanding, as *sans un nuage* is not literal
20	After six years, what happened?	D	(A) "The husband of the narrator left." (B) "The good weather changed.": *sans un nuage* is not literal (C) "The narrator decided to leave." **(D) "The narrator found a lover.": see** *j'ai rencontré celui que je devais aimer.*

Question		Answer	Explanation
21	It is understood that Antoine Lemurier	D	(A) "is dead" (B) "missed the train" (C) "left his work" **(D) "nearly succumbed to an illness": see _avait manqué mourir_ (almost died)**
22	What did the neighbors think of Lemurier's illness?	A	**(A) "They expected an interesting end to the tragedy.": see _ils vivaient anxieusement dans l'attente d'un dénouement qui fût digne de la pièce_** (B) "They were sad." (C) "They were angry with Lemurier." (D) "They fell ill."
23	According to the neighbors, what would have been a fitting end to the situation?	C	(A) "Mr. Lemurier loses his job." (B) "Mr. Lemurier completely recovers." **(C) "Mrs. Lemurier is without shelter.": see _la femme à la rue_** (D) "Mrs. Lemurier sells the house.": close, but the phrase is _le mobilier être vendu_

Part V
Practice Test 2

Practice Test 2
Practice Test 2: Answers and Explanations

Practice Test 2

FRENCH SUBJECT TEST 2

When your supervisor gives the signal, turn the page and begin the SAT Subject Test in French.

FRENCH SUBJECT TEST 2

Part A

Directions: This part consists of a number of incomplete statements, each having four suggested completions. Select the most appropriate completion and fill in the corresponding circle on the answer sheet.

1. Les étudiants sont . . . avec l'enseignant sur l'explication de l'examen.

   (A) en retard
   (B) d'accord
   (C) à l'heure
   (D) avant de

2. N'oublie pas ton parapluie; il va . . . ce soir.

   (A) pleurer
   (B) faire froid
   (C) ouvrir
   (D) pleuvoir

3. Il n'y a plus rien dans le réfrigérateur. Il faut que j'aille . . .

   (A) prendre une douche
   (B) tondre le gazon
   (C) faire les courses
   (D) mettre le couvert

4. J'ai mal à . . . d'avoir tapé à l'ordinateur toute la journée.

   (A) la main
   (B) le pied
   (C) l'oreille
   (D) la barbe

5. Sa voiture est toujours en panne et il en a vraiment . . .

   (A) marre
   (B) mer
   (C) miel
   (D) dégoûté

6. Au crépuscule, le ciel . . . de mille feux.

   (A) éteignait
   (B) disparaissait
   (C) tombait
   (D) brillait

7. Les engagements . . . doivent être honorés; sinon les gens ne vont pas avoir confiance en vous.

   (A) être pauvre
   (B) reçu
   (C) pris
   (D) recueillir

8. Jean va acheter des livres à la . . .

   (A) boucherie
   (B) librairie
   (C) pâtisserie
   (D) bibliothèque

9. Elle est si allergique à la poussière qu'elle . . . sans arrêt.

   (A) éclate
   (B) salue
   (C) éternue
   (D) respire

10. J'ai ouvert une nouvelle . . . dans le centre-ville où je vends des gâteaux.

   (A) entreprise
   (B) gare
   (C) chambre
   (D) voiture

GO ON TO THE NEXT PAGE

11. Il s'est évanoui en apprenant . . .

    (A) la nouvelle
    (B) la leçon
    (C) le fauteuil
    (D) la poubelle

12. Personne ne répond à la porte; elle n'est probablement pas . . .

    (A) là
    (B) dessus
    (C) dessous
    (D) à côté

13. Je suis très . . . que le garçon prenne tellement de temps avec ma commande.

    (A) heureux
    (B) satisfait
    (C) fâché
    (D) ravi

14. Ils ont choisi d'habiter . . . avec leurs trois petits enfants.

    (A) en banlieue
    (B) en chemin
    (C) en cachette
    (D) en retard

15. Ils sont pleins d'énergie et sont . . . tous les matins à 6 heures.

    (A) étendus
    (B) assis
    (C) debout
    (D) fâchés

16. Je n'ai pas . . . d'acheter une nouvelle voiture; je peux me déplacer à vélo en ville.

    (A) hésiter
    (B) espoir
    (C) hésiter
    (D) besoin

17. Pour son entrevue avec son futur employeur demain, elle va mettre . . .

    (A) un soulier
    (B) un tailleur
    (C) un costume
    (D) un portemanteau

18. Elle a . . . beaucoup d'argent pour acheter sa maison.

    (A) prêté
    (B) renversé
    (C) emprunté
    (D) vendu

19. Je suppose que vous . . . parce que la journée a été très chaude.

    (A) avez soif
    (B) avez progreseé
    (C) avez détruit
    (D) avez évoqué

20. Il est exténué; il a . . . travaillé.

    (A) peu
    (B) bientôt
    (C) souvent
    (D) trop

21. Les trains passent moins souvent les jours . . .

    (A) normaux
    (B) libres
    (C) fériés
    (D) courants

22. Cette ancienne carte va nous . . . où le trésor est enterré.

    (A) masquer
    (B) montrer
    (C) rappeler
    (D) demander

GO ON TO THE NEXT PAGE

23. Des années d'usage vont . . . le cuir de ces bottes.

 (A) assiéger
 (B) réduire
 (C) assouplir
 (D) surprendre

24. Si je pars maintenant, je peux . . . les embouteillages.

 (A) estimer
 (B) revoir
 (C) arranger
 (D) éviter

GO ON TO THE NEXT PAGE →

| For more free content, visit <u>PrincetonReview.com</u>

Part B

Directions: Each of the following sentences contains a blank. From the four choices given, select the one that can be inserted in the blank to form a grammatically correct sentence and fill in the corresponding circle on the answer sheet. Choice (A) may consist of dashes that indicate that no insertion is required to form a grammatically correct sentence.

25. Le paquet ------- mon père a signé est sur la table de la cuisine.

    (A) que
    (B) à qui
    (C) pour lequel
    (D) dont

26. Je suis passée à la maison ------- prendre mon parapluie.

    (A) à
    (B) pour
    (C) parce que
    (D) après

27. Mon père revenait toujours ------- à la maison entre midi et deux heures.

    (A) déjeuner
    (B) déjeuné
    (C) déjeunait
    (D) déjeunant

28. Les chocolats ------- Belgique sont les meilleurs au monde.

    (A) de
    (B) dans
    (C) aux
    (D) du

29. Elle dessine beaucoup ------- que son frère.

    (A) bien
    (B) meilleur
    (C) mal
    (D) mieux

30. La robe qu'elle a ------- hier n'est vraiment pas à la mode.

    (A) mise
    (B) acheté
    (C) mis
    (D) enfiler

31. Je vais faire des courses -------- tu aimerais mieux.

    (A) avant que
    (B) puisque
    (C) selon que
    (D) à moins que

32. Regarde ------- tu mets les pieds quand tu marches.

    (A) là
    (B) où
    (C) vers
    (D) près de

GO ON TO THE NEXT PAGE

33. Appelle-moi ------- prendre une décision.

    (A) en
    (B) pendant
    (C) avant de
    (D) à

34. ------- mieux prendre des vacances plutôt que de rester à la maison en hiver.

    (A) Je vais aimer
    (B) J'aimais
    (C) J'aimerais
    (D) Que j'aime

35. Est-ce que tu veux un bonbon? Oui, j'en veux bien -------.

    (A) quelque
    (B) peu
    (C) un peu
    (D) un

36. Est-ce que Marie est déjà partie à la poste? Non, mais elle va ------- aller tout de suite.

    (A) y
    (B) en
    (C) toujours
    (D) demain

37. Il ------- tous les jours avant de déjeuner quand il était en vacances.

    (A) va nager
    (B) avait nagé
    (C) a nagé
    (D) serait nager

38. Il faut que ------- à la banque demain matin pour retirer de l'argent.

    (A) j'allais
    (B) j'aille
    (C) j'irai
    (D) j'irais

GO ON TO THE NEXT PAGE

Part C

Directions: The paragraphs below contain blank spaces indicating omissions in the text. For some blanks, it is necessary to choose the completion that is most appropriate to the meaning of the passage; for other blanks, to choose the one completion that forms a grammatically correct sentence. In some instances, choice (A) may consist of dashes that indicate that no insertion is required to form a grammatically correct sentence. In each case, indicate your answer by filling in the corresponding circle on the answer sheet. Be sure to read the paragraph completely before answering the questions related to it.

In n'avait pas mangé __(39)__ le matin. Les cafés qu'il rencontrait à __(40)__ pas l'intimidaient et le __(41)__ , à cause de la foule qui __(42)__ était __(43)__ . Il s'adressa __(44)__ un gendarme. Mais il était si lent à __(45)__ ses mots que l'autre ne se donna même pas la peine de l'écouter __(46)__ bout et __(47)__ tourna le dos au milieu de la phrase, en __(48)__ les épaules. Il continua machinalement __(49)__ marcher.

39. (A) après
    (B) depuis
    (C) pour
    (D) dans

40. (A) tous
    (B) chacun
    (C) chaque
    (D) quelque

41. (A) discutaient
    (B) salivaient
    (C) dégoûtaient
    (D) aimaient

42. (A) en
    (B) y
    (C) dans
    (D) où

43. (A) entassé
    (B) entasser
    (C) entassées
    (D) entassée

44. (A) à
    (B) vers
    (C) avec
    (D) pour

45. (A) trouvé
    (B) trouver
    (C) trouvés
    (D) trouvait

46. (A) à travers
    (B) jusque-là
    (C) au
    (D) jusqu'au

47. (A) leur
    (B) lui
    (C) le
    (D) la

48. (A) tirant
    (B) portant
    (C) haussant
    (D) passant

49. (A) -------
    (B) pour
    (C) à
    (D) en

GO ON TO THE NEXT PAGE

Cher Monsieur,

La lettre __(50)__ je vous __(51)__ adressée le 1er juillet __(52)__ restée sans réponse, je me permets de vous écrire pour __(53)__ prier de prendre ma requête __(54)__ considération.

50. (A) -------
    (B) laquelle
    (C) dont
    (D) que

51. (A) aie
    (B) ai
    (C) aurai
    (D) avait

52. (A) ayant
    (B) avant
    (C) étant
    (D) était

53. (A) te
    (B) me
    (C) vous
    (D) le

54. (A) en
    (B) avec
    (C) par
    (D) comme

Quand j'étais petit, mes parents __(55)__ emmenaient __(56)__ nager à la piscine municipale de Roubaix.

55. (A) leur
    (B) te
    (C) s'
    (D) m'

56. (A) peut-être
    (B) pourtant
    (C) une fois
    (D) souvent

GO ON TO THE NEXT PAGE

Part D

Directions: Read the following texts carefully for comprehension. Each is followed by a number of questions or incomplete statements. Select the completion or answer that is best according to the text and fill in the corresponding circle on the answer sheet.

"L'été est trop long," disait la grand-mère qui accueillait du même soupir soulagé la pluie d'automne et le départ de Jacques, dont les piétinements d'ennui
Ligne au long des journées torrides, dans les pièces aux
5 persiennes closes, ajoutaient encore à son énervement.
Elle ne comprenait pas d'ailleurs qu'une période de l'année fût plus spécialement désignée pour n'y rien faire. "Je n'ai jamais eu de vacances, moi," disait-elle, et c'était vrai, elle n'avait connu ni l'école
10 ni le loisir, elle avait travaillé enfant, et travaillé sans relâche. Elle admettait que, pour un bénéfice plus grand, son petit-fils pendant quelques années ne rapporte pas d'argent à la maison. Mais, dès le premier jour, elle avait commencé de ruminer sur
15 ces trois mois perdus, et, lorsque Jacques entra en troisième, elle jugea qu'il était temps de lui trouver l'emploi de ses vacances. "Tu vas travailler cet été," lui dit-elle à la fin de l'année scolaire, "et rapporter un peu d'argent à la maison. Tu ne peux pas rester
20 comme ça sans rien faire."

(Albert Camus, *Le premier homme*, Folio)

57. Quand arrivait la pluie d'automne, la grand-mère était

    (A) énervée
    (B) triste
    (C) contente
    (D) fière

58. Pendant les mois d'été, Jacques

    (A) travaillait beaucoup
    (B) passait son temps à lire
    (C) s'amusait sans arrêt
    (D) ne savait pas comment se distraire

59. Quand elle était petite, la grand-mère

    (A) avait de moins longues vacances que Jacques
    (B) dessinait pendant ses loisirs
    (C) passait tout son temps au travail
    (D) ne faisait jamais rien

60. D'après le texte, on comprend que

    (A) Jacques poursuit ses études
    (B) la grand-mère ne veut pas que Jacques aille encore à l'école
    (C) la grand-mère refuse que Jacques travaille pendant l'été
    (D) Jacques est le troisième de sa classe

61. La grand-mère veut que Jacques ait un emploi pour qu'il

    (A) ait un peu d'argent de poche
    (B) puisse payer ses études
    (C) contribue aux dépenses de la famille
    (D) apprenne un métier

GO ON TO THE NEXT PAGE

Avant de venir au Central, lisait-il, je viens
d'assister à une scène d'une atroce beauté.
Ligne   On a trouvé cette nuit près de la Puerta del Sol un
enfant de trois ans qui pleurait perdu, dans les ténèbres.
5 Or, une des femmes réfugiées dans les sous-sols de
la Gran Via ignorait ce qu'était devenu son enfant,
un petit garçon du même âge, blond comme l'enfant
trouvé dans la Puerta del Sol. On lui donne la nouvelle.
Elle court à la maison où l'on garde l'enfant, calle
10 Montera. Dans la demi-obscurité d'une boutique aux
rideaux baissés, l'enfant suce un morceau de chocolat.
La mère s'avance vers lui, les bras tendus, mais
ses yeux s'agrandissent, prennent une fixité terrible,
démente.
15   Ce n'est pas son enfant.
Elle reste immobile de longues minutes. L'enfant
perdu lui sourit. Alors elle se précipite sur lui, le serre
contre elle, l'emporte en pensant à l'enfant qu'on n'a
pas retrouvé.

(André Malraux, *L'espoir*, Folio Plus)

62. L'enfant de trois ans pleure parce qu'

(A) il a perdu son morceau de chocolat
(B) il s'est fait mal
(C) il ne sait pas où est sa famille
(D) il fait nuit

63. Les rideaux de la boutique sont

(A) ouverts
(B) levés
(C) descendus
(D) déchirés

64. La femme "se précipite sur lui" veut dire qu'elle
va vers l'enfant

(A) en courant
(B) à pas lents
(C) en pleurant
(D) avec nonchalance

65. Elle "le serre contre elle" signifie qu'elle

(A) le repousse
(B) l'embrasse
(C) lui sourit
(D) le frappe

66. A qui la femme pense-t-elle en emportant l'enfant?

(A) à son propre fils
(B) au fils d'une des refugiées
(C) au fils du lecteur
(D) au fils d'un garde

GO ON TO THE NEXT PAGE

TRAIN + VOITURE: EN TOUTE LIBERTÉ

Evitez les bouchons des grands départs!

En choisissant la formule "Train + Location de voitures," vous êtes sûrs de bénéficier de tous les avantages: le confort du train, la liberté de la voiture … Tout en réalisant de vraies **économies**!

Pratique: à la descente du train, votre voiture vous attend en gare.

Economique: vous bénéficiez d'une réduction importante sur votre location.

Efficace: vous réservez votre voiture en même temps que votre train.

Pour profiter de cette offre:

– Réservez votre place.

– En fin de commande, cliquez sur "AJOUTER UNE VOITURE."

– Choisissez l'offre "Train + Location de Voitures."

67. Les bouchons dont il est question dans le texte

(A) servent à boucher les bouteilles
(B) sont des embouteillages
(C) retardent les trains
(D) évitent de perdre du temps

68. D'après le texte, la solution Train + Location de Voitures

(A) revient plus cher
(B) coûte trop cher
(C) n'est guère pratique
(D) est une bonne affaire

GO ON TO THE NEXT PAGE

Heureusement, [l'Etablissement français du sang] nous ne manquons jamais de stocks de sang à court terme. Nous avons besoin d'environ 10 000 dons par jour, qui permettent de pourvoir aux besoins d'un million de personnes chaque année. Quelque 500 000 personnes profitent des produits que nous collectons et 500 000 autres sont soignées grâce à des médicaments à base de dérivés de sang. Nos appels réguliers aux dons sont liés au fait que la durée de vie des produits sanguins est limitée, de 5 jours pour les palettes à cause de la coagulation à 42 jours pour les globules rouges.

Cette journée mondiale des donneurs de sang est d'autant plus importante que le nombre de dons a chuté, comme chaque année, durant les mois d'avril et de mai, à cause des jours fériés. Il faut aussi prévoir une baisse de fréquentation pendant les vacances d'été. A cette période, les gens sont loin de chez eux et n'y pensent pas. C'est pour cela que nous essayons d'organiser des opérations mobiles, notamment sur les plages, pour leur rappeler l'importance du don. Le phénomène est le même en hiver, surtout lors des vacances de Noël. Sauf qu'à cette période-là, c'est en raison des maladies, comme les rhumes et les gastros, que les dons diminuent.

From *Le Monde,* June 14, 2017 article titled, « Journée mondiale des donneurs de sang : appel aux jeunes générations » by Camille Mordelet.

69. D'après cet article, l'établissement

(A) reçoit 10 000 dons chaque jour
(B) ne reçoit jamais 10 000 dons en un seul jour
(C) un besoin immédiat de sang
(D) a assez de sang pour le futur imminent

70. Les appels réguliers aux dons

(A) sont nécessaires pour plusieurs raisons.
(B) prennent rendez-vous par téléphone
(C) n'ont guère d'intérêt
(D) sont faits tous les 42 jours

71. Cette journée mondiale des donneurs du sang est importante parce que

(A) c'est une bonne fête
(B) il y a eu moins de donneurs au printemps comme d'habitude
(C) les donneurs du sang sont partis en vacances d'été
(D) c'était durant les mois d'avril et de mai

72. « …n'y pensent pas » signifie que les gens

(A) n'organisent pas souvent leur vacances
(B) sont souvent blessés en vacances
(C) visitent des endroits à l'étranger
(D) ne se souviennent pas de faire un don

73. « Le phénomène » représente

(A) une chose extraordinaire
(B) les vacances de Noël
(C) une baisse de dons en décembre et janvier
(D) les maladies fréquentes dans l'hiver

GO ON TO THE NEXT PAGE

Voici la recette des madeleines, ces petits gâteaux de forme ovale au ventre bombé, si chers à Marcel Proust:

La veille, mélangez soigneusement les ingrédients suivants jusqu'à l'obtention d'une pâte parfaitement lisse:

Madeleines

Farine	90 gr
Sucre	90 gr
Levure	2 gr
Miel de Provence	10 gr
Oeufs	2
Beurre fondu	90 gr
Le zeste d'un citron	
Pastis (facultatif)	1 cl

Conservez cette pâte au réfrigérateur.

Le lendemain, distribuez la pâte dans 12 moules à madeleines beurrés. Enfournez à four moyen et laissez cuire jusqu'à ce que les gâteaux aient une belle couleur dorée. Démoulez sur une grille à la sortie du four, laissez refroidir, et dégustez!

74. Quand faut-il préparer la pâte des madeleines?

(A) le lendemain
(B) le jour précédent
(C) deux heures à l'avance
(D) hier

75. D'après la recette, le pastis est un ingrédient

(A) indispensable
(B) sucré
(C) optionnel
(D) parfumé

GO ON TO THE NEXT PAGE

Le bossu reparut, une brochure à la main. Il s'installa commodément, les coudes sur la table, son menton entre ses mains.

Ligne
"Je vous ai déjà laissé entendre, dit-il, que j'avais
5 des projets d'une assez grande envergure."

"De vastes projets."

"C'est cela même, et je vais vous les révéler aujourd'hui." Il prit le ton d'un conférencier.

"Ce qui m'a attiré ici, c'est d'abord mon amour
10 de la nature. Mais quoique je ne manque pas d'argent en ce moment, j'ai une famille à nourrir, et je dois assurer l'avenir de ma fillette: c'est pourquoi le philosophe que je suis a voulu concilier son désir de la vie naturelle et l'obligation où il se trouve de faire
15 fortune."

De ce discours, Ugolin ne retint que les derniers mots. Il avait l'intention de "faire fortune." Faire fortune aux Romarins! Avec quoi? Sûrement pas avec ces oliviers à demi morts, ni ces amandiers à l'agonie;
20 ni avec des légumes, ni avec du blé, ni avec du vin. Il connaissait donc la source, et il voulait peut-être planter des œillets! C'est pourquoi, par une contre-attaque désespérée, il dit: "Vous savez ici, les fleurs, même si vous aviez une belle source . . ."
25 "Quelles fleurs?" dit le bossu d'un air surpris. "Croyez-vous que j'espère faire fortune en vendant des églantines ou des chardons? Et quelle source? Vous savez que celle que je possède est bien loin d'ici!"

(Coll Fortunio, Editions de Fallois © Marcel Pagnol, 2004)

76. "Je vous ai déjà laissé entendre" signifie "je vous ai déjà"

   (A) dit
   (B) répété
   (C) suggéré
   (D) menti

77. Le bossu a de "vastes projets" parce qu'il

   (A) a besoin d'argent tout de suite
   (B) pense à l'avenir de sa fille
   (C) est philosophe
   (D) aime beaucoup l'argent

78. Du discours du bossu, Ugolin se souvient

   (A) uniquement des derniers mots
   (B) peut-être des premiers mots
   (C) toujours de la dernière phrase
   (D) de tout sauf de la fin

79. Aux lignes 18–23, après l'annonce des projets du bossu, Ugolin est

   (A) amusé
   (B) très inquiet
   (C) rempli de joie
   (D) rassuré

80. Ugolin cherche à savoir si le bossu

   (A) va planter des vignes
   (B) va sauver les oliviers et les amandiers
   (C) compte vendre des chardons
   (D) connaît l'existence de la source

GO ON TO THE NEXT PAGE

Ligne

Vous comprenez tout de suite que la vraie ville est l'arsenal, que l'autre ne vit que par lui, qu'il déborde sur elle. Sous toutes les formes, en tous lieux, à tous les coins réapparaissent l'administration, la discipline,

5 la feuille de papier rayé, le cadre, la règle. On admire beaucoup la symétrie factice et la propreté imbécile. A l'hôpital de la marine, par exemple, les salles sont cirées de telle façon qu'un convalescent, essayant de marcher sur sa jambe remise, doit se casser l'autre

10 en tombant. Mais c'est beau, ça brille, on s'y mire. Entre chaque salle est une cour, mais où le soleil ne vient jamais et dont soigneusement on arrache l'herbe. Les cuisines sont superbes, mais à une telle distance, qu'en hiver tout doit parvenir glacé aux malades. Il

15 s'agit bien d'eux! Les casseroles ne sont-elles pas luisantes? Nous vîmes un homme qui s'était cassé le crâne en tombant d'une frégate et qui depuis dix-huit heures n'avait pas encore reçu de secours; mais ses draps étaient très blancs, car la lingerie est fort bien

20 tenue.

(Gustave Flaubert, *Notes de voyage*, L'Intégrale)

81. "En tous lieux" signifie

(A) nulle part
(B) partout
(C) ailleurs
(D) quelque part

82. Le convalescent risque de se casser l'autre jambe parce que le sol est

(A) mouillé
(B) inégal
(C) plein de trous
(D) glissant

83. La cour entre chaque salle est

(A) inondée de soleil
(B) privée d'ombre
(C) ensoleillée
(D) privée de soleil

84. En hiver les repas sont servis aux malades

(A) brûlants
(B) tièdes
(C) à point
(D) très froids

85. Le ton de Flaubert dans ce passage est

(A) sarcastique
(B) sérieux
(C) enjoué
(D) tragique

S T O P
If you finish before time is called, you may check your work on this test only.
Do not work on any other test in this book.

Practice Test 2:
Answers and
Explanations

PRACTICE TEST 2 ANSWER KEY

Question number	Correct answer	Right	Wrong
1.	B	_____	_____
2.	D	_____	_____
3.	C	_____	_____
4.	A	_____	_____
5.	A	_____	_____
6.	D	_____	_____
7.	C	_____	_____
8.	B	_____	_____
9.	C	_____	_____
10.	A	_____	_____
11.	A	_____	_____
12.	A	_____	_____
13.	C	_____	_____
14.	A	_____	_____
15.	C	_____	_____
16.	D	_____	_____
17.	B	_____	_____
18.	C	_____	_____
19.	A	_____	_____
20.	D	_____	_____
21.	C	_____	_____
22.	B	_____	_____
23.	C	_____	_____
24.	D	_____	_____
25.	C	_____	_____
26.	B	_____	_____
27.	A	_____	_____
28.	A	_____	_____
29.	D	_____	_____
30.	A	_____	_____
31.	D	_____	_____
32.	B	_____	_____
33.	C	_____	_____
34.	C	_____	_____
35.	D	_____	_____

Question number	Correct answer	Right	Wrong
36.	A	_____	_____
37.	B	_____	_____
38.	B	_____	_____
39.	B	_____	_____
40.	C	_____	_____
41.	C	_____	_____
42.	B	_____	_____
43.	D	_____	_____
44.	A	_____	_____
45.	B	_____	_____
46.	D	_____	_____
47.	B	_____	_____
48.	C	_____	_____
49.	C	_____	_____
50.	D	_____	_____
51.	B	_____	_____
52.	C	_____	_____
53.	C	_____	_____
54.	A	_____	_____
55.	D	_____	_____
56.	D	_____	_____
57.	C	_____	_____
58.	D	_____	_____
59.	C	_____	_____
60.	A	_____	_____
61.	C	_____	_____
62.	C	_____	_____
63.	C	_____	_____
64.	A	_____	_____
65.	B	_____	_____
66.	A	_____	_____
67.	B	_____	_____
68.	D	_____	_____
69.	D	_____	_____
70.	A	_____	_____

Question number	Correct answer	Right	Wrong
71.	B	_____	_____
72.	D	_____	_____
73.	C	_____	_____
74.	B	_____	_____
75.	C	_____	_____
76.	C	_____	_____
77.	B	_____	_____
78.	A	_____	_____
79.	B	_____	_____
80.	D	_____	_____
81.	B	_____	_____
82.	D	_____	_____
83.	D	_____	_____
84.	D	_____	_____
85.	A	_____	_____

PRACTICE TEST 2 EXPLANATIONS

The possible choices are examined for clues that should have indicated the correct answer. To help explain why a choice is right or wrong, resemblances between English and French words are noted, grammatical explanations are given, and an analysis of the comprehension questions is provided.

Part A

1. **B** The sentence says, "The students are…with the teacher's explanation of the test." The key phrase is *avec l'enseignant*. A proper vocabulary word should show agreement with the teacher. Choice (A) means behind. Choice (B) means in agreement with. Choice (C) means on time. Choice (D) means ahead of. The answer is (B).

2. **D** The sentence says, "Don't forget your umbrella; it's going to…tonight." The key phrase is *parapluie*. A proper vocabulary word is rain. Choice (A) means to cry. Choice (B) means be cold. Choice (C) means to open. Choice (D) means to rain. The answer is (D).

3. **C** The sentence says, "There is nothing in the refrigerator. I have to go…" The key phrase is *rien dans le réfrigérateur*. A proper vocabulary word would be buy some food. Choice (A) means take a shower. Choice (B) means mow the lawn. Choice (C) means go shopping. Choice (D) means set the table. The answer is (C).

4. **A** The sentence says, "My…hurts from having typed on the computer all day." The key phrase is *d'avoir tapé à l'ordinateur*. A proper vocabulary word would be finger. Choice (A) means hand. Choice (B) means foot. Choice (C) means ear. Choice (D) means beard. The correct answer is (A).

5. **A** The sentence says, "His car is always broken down, and he has really…" The key phrase is *est toujours en panne*. A proper vocabulary word would be annoyed or fed up. Choice (A) is part of the idiomatic expression *en avoir marre*, which means to be fed up with. Using process of elimination helps with idiomatic expression. Choice (B) means ocean. Choice (C) means honey. Choice (D) means disgusted. Choice (D) might work, but *dégoûté* requires the verb être (*il est dégouté*) rather than the verb *avoir* (*il a…*). The answer is (A).

6. **D** The sentence says, "At dusk, the sky…with a thousand lights." The key phrase is *de mille feux*. A proper vocabulary word would be glows. Choice (A) means turned off. Choice (B) means disappeared. Choice (C) means fell. Choice (D) means shined. The answer is (D).

7. **C** The sentence says, "Meetings…must be honored; otherwise people will not trust you." The key phrase is *sinon les gens ne vont pas avoir confiance en vous*. A proper vocab word would explain what kind of non-honored meetings would cause people to mistrust someone, such as scheduled. Choice (A) means to be poor. Choice (B) means received. Choice (C) means made or scheduled. Choice (D) means to collect. The answer is (C).

8. **B** The sentence says, "John is going to buy books at the..." The key phrase is *va acheter des livres*. A proper vocabulary word would be bookstore. Choice (A) means butcher. Choice (B) means bookstore. Choice (C) means baker (of desserts). Choice (D) means library. Be careful to not eliminate (B): *librarie* and *bibliothèque* are *faux-amis*. The answer is (B).

9. **C** The sentence says, "She is so allergic to dust that she...without stopping." The key phrase is *si allergique*. A proper vocabulary word would be something that indicated an allergic reaction, such as sneezed or itched. Choice (A) means burst. Choice (B) means greeted. Choice (C) means sneezed. Choice (D) means breathed. The answer is (C).

10. **A** The sentence says, "I opened a new...in the center of town where I sell cakes. The key phrase is *où je vends des gâteaux*. A proper vocabulary word would be bakery. Choice (A) means business. Choice (B) means a train station. Choice (C) means a bedroom. Choice (D) means a car. The answer is (A).

11. **A** The sentence says, "He fainted upon learning..." The key phrase is *apprenant*. A proper vocabulary word would be news or information. Choice (A) means the news. Choice (B) means the lesson. Choice (C) means the armchair. Choice (D) means the trashcan. The answer is (A).

12. **A** The sentence says, "Nobody is answering the door; she is probably not..." The phrase is *Personne ne répond*. A proper vocabulary phrase would be not home. Choice (A) means there. Choice (B) means above. Choice (C) means below. Choice (D) means to the side. The answer is (A).

13. **C** The sentence says, "I am very...that the waiter is taking so long with my order." The key phrase is *prenne tellement de temps*. A proper vocabulary word would be upset. Choice (A) means happy. Choice (B) means satisfied. Choice (C) means angry. Choice (D) means delighted. The answer is (C).

14. **A** The sentence says, "They have chosen to live...with their three young children." The key phrase is *habiter*. A proper vocabulary word would be a word that describes a place a family lives, such as in the countryside. Choice (A) means in a suburb. Choice (B) means on the way. Choice (C) means in a hiding place. Choice (D) means late. The answer is (A).

15. **C** The sentence says, "They are full of energy and are...every morning at 6." The key phrase is *pleins d'énergie*. A proper vocabulary word would be awake. Choice (A) means heard. Choice (B) means seated. Choice (C) means up. Choice (D) means angry. The answer is (C).

16. **D** The sentence says, "I don't have...to buy a new car; I can ride my bicycle into town." The key phrase is *n'ai pas...d'acheter*. A proper vocabulary word would be a desire. Choice (A) means hesitation. Choice (B) means hope. Choice (C) means hesitation. Choice (D) means a need. The answer is (D).

17. **B** The sentence says, "For her interview with her future boss tomorrow, she is going to wear..." The key phrases are *son entrevue* and *elle va mettre*. A proper vocabulary word would be business clothes.

Choice (A) means flat-heeled shoes. Choice (B) means a woman's business suit. Choice (C) means a man's business suit. Choice (D) means a coatrack. The answer is (B).

18. **C** The sentence says, "She has…a lot of money to buy her house." The key phrase is *pour acheter sa maison*. A proper vocabulary word would explain what action the woman took with money to buy her house, such as paid or borrowed. Choice (A) means lent. Choice (B) means returned. Choice (C) means borrowed. Choice (D) means sold. Be careful about the trap in (D). Selling is something one does with one's house, but not with the money for the house. The answer is (C).

19. **A** The sentence says, "I suppose that you…since the day was very hot." The key phrase is *la journée a été très chaude*. A proper vocabulary word would be thirsty. Choice (A) means are thirsty. Choice (B) means have progressed. Choice (C) means have destroyed. Choice (D) means have evoked. The answer is (A).

20. **D** The sentence says, "He is exhausted; he has worked…" The key phrase is *exténué*. A proper vocabulary word would be too much. Choice (A) means little. Choice (B) means soon. Choice (C) means often. Choice (D) means too much. Choice (C) is close, but often working does not necessarily mean he will be exhausted. Working too much better matches the tone of the sentence. The answer is (D).

21. **C** The sentence says, "Trains run less often on…days." The key phrase is *passent moins souvent*. A proper vocabulary word would describe a type of day on which a train schedule would be less regular, such as holidays. Choice (A) means normal. Choice (B) means free. Choice (C) means festival. Choice (D) means current. The answer is (C).

22. **B** The sentence says, "This ancient map is going to…us where the treasure is buried." The key phrase is *où le trésor est enterré*. A proper vocabulary word would be show. Choice (A) means hide. Choice (B) means show. Choice (C) means remind. Choice (D) means ask. Choice (C) is possible, but there is no evidence in the sentence that the speakers had once known the location of the treasure. The answer is (B).

23. **C** The sentence says, "Years of use will…the leather of these boots." The key phrase is *Des années d'usage* and *cuir*. A proper vocabulary word would describe what might happen to leather after years of use, such as wear out. Choice (A) means to besiege. Choice (B) means to reduce. Choice (C) means to soften leather or to make supple. Choice (D) means to surprise. Choice (B) is close, but does not mean the same thing as wear out. The answer is (C).

24. **D** The sentence says, "If I leave now, I can…the traffic jams." The key phrase is *les embouteillages*. A proper vocabulary word would be avoid. Choice (A) means praise. Choice (B) means see again. Choice (C) means arrange. Choice (D) means avoid. The answer is (D).

Part B

25. **C** *Pronouns*

The sentence says, "The parcel-------my dad signed is on the kitchen table." The question is testing the best pronoun that logically completes the sentence. Since the pronoun follows the subject, a pronoun that can refer to a thing is needed. Choice (A) means which but is only used as a direct object pronoun. Choice (B) means to whom and refers to a person. Choice (C) means for which, and *lequel,* can refer to parcel. Choice (D) means of which or of what, but sign for is *signer pour.* The answer is (C).

26. **B** *Prepositions*

The sentence says, "I went by the house--------to get my umbrella. This question is testing the correct way to describe why the person went by the house. Choice (A) means at. Choice (B) means in order to. Choice (C) means because. Choice (D) means after. Choice (C) must be followed by a subject (*parce que je…*) in order to be correct. The answer is (B).

27. **A** *Verbs*

The sentence says, "My father returned home every day -------between noon and 2 pm. The question is testing the correct form of the verb *déjeunner* that follows *revenait.* Choice (A) means to eat lunch and is infinitive, which is typically required when one verb follows another. Choice (B) is the past participle which would require an auxiliary verb. Choice (C) means was eating in the imperfect. While it matches the verb tense of *revenir,* it is not the correct form since there is no linking word, such as *et.* Choice (D) means eating and is the gerund form. The answer is (A).

28. **A** *Prepositions*

The sentence says, "Chocolates-------Belgium are the best in the world. The question is testing the best preposition to describe that the chocolates are from Belgium. Choice (A) means from. Choice (B) means in. Choice (C) means to the. Choice (D) means from but is masculine. The answer is (A).

29. **D** *Odds and Ends: Adverbs*

The sentence says, "She draws much-------than her brother." The question is testing the best way to compare how she draws. Choice (A) means good and is not a comparison. Choice (B) means best and is superlative, not comparative. Choice (C) means bad and is not a comparison. Choice (D) means better and is a comparison. The answer is (D).

30. **A** *Verbs*

The sentence says, "The dress that she-------yesterday is not really fashionable." The question is testing the proper word to complete the sentence and whether the participle should agree. In general, when the *passé composé* is made with the verb *avoir,* participles do not agree. However, one exception to this rule is when the direct object comes before the verb. In this sentence, the direct object, the dress, comes before the verb, so the participle form must match gender and number. *La robe* is singular feminine, so the participle must be also. Choice (A) means put on and is singular feminine. Choice (B) means bought and is singular masculine. Choice (C) means put on and is singular masculine. Choice (D) means to slip into (some clothes) and is infinitive form. The answer is (A).

31. **D**   *Prepositions*

The sentence says, "I am going to go shopping-------you'd rather go." The question is testing for the word that logically connects the two phrases. Choice (A) means before. Choice (B) means since. Choice (C) means according to. Choice (D) means unless. Choice (A) might work, but *avant que* would require the subjunctive tense rather than the conditional. The answer is (D).

32. **B**   *Prepositions/Pronouns*

The sentence says, "Watch------you put your feet when you walk." The question is testing which is the best preposition or pronoun to logically complete the sentence. Choice (A) is a pronoun and means there. Choice (B) is a pronoun and means where. Choice (C) is a preposition and means toward. Choice (D) is a preposition and means near. The answer is (B).

33. **C**   *Prepositions*

The sentence says, "Call me-------making the decision." The question is testing which preposition would most logically complete the sentence. Choice (A) means in. Choice (B) means while. Choice (C) means before. Choice (D) means at. Choice (B) might seem possible, but in order to link two verbs, the phrase would need a subject and verb (*pendant que tu prends*) The answer is (C).

34. **C**   *Verbs*

The sentence says, "-------better to take vacation than to remain at the house all winter." The question is testing what the correct form of the verb is when discussing a hypothetical situation. In this case, the conditional tense is used. Choice (A) means I will like and is proximate (near) future. Choice (B) means I liked and is in the imperfect tense. Choice (C) means I would like and is in the conditional tense. Choice (D) means that I like. It is the present tense and adds an unnecessary word. The answer is (C).

35. **D**   *Pronouns*

The sentence says, "Would you like a candy? Yes, I would like-------of them." The question is testing the correct way to refer to a specific number of things when using the pronoun *en*. Here, the number of things follows the verb. Since *un bonbon* is singular masculine, the number one is needed and must be masculine. Choice (A) means some. Choice (B) means little. Choice (C) means a little. Choice (D) means one and is masculine singular. While the English translation would make it appear that all of these would work, the correct expression requires a number. The answer is (D).

36. **A** *Pronouns*

The sentence says, "Did Marie already leave for the post office? No, but she is going to go-------soon." The question is testing the correct pronoun for referring to a location. Choice (A) means there and is used for location when the original phrase used the pronoun *à*. Choice (B) could mean there but can only replace phrases that begin with *de*. Choice (C) means always. Choice (D) means tomorrow. The answer is (A).

37. **B** *Verbs*

The sentence says, "He-------every day before lunch when he was on vacation." The question is testing the correct form of the verb that would describe a past action done before another past action. This is known as the past perfect or *plus-que-parfait* in French. Choice (A) means will swim and is future tense. Choice (B) means had swum and is past perfect. Choice (C) means swam and is *passé composé*. Choice (D) means would swim and is conditional. The answer is (B).

38. **B** *Verbs*

The sentence says, "It's necessary that-------to the bank tomorrow to withdraw some money." The question is testing the correct form of the verb *aller* that follows the phrase *il faut que*. This phrase requires the use of the subjunctive. Choice (A) means I went and is the imperfect. Choice (B) means I (will) go and is the subjunctive. Choice (C) means I will go and is future tense. This may seem correct when translated, but the French phrase requires subjunctive. Choice (D) means I would go and is conditional. The answer is (B).

Part C

The following translation is for questions 39–49.

He had not eaten __(39)__ morning. The cafés that he came across with __(40)__ step intimidated him and __(41)__ him, due to the crowd that __(42)__ was __(43)__ . He spoke __(44)__ a watchman. However, he was so slow to __(45)__ his words that the other did not even bother to listen to him __(46)__ end and __(47)__ turned his back, in the middle of the sentence, while __(48)__ his shoulders. He continued __(49)__ march mechanically.

39. **B** *Vocabulary*

The question is testing the word that most logically completes the phrase. Choice (A) means after. Choice (B) means since. Choice (C) means for. Choice (D) means in, but *dans* is not used before *le matin*. The answer is (B).

40. **C** *Vocabulary*

The question is testing which pronoun can be used to describe his steps. Choice (A) means all, but would require the article *les*. Choice (B) means each one. Choice (C) means each. Choice (D) means some. The answer is (C).

41. **C** *Vocabulary*

The question is testing which word best completes the phrase intimidated. Choice (A) means discussed. Choice (B) means drooled. Choice (C) means disgusted. Choice (D) means liked. The answer is (C).

42. **B** *Pronouns*

The question is testing which pronoun can be used to refer to *les cafés* and can be used with the verb être. Choice (A) means from there. Choice (B) means there. Choice (C) means in. Choice (D) means where. The answer is (B).

43. **D** *Verbs*

The question is testing the correct form of the verb *entasser*, which means crowded into. The word will follow the verb *être*, so the past participle must match the number and gender of *la foule*, which is singular feminine. Choice (A) is the singular masculine participle. Choice (B) is the infinitive form. Choice (C) is the plural feminine. Choice (D) is the singular feminine. The answer is (D).

44. **A** *Prepositions*

The question is testing the word that most logically completes the sentence. Choice (A) means to. Choice (B) means toward, but indicates movement. Choice (C) means with, but in French the preposition *à* is used when addressing a person. Choice (D) means for. The answer is (A).

45. **B** *Verbs*

The question is testing the correct form of *trouver*, to find. The verb will follow the preposition *à* and so needs to be in the infinitive form. Choice (A) is the past participle. Choice (B) is the infinitive. Choice (C) is the plural past participle. Choice (D) is the imperfect form. The answer is (B).

46. **D** *Prepositions*

The question is testing the word that most logically completes the phrase. Choice (A) means through. Choice (B) means up to there. Choice (C) means at the. Choice (D) means until the. The answer is (D).

47. **B** *Pronouns*

The question is testing the correct form of the pronoun. Since the watchman turned his back on the man, a singular indirect object pronoun is needed. Choice (A) is the plural indirect object pronoun. Choice (B) is a singular indirect object pronoun. Choice (C) is the masculine direct object pronoun. Choice (D) is the feminine direct object pronoun. The answer is (B).

48. **C** *Vocabulary*

The question is testing the word that most logically describes what the watchman does with his shoulders. Choice (A) means pulling. Choice (B) mean carrying. Choice (C) means shrugging. Choice (D) means passing. The answer is (C).

49. **C** *Prepositions*

The question is testing the correct preposition to follow *continuer* and precede *marcher*. Choice (A) is null but *continuer* needs a pronoun. Choice (B) means for. Choice (C) means to. Choice (D) means in. The answer is (C).

The following translation is for questions 50–54.

The letter __(50)__ I __(51)__ you, addressed July 1st, __(52)__ remained unanswered, I am thus writing you to implore __(53)__ to take my request __(54)__ consideration.

50. **D** *Pronouns*

This question is testing which relative pronoun most logically completes the phrase. Choice (A) omits the pronoun, which is not permissible in French. Choice (B) means that which and should not follow a noun directly. Choice (C) is an indirect object pronoun meaning for which. The verb *adresser* takes a direct object pronoun. Choice (D) means that and is a direct object pronoun. The answer is (D).

51. **B** *Verbs*

This question is testing the correct form of *avoir* to logically complete the sentence. The context of the letter shows that the first letter was written in the past. Choice (A) is the subjunctive. Choice (B) is the *passé composé*. Choice (C) is the future tense. Choice (D) is imperfect, but it is in the third person (*il avait* instead of *j'avais*). The answer is (B).

52. **C** *Verbs*

This question is testing both the correct verb to combine with the participle *restée* and the form that verb should take. In the participle form, *rester* needs *être*. Choice (A) is the gerund form of *avoir*. Choice (B) means before. Choice (C) is the gerund form of *être*. Choice (D) is the imperfect form; however, when combined with the participle forms the past perfect (*plus-que-parfait*) tense. This tense does not make sense in this context. The answer is (C).

53. **C** *Pronouns*

This question is testing the correct pronoun to use to refer to the addressee of the letter. All the pronouns are in the direct object case, so this is more of a vocabulary question. Choice (A) is the informal you. Choice (B) is me. Choice (C) is the formal you. Choice (D) is him. Since this is a business letter, formal language is needed, as has already been used earlier in the letter. The answer is (C).

54.   **A**   *Prepositions*

This question is testing which pronoun correctly matches with the verb *prendre*. This is an idiomatic expression. Choice (A) is *prendre en*, which means take into. Choice (B) means with. Choice (C) means by. Choice (D) means as. The answer is (A).

The following translation is for questions 55–56.

When I was young, my parents took __(55)__ swimming __(56)__ at Roubaix municipal pool.

55.   **D**   *Pronouns*

This question is testing the correct form and use of pronouns with the verb *emmener*. This verb requires a direct object pronoun. Choice (A) is an indirect object pronoun. Choice (B) is a direct object pronoun meaning you. Choice (C) is a reflexive pronoun meaning himself. Choice (D) is a direct object pronoun meaning me. The answer is (D).

56.   **D**   *Odds and Ends: Adverbs*

This question is testing the adverb that best matches the context of the sentence. Choice (A) means maybe. Choice (B) means yet. Choice (C) means once. Choice (D) means often. Choice (C) might seem plausible, but the verb *emmener* is in the imperfect form, which indicates ongoing action in the past. The phrase *une fois* would require the use of *passé composé*.

Part D
The following translation is for questions 57–61.

"Summer is too long" said the grandmother who welcomed the autumn rain with the same sigh of relief as she did when Jacques left, whose stampings of boredom in rooms with closed shutters during the long sweltering days added to her annoyance.

Besides, she had never understood why a period of each year was specially designed for doing nothing. "I myself never had vacations," she said, and this was true, she had not known either school or free time, she had worked from infancy, and worked without ceasing. She had accepted that, for a greater good, her grandson would not bring money into the house for several years. But from the first day of summer, she had begun grumbling about these three lost months, and, ever since Jacques had begun 9th grade, she had deemed that it was time for him to find work during vacation. "You are going to work this summer," she told him at the end of the school year, "and bring a little bit of money back into this household." You cannot lie around like that doing nothing.

57. **C** The question asks, "When the autumn rain arrived, the grandmother was:"

(A) No. "Annoyed." This is a familiar word—wrong context. She was annoyed at Jacques during the summer.

(B) No. "Sad." There is no evidence of this in the text.

(C) Yes. "Glad." According to the text the grandmother *du même soupir soulagé...le départ de Jacques*.

(D) No. "Proud." There is no evidence of this in the text.

58. **D** The question asks, "During the summer months, Jacques:"

(A) No. "Worked a lot." These are familiar words—wrong context.

(B) No. "Spent his time reading." There is no support for this in the text."

(C) No. "Never stopped having fun." This is opposite the passage which says *les piétinements d'ennui*.

(D) Yes. "Did not know how to entertain himself." This is supported by the passage which says *les piétinements d'ennui*.

59. **C** The question asks, "When she was a little girl, the grandmother:"

(A) No. "Had a shorter vacation than Jacques." Careful with the negation in the French. According to the passage, the grandmother never had vacation: *je n'ai jamais eu de vacances*.

(B) No. "Used to draw pictures during her free time." There is no evidence for this in the passage. Additionally, the grandmother *n'avait connu...le loisir*.

(C) Yes. "Spent all her time working." This is supported by the passage which says *elle avait travaillé enfant, et travaillé sans relâche*.

(D) No. "Never did anything." This is directly contradicted by the passage, which mentions that she was working all the time.

60. **A** The question asks, "According to the passage, it is understood that:"

(A) Yes. "Jacques is attending school." This is supported by the passage which says *Jacques entra en troisième*.

(B) No. "The grandmother does not want Jacques to return to school." This is contradicted by the text, which says *Elle admettait, pour un bénéfice plus grand*.

(C) No. "The grandmother is opposed to Jacques having a summer job." This is contradicted by the text, which says *tu vas travailler cet* été.

(D) No. "Jacques is the third in his class." These are familiar words—wrong context.

61. **C** The question asks, "The grandmother wants Jacques to have a job so that he:"

(A) No. "Might have some spending money." These are familiar words—wrong context.

(B) No. "Might be able to pay for his studies." These are familiar words—wrong context.

(C) Yes. "Might contribute to the family expenses." This is supported by the text, which says *rapporter un peu d'argent à la maison*.

(D) No. "Might learn a trade." There is no evidence for this in the passage.

The following translation is for questions 62–66.

Before coming to Central, he read, I had witnessed a scene of atrocious beauty.

We found that night near the Puerta del Sol a lost three-year-old child who was crying in the shadows. Now, one of the refugee women living in the basement of the Gran Via had no idea what had happened to her own son, a little boy of the same age, blond like the child found in the Puerta del Sol. We tell her the news. She runs to the house where we were keeping the boy, on Calle Montera. In the half-dark of a store with lowered blinds, the boy sucks on a piece of chocolate. The woman approaches him, her arms outstretched, but her eyes grow large, taking on a terrible, demented stare.

This isn't her son.

She stays very still for several minutes. The lost boy smiles at her. Then she rushes at him, clutches him to her, and takes him away, thinking about the child whom we never found.

62. **C** The question asks, "The three year old child is crying because:"

(A) No. "He has lost his piece of chocolate." These are familiar words—wrong context.

(B) No. "He has hurt himself." There is no evidence of this in the text.

(C) Yes. "He does not know where his family is." This is supported by the text that says *qui pleurait perdu*.

(D) No. "It is dark." These are familiar words—wrong context. There is no explanation of why there are shadows (*ténèbres*).

63. **C** The question asks, "The shutters of the store are:"

(A) No. "Open." This is contradicted by the passage that says *baissés*.

(B) No. "Up." This is contradicted by the passage that says *baissés*.

(C) Yes. "Lowered." This is supported by the passage that says *baissés*.

(D) No. "Torn." There is no evidence of this in the passage.

64. **A** The question asks, "The woman 'rushes toward him' means that she goes toward the child:"

(A) Yes. "Running." This is the meaning of *se précipite sur lui*.

(B) No. "Slowly." No this is contradicted by the passage.

(C) No. "Crying." This is a familiar word—wrong context.

(D) No. "Unconcerned." There is no evidence of this in the text.

65. **B** The question asks, "She 'clutches him to her' means that she:"

(A) No. "Pushes him away." This is contradicted by the passage that says *l'emporte*.

(B) Yes. "Hugs him." This is supported by the passage that says *l'emporte*.

(C) No. "Smiles at him." These are familiar words—wrong context.

(D) No. "Hits him." There is no evidence of this in the text.

66. **A** The question asks, "Who does the woman think of as she carries the child away?"

(A) Yes. "Her own son." This is supported by the passage that says *en pensant à l'enfant qu'on n'a pas retrouvé*.

(B) No. "The son of one of the refugees." These are familiar words—wrong context.

(C) No. "The reader's son." These are familiar words—wrong context.

(D) No. "The son of a guard." This is a misunderstanding of *on garde* which means we kept.

The following translations is for questions 67–68.

Train + Car: in complete liberty

Avoid the traffic delays of long trips! Choosing the formula "Train + Car Rental" will guarantee that you can benefit from all the advantages: the comfort of the train, the freedom of the car…All while getting genuine savings! Practical: When you get off the train, a car is right there waiting in the station. Economical: you will benefit from a great reduction of rental costs. Efficient: you will reserve your car at the same time as your train ticket. To take advantage of this offer: make a reservation for the train, at the purchase click on "ADD A CAR," and choose the offer "Train + Car Rental."

67.   **B**   The question asks, "The delays mentioned in the text:"

   (A)   No. "Are used to cork a bottle." This is a second definition of *boucher*.

   (B)   Yes. "Are traffic jams." In the context of the text *les bouchons* is synonymous with *les embouteillages*.

   (C)   No. "Delay the trains." This is not supported by the passage.

   (D)   No. "Avoid wasting time." This is not supported by the passage.

68.   **D**   The question asks, "According to the text, the combination Train + Car Rental:"

   (A)   No. "Is more expensive." This is contradicted by the text that says *tout en réalisant de vraies économies*.

   (B)   No. "Is too expensive." This is not supported by the text.

   (C)   No. "Is not very convenient." This is contradicted by the passage that says *tous les avantages*.

   (D)   Yes. "Is a good deal." This is supported by the text that says *tout en réalisant de vraies économies*.

The following translation is for questions 69–73.

> Happily, (the French blood bank) we are never in desperate need of blood supplies for the short term. We need about 10,000 donations every day, which enable us to see to the needs of a million people each year. Some 500,000 are helped directly by the products we collect and 500,000 more are saved thanks to medications that are derived from blood products. Our repeated appeals to donors are due to the fact that the shelf life of blood products is limited to five days for platelets due to coagulation and to 42 days for blood cells.
>
> This worldwide day of blood donors is even more important since the number of donors has fallen, as it does every year, during the months of April and May, due to the many holidays. It is also necessary to prepare for a decreased frequency of donations during summer vacations. At this time, people are often far from home and don't think about it. For this reason, we try to organize mobile operations, notably at the beach, to remind them of the importance of donating blood. The phenomenon is the same in winter, especially during the Christmas holidays. However, the decrease in donations during this period can be attributed to illness, such as flu and gastrointestinal problems.

69.   **D**   The question asks, "According to the article, the organization:"

   (A)   No. "Receives 10,000 donations every day." These are familiar words—wrong context. The organization needs that many, but there is no proof that they get that many.

   (B)   No. "Has never received 10,000 donations in a single day." These are familiar words—wrong context.

   (C)   No. "Has an immediate need for blood." This is contradicted by the passage that says *nous ne manquons jamais de stocks de sang à court terme*.

   (D)   Yes. "Has enough blood for the immediate future." This is supported by the passage that says *nous ne manquons jamais de stocks de sang à court terme*.

70. **A** The question asks, "The regular appeals to donors:"

(A) Yes. "Are necessary for several reasons." This is supported by the text that says *la durée de vie des produits sanguins est limitée*.

(B) No. "Make appointments over the telephone." This is confusion over the meaning of *les appels* in the context of the passage.

(C) No. "Are of little interest." This is not supported by the passage.

(D) No. "Are made every 42 days." These are familiar words—wrong context.

71. **B** The question asks, "This worldwide blood donor's day is important because:"

(A) No. "There was a big festival." These are familiar words—wrong context.

(B) Yes. "As usual, there are fewer donors in springtime." This is supported by the passage that says, *le nombre de dons a chuté, comme chaque année, durant les mois d'avril et de mai*.

(C) No. "Blood donors have whispered to one another." This is confusion between the words *chuter* and *chuchoter*.

(D) No. "It was during the months of April and May." These are familiar words—wrong context."

72. **D** The question asks, "The phrase 'don't think about it' means that people:"

(A) No. "Don't often plan their vacations." These are familiar words—wrong context.

(B) No. "Are often wounded on vacation." These are familiar words—wrong context.

(C) No. "Travel to foreign countries." These are familiar words—wrong context.

(D) Yes. "Don't remember to give blood." This is supported by the pronoun *y* which refers to that which people think about (*penser à*).

73. **C** The question asks, "'The phenomenon' refers to:"

(A) No. "An extraordinary thing." This is a different meaning of the word.

(B) No. "The Christmas holidays." These are familiar words—wrong context.

(C) Yes. "A decrease in donations in December and January." This is supported by the passage that says, *est le même en hiver*.

(D) No. "The frequent illnesses of winter." These are familiar words—wrong context.

The following translation is for questions 74–75.

Here is the recipe for Madeleines, those little oval cookies with a plump center, so dear to Marcel Proust.

The day before, carefully mix the following ingredients until obtaining a perfectly smooth dough:

Madeleines

Flour	90g
Sugar	90g
Yeast	2g
Natural Honey	10g
Eggs	2
Melted Butter	90g
Lemon Zest	
Anise (optional)	1 clove

Store the dough in the refrigerator.

The next day, distribute the dough into 12 buttered madeleine molds. Bake in an oven on medium heat until the cookies reach a beautiful golden color. Place them on a cooling rack as soon as you remove them from the oven, let them cool, and enjoy!

74. **B** The question asks, "When do you have to prepare the dough for the madeleines?"

(A) No. "The next day." These are familiar words—wrong context.

(B) Yes. "The day before." This is supported by the text that says *la veille*.

(C) No. "Two hours ahead of time." There is no support for this in the passage.

(D) No. "Yesterday." This is too literal.

75. **C** The question asks, "According to the recipe, anise is an ingredient which is:"

(A) No. "Necessary." This is contradicted by the passage that says *facultatif*.

(B) No. "Sweet." This is not supported by the passage.

(C) Yes. "Optional." This is a synonym of the word *facultatif*.

(D) No. "Fragrant." While this may be true, this is not supported by the passage.

The following translation is for questions 76–80.

> The hunchback reappeared, a brochure in his hands. He settled himself comfortably, elbows on the table, his chin in his hands.
>
> "I already hinted to you," he said, "that I had some really large projects in the works."
>
> "Huge projects."
>
> "It is that exact thing, and I'm going to reveal it to you today." He took on a confidential tone.
>
> "That which brought me here is, above all else, my love of nature. But even though I don't lack money at the moment, I have a family to feed, and I must think about the future of my little girl: this is why, the philosopher in me wanted to reconcile its desire for a natural life and the obligation of figuring out how to earn a fortune.
>
> Throughout this discourse, Ugolin remembered only the last few words. He had the intention of "earning a fortune." Leave earning fortunes to the Romarins! With what? Surely not with these half dead olive trees, nor these agonized almond trees; nor with the vegetables, the wheat, or the wine. Thus he knew about the spring, and he wanted perhaps to plant carnations! That is why, as a hopeless counterattack, he said, "You know, these flowers here, even if you have a good artesian spring…"
>
> "What flowers?" said the hunchback in a surprised tone. You think I want to make it rich selling wild roses and thistles? And what spring? You know that mine is pretty far from here.

76.   **C**   The question asks, "I already hinted to you" means that "I have already":

(A)   No. "Told you." This is too explicit.

(B)   No. "Repeated to you." This is too explicit.

(C)   Yes. "Suggested to you." This is supported by the passage *je vais vous le révéler.*

(D)   No. "Lied to you." There is no support for this in the passage.

77.   **B**   The question asks, "The hunchback has big plans because:"

(A)   No. "He needs money right away." This is contradicted by the passage that says *je ne manque pas d'argent en ce moment.*

(B)   Yes. "He thinks about his daughter's future." This is supported by the passage that says *je dois assurer l'avenir de ma fillette.*

(C)   No. "He is a philosopher." These are familiar words—wrong context.

(D)   No. "He loves money." These are familiar words—wrong context.

78.   **A**   The question asks, "From the hunchback's speech, Ugolin remembers:"

(A)   Yes. "Only the last words." This is supported by the passage that says *De ce discours, Ugolin ne retint que les derniers mots.*

(B)   No. "Maybe the first words." This is contradicted in the passage that says *que les derniers mots.*

(C)   No. "Always the last sentence." These are familiar words—wrong context.

(D)   No. "Everything but the end." These are familiar words—wrong context.

79.   **B**   The question asks, "In lines 18-23, after hearing the hunchback's plans, Ugolin is:"

(A)   No. "Amused." This is not supported by the passage.

(B)   Yes. "Very worried." This is supported by the passage *Avec quoi?...par une contreattaque désespérée.*

(C)   No. "Full of joy." This is contradicted by the passage that says *désespérée.*

(D)   No. "Reassured." This is contradicted by the passage that says *désespérée.*

80.   **D**   The question asks, "Ugolin is trying to find out whether the hunchback:"

(A)   No. "Is going to plant a vineyard." These are familiar words—wrong context.

(B)   No. "Will save the olive trees and the almond trees." These are familiar words—wrong context.

(C)   No. "Is planning to sell thistles." These are familiar words—wrong context.

(D)   Yes. "Knew about the existence of the spring." This is supported by the passage that says *il connaissait donc la source.*

The following translation is for questions 81–85.

> You understand all of a sudden that the real city is the naval docks, that the city does not exist except to serve it, that the docks overflow into it. Under all forms, in all places, and in all corners reappears the administration, the discipline, the sheet of lined paper, the framework, the rules. One greatly admires the artificial symmetry and the idiotic cleanliness. At the maritime hospital, for example, the rooms are polished to such an extent that a convalescent, trying to walk on his still healing leg, would break the other by falling down. But it's beautiful, it shines, and one gazes at oneself in it. Between each room is a courtyard, but one in which the sun never shines and where the grass is carefully pulled up. The kitchens are truly superb, but at a distance, such that in winter, everything must be icy cold by the time it gets to the patients. It is really all about them! Aren't the casseroles shiny? We saw a man who had cracked his skull by falling from a frigate and who still had not been treated after eighteen hours; but the linens were very white because the linen closet is very well kept.

81.   **B**   The question asks, "'In every place' means:"

(A)   No. "Nowhere." This is opposite what the phrase means.

(B)   Yes. "Everywhere." This is a synonym of *en tous lieux*.

(C)   No. "Somewhere else." This is not supported by the passage.

(D)   No. "Somewhere." This is not supported by the passage.

82.   **D**   The question asks, "The convalescent runs the risks of breaking his other leg because the floor is:"

(A)   No. "Wet." This is a misunderstanding of the passage. It is slippery due to wax, not liquid.

(B)   No. "Uneven." This is not supported by the passage.

(C)   No. "Full of holes." This is not supported by the passage.

(D)   Yes. "Slippery." This is supported by the passage that says *les salles sont cirées de telle façon… doit se casser l'autre.*

83.   **D**   The question asks, "The courtyard between every room is:"

(A)   No. "Full of sun." This is contradicted by the passage that says *le soleil ne vient jamais.*

(B)   No. "Without any shade." This is contradicted by the passage that says *le soleil ne vient jamais.*

(C)   No. "Sunny." This is contradicted by the passage that says *le soleil ne vient jamais.*

(D)   Yes. "Without any sun." This is supported by the passage that says *le soleil ne vient jamais.*

84.   **D**   The question asks, "In winter the patients' meals are served:"

(A)   No. "Piping hot." This is contradicted by the passage that says *glacé.*

(B)   No. "Lukewarm." This is contradicted by the passage that says *glacé.*

(C)   No. "At the right temperature." This is contradicted by the passage that says *glacé.*

(D)   Yes. "Very cold." This is supported by the passage that says *glacé.*

85.   **A**   The question asks, "Flaubert's tone in this passage is:"

(A)   Yes. "Sarcastic." This is supported throughout the passage, such as when it says *la symétrie factice* or *la propreté imbécile.*

(B)   No. "Serious." This is opposite the tone of the passage.

(C)   No. "Playful." This is not strong enough.

(D)   No. "Tragic." There is no evidence of this in the passage.

HOW TO SCORE PRACTICE TEST 2

When you take the real exam, the proctors will collect your test booklet and bubble sheet and send your answer sheet to a processing center where a computer looks at the pattern of filled-in ovals on your answer sheet and gives you a score. We are providing you, however, with this more primitive way of scoring your exam.

Determining Your Score

STEP 1   Using the answer key, determine how many questions you got right and how many you got wrong on the test. Remember: Questions that you do not answer do not count as either right answers or wrong answers.

STEP 2   Write the number of correct answers on line A.   (A) _____

STEP 3   Write the number of wrong answers on line B. Divide that number by 3.   (B) _____ ÷ 3 = _____

STEP 4   Subtract the number of wrong answers divided by 3 on line B from the number of correct answers on line A, and round to the nearest whole number. (C) is your **raw score**.   (A) _____ – (B) _____ = (C) _____

STEP 5   To determine your **real score**, look up your raw score in the left column of the Score Conversion Table on the next page; the corresponding score on the right is the score you earned on the exam.

PRACTICE TEST 2
SCORE CONVERSION TABLE

Raw score	Scaled score	Raw score	Scaled score	Raw score	Scaled score
85	800	45	630	5	410
84	800	44	620	4	410
83	800	43	620	3	400
82	800	42	610	2	400
81	800	41	610	1	390
80	800	40	600	0	390
79	800	39	600	−1	380
78	800	38	590	−2	380
77	800	37	580	−3	370
76	790	36	580	−4	360
75	790	35	570	−5	360
74	780	34	570	−6	350
73	780	33	560	−7	350
72	770	32	560	−8	340
71	770	31	550	−9	340
70	760	30	550	−10	330
69	760	29	540	−11	330
68	750	28	540	−12	320
67	740	27	530	−13	320
66	740	26	530	−14	310
65	730	25	520	−15	300
64	730	24	520	−16	290
63	720	23	510	−17	290
62	720	22	500	−18	280
61	710	21	500	−19	280
60	710	20	490	−20	270
59	700	19	490	−21	270
58	700	18	480	−22	260
57	690	17	480	−23	260
56	690	16	470	−24	250
55	680	15	470	−25 through −28	240
54	680	14	460		
53	670	13	460		
52	660	12	450		
51	660	11	450		
50	650	10	440		
49	650	9	430		
48	640	8	430		
47	640	7	420		
46	630	6	420		

Completely darken bubbles with a No. 2 pencil. If you make a mistake, be sure to erase mark completely. Erase all stray marks.

1.

YOUR NAME: _____
(Print)   Last   First   M.I.

SIGNATURE: _____   DATE: ___ / ___ / ___

HOME ADDRESS: _____
(Print)   Number and Street

_____
City   State   Zip Code

PHONE NO.: _____
(Print)

IMPORTANT: Please fill in these boxes exactly as shown on the back cover of your test book.

2. TEST FORM

_____

6. DATE OF BIRTH

Month		Day		Year	
◯ JAN					
◯ FEB	⓪	⓪	⓪	⓪	
◯ MAR	①	①	①	①	
◯ APR	②	②	②	②	
◯ MAY	③	③	③	③	
◯ JUN		④	④	④	
◯ JUL		⑤	⑤	⑤	
◯ AUG		⑥	⑥	⑥	
◯ SEP		⑦	⑦	⑦	
◯ OCT		⑧	⑧	⑧	
◯ NOV		⑨	⑨	⑨	
◯ DEC					

3. TEST CODE

⓪	Ⓐ	Ⓙ	⓪	⓪
①	Ⓑ	Ⓚ	①	①
②	Ⓒ	Ⓛ	②	②
③	Ⓓ	Ⓜ	③	③
④	Ⓔ	Ⓝ	④	④
⑤	Ⓕ	Ⓞ	⑤	⑤
⑥	Ⓖ	Ⓟ	⑥	⑥
⑦	Ⓗ	Ⓠ	⑦	⑦
⑧	Ⓘ	Ⓡ	⑧	⑧
⑨			⑨	⑨

4. REGISTRATION NUMBER

⓪	⓪	⓪	⓪	⓪	⓪	⓪
①	①	①	①	①	①	①
②	②	②	②	②	②	②
③	③	③	③	③	③	③
④	④	④	④	④	④	④
⑤	⑤	⑤	⑤	⑤	⑤	⑤
⑥	⑥	⑥	⑥	⑥	⑥	⑥
⑦	⑦	⑦	⑦	⑦	⑦	⑦
⑧	⑧	⑧	⑧	⑧	⑧	⑧
⑨	⑨	⑨	⑨	⑨	⑨	⑨

7. SEX

◯ MALE
◯ FEMALE

5. YOUR NAME

First 4 letters of last name				FIRST INIT	MID INIT
Ⓐ	Ⓐ	Ⓐ	Ⓐ	Ⓐ	Ⓐ
Ⓑ	Ⓑ	Ⓑ	Ⓑ	Ⓑ	Ⓑ
Ⓒ	Ⓒ	Ⓒ	Ⓒ	Ⓒ	Ⓒ
Ⓓ	Ⓓ	Ⓓ	Ⓓ	Ⓓ	Ⓓ
Ⓔ	Ⓔ	Ⓔ	Ⓔ	Ⓔ	Ⓔ
Ⓕ	Ⓕ	Ⓕ	Ⓕ	Ⓕ	Ⓕ
Ⓖ	Ⓖ	Ⓖ	Ⓖ	Ⓖ	Ⓖ
Ⓗ	Ⓗ	Ⓗ	Ⓗ	Ⓗ	Ⓗ
Ⓘ	Ⓘ	Ⓘ	Ⓘ	Ⓘ	Ⓘ
Ⓙ	Ⓙ	Ⓙ	Ⓙ	Ⓙ	Ⓙ
Ⓚ	Ⓚ	Ⓚ	Ⓚ	Ⓚ	Ⓚ
Ⓛ	Ⓛ	Ⓛ	Ⓛ	Ⓛ	Ⓛ
Ⓜ	Ⓜ	Ⓜ	Ⓜ	Ⓜ	Ⓜ
Ⓝ	Ⓝ	Ⓝ	Ⓝ	Ⓝ	Ⓝ
Ⓞ	Ⓞ	Ⓞ	Ⓞ	Ⓞ	Ⓞ
Ⓟ	Ⓟ	Ⓟ	Ⓟ	Ⓟ	Ⓟ
Ⓠ	Ⓠ	Ⓠ	Ⓠ	Ⓠ	Ⓠ
Ⓡ	Ⓡ	Ⓡ	Ⓡ	Ⓡ	Ⓡ
Ⓢ	Ⓢ	Ⓢ	Ⓢ	Ⓢ	Ⓢ
Ⓣ	Ⓣ	Ⓣ	Ⓣ	Ⓣ	Ⓣ
Ⓤ	Ⓤ	Ⓤ	Ⓤ	Ⓤ	Ⓤ
Ⓥ	Ⓥ	Ⓥ	Ⓥ	Ⓥ	Ⓥ
Ⓦ	Ⓦ	Ⓦ	Ⓦ	Ⓦ	Ⓦ
Ⓧ	Ⓧ	Ⓧ	Ⓧ	Ⓧ	Ⓧ
Ⓨ	Ⓨ	Ⓨ	Ⓨ	Ⓨ	Ⓨ
Ⓩ	Ⓩ	Ⓩ	Ⓩ	Ⓩ	Ⓩ

The **Princeton** Review®

1. Ⓐ Ⓑ Ⓒ Ⓓ
2. Ⓐ Ⓑ Ⓒ Ⓓ
3. Ⓐ Ⓑ Ⓒ Ⓓ
4. Ⓐ Ⓑ Ⓒ Ⓓ
5. Ⓐ Ⓑ Ⓒ Ⓓ
6. Ⓐ Ⓑ Ⓒ Ⓓ
7. Ⓐ Ⓑ Ⓒ Ⓓ
8. Ⓐ Ⓑ Ⓒ Ⓓ
9. Ⓐ Ⓑ Ⓒ Ⓓ
10. Ⓐ Ⓑ Ⓒ Ⓓ
11. Ⓐ Ⓑ Ⓒ Ⓓ
12. Ⓐ Ⓑ Ⓒ Ⓓ
13. Ⓐ Ⓑ Ⓒ Ⓓ
14. Ⓐ Ⓑ Ⓒ Ⓓ
15. Ⓐ Ⓑ Ⓒ Ⓓ
16. Ⓐ Ⓑ Ⓒ Ⓓ
17. Ⓐ Ⓑ Ⓒ Ⓓ
18. Ⓐ Ⓑ Ⓒ Ⓓ
19. Ⓐ Ⓑ Ⓒ Ⓓ
20. Ⓐ Ⓑ Ⓒ Ⓓ
21. Ⓐ Ⓑ Ⓒ Ⓓ

22. Ⓐ Ⓑ Ⓒ Ⓓ
23. Ⓐ Ⓑ Ⓒ Ⓓ
24. Ⓐ Ⓑ Ⓒ Ⓓ
25. Ⓐ Ⓑ Ⓒ Ⓓ
26. Ⓐ Ⓑ Ⓒ Ⓓ
27. Ⓐ Ⓑ Ⓒ Ⓓ
28. Ⓐ Ⓑ Ⓒ Ⓓ
29. Ⓐ Ⓑ Ⓒ Ⓓ
30. Ⓐ Ⓑ Ⓒ Ⓓ
31. Ⓐ Ⓑ Ⓒ Ⓓ
32. Ⓐ Ⓑ Ⓒ Ⓓ
33. Ⓐ Ⓑ Ⓒ Ⓓ
34. Ⓐ Ⓑ Ⓒ Ⓓ
35. Ⓐ Ⓑ Ⓒ Ⓓ
36. Ⓐ Ⓑ Ⓒ Ⓓ
37. Ⓐ Ⓑ Ⓒ Ⓓ
38. Ⓐ Ⓑ Ⓒ Ⓓ
39. Ⓐ Ⓑ Ⓒ Ⓓ
40. Ⓐ Ⓑ Ⓒ Ⓓ
41. Ⓐ Ⓑ Ⓒ Ⓓ
42. Ⓐ Ⓑ Ⓒ Ⓓ

43. Ⓐ Ⓑ Ⓒ Ⓓ
44. Ⓐ Ⓑ Ⓒ Ⓓ
45. Ⓐ Ⓑ Ⓒ Ⓓ
46. Ⓐ Ⓑ Ⓒ Ⓓ
47. Ⓐ Ⓑ Ⓒ Ⓓ
48. Ⓐ Ⓑ Ⓒ Ⓓ
49. Ⓐ Ⓑ Ⓒ Ⓓ
50. Ⓐ Ⓑ Ⓒ Ⓓ
51. Ⓐ Ⓑ Ⓒ Ⓓ
52. Ⓐ Ⓑ Ⓒ Ⓓ
53. Ⓐ Ⓑ Ⓒ Ⓓ
54. Ⓐ Ⓑ Ⓒ Ⓓ
55. Ⓐ Ⓑ Ⓒ Ⓓ
56. Ⓐ Ⓑ Ⓒ Ⓓ
57. Ⓐ Ⓑ Ⓒ Ⓓ
58. Ⓐ Ⓑ Ⓒ Ⓓ
59. Ⓐ Ⓑ Ⓒ Ⓓ
60. Ⓐ Ⓑ Ⓒ Ⓓ
61. Ⓐ Ⓑ Ⓒ Ⓓ
62. Ⓐ Ⓑ Ⓒ Ⓓ
63. Ⓐ Ⓑ Ⓒ Ⓓ

64. Ⓐ Ⓑ Ⓒ Ⓓ
65. Ⓐ Ⓑ Ⓒ Ⓓ
66. Ⓐ Ⓑ Ⓒ Ⓓ
67. Ⓐ Ⓑ Ⓒ Ⓓ
68. Ⓐ Ⓑ Ⓒ Ⓓ
69. Ⓐ Ⓑ Ⓒ Ⓓ
70. Ⓐ Ⓑ Ⓒ Ⓓ
71. Ⓐ Ⓑ Ⓒ Ⓓ
72. Ⓐ Ⓑ Ⓒ Ⓓ
73. Ⓐ Ⓑ Ⓒ Ⓓ
74. Ⓐ Ⓑ Ⓒ Ⓓ
75. Ⓐ Ⓑ Ⓒ Ⓓ
76. Ⓐ Ⓑ Ⓒ Ⓓ
77. Ⓐ Ⓑ Ⓒ Ⓓ
78. Ⓐ Ⓑ Ⓒ Ⓓ
79. Ⓐ Ⓑ Ⓒ Ⓓ
80. Ⓐ Ⓑ Ⓒ Ⓓ
81. Ⓐ Ⓑ Ⓒ Ⓓ
82. Ⓐ Ⓑ Ⓒ Ⓓ
83. Ⓐ Ⓑ Ⓒ Ⓓ
84. Ⓐ Ⓑ Ⓒ Ⓓ
85. Ⓐ Ⓑ Ⓒ Ⓓ

Completely darken bubbles with a No. 2 pencil. If you make a mistake, be sure to erase mark completely. Erase all stray marks.

1.

YOUR NAME: _____
(Print)
                  Last   First   M.I.

SIGNATURE: _____   DATE: ___ / ___ / ___

HOME ADDRESS: _____
(Print)
                Number and Street

_____
   City   State   Zip Code

PHONE NO.: _____
(Print)

IMPORTANT: Please fill in these boxes exactly as shown on the back cover of your test book.

2. TEST FORM

_____

6. DATE OF BIRTH

Month	Day		Year	
⟨⟩ JAN				
⟨⟩ FEB	⓪	⓪	⓪	⓪
⟨⟩ MAR	①	①	①	①
⟨⟩ APR	②	②	②	②
⟨⟩ MAY	③	③	③	③
⟨⟩ JUN		④	④	④
⟨⟩ JUL		⑤	⑤	⑤
⟨⟩ AUG		⑥	⑥	⑥
⟨⟩ SEP		⑦	⑦	⑦
⟨⟩ OCT		⑧	⑧	⑧
⟨⟩ NOV		⑨	⑨	⑨
⟨⟩ DEC				

3. TEST CODE

⓪	Ⓐ	Ⓙ	⓪	⓪
①	Ⓑ	Ⓚ	①	①
②	Ⓒ	Ⓛ	②	②
③	Ⓓ	Ⓜ	③	③
④	Ⓔ	Ⓝ	④	④
⑤	Ⓕ	Ⓞ	⑤	⑤
⑥	Ⓖ	Ⓟ	⑥	⑥
⑦	Ⓗ	Ⓠ	⑦	⑦
⑧	Ⓘ	Ⓡ	⑧	⑧
⑨			⑨	⑨

4. REGISTRATION NUMBER

⓪	⓪	⓪	⓪	⓪	⓪
①	①	①	①	①	①
②	②	②	②	②	②
③	③	③	③	③	③
④	④	④	④	④	④
⑤	⑤	⑤	⑤	⑤	⑤
⑥	⑥	⑥	⑥	⑥	⑥
⑦	⑦	⑦	⑦	⑦	⑦
⑧	⑧	⑧	⑧	⑧	⑧
⑨	⑨	⑨	⑨	⑨	⑨

7. SEX

⟨⟩ MALE
⟨⟩ FEMALE

The Princeton Review®

5. YOUR NAME

First 4 letters of last name				FIRST INIT	MID INIT
Ⓐ	Ⓐ	Ⓐ	Ⓐ	Ⓐ	Ⓐ
Ⓑ	Ⓑ	Ⓑ	Ⓑ	Ⓑ	Ⓑ
Ⓒ	Ⓒ	Ⓒ	Ⓒ	Ⓒ	Ⓒ
Ⓓ	Ⓓ	Ⓓ	Ⓓ	Ⓓ	Ⓓ
Ⓔ	Ⓔ	Ⓔ	Ⓔ	Ⓔ	Ⓔ
Ⓕ	Ⓕ	Ⓕ	Ⓕ	Ⓕ	Ⓕ
Ⓖ	Ⓖ	Ⓖ	Ⓖ	Ⓖ	Ⓖ
Ⓗ	Ⓗ	Ⓗ	Ⓗ	Ⓗ	Ⓗ
Ⓘ	Ⓘ	Ⓘ	Ⓘ	Ⓘ	Ⓘ
Ⓙ	Ⓙ	Ⓙ	Ⓙ	Ⓙ	Ⓙ
Ⓚ	Ⓚ	Ⓚ	Ⓚ	Ⓚ	Ⓚ
Ⓛ	Ⓛ	Ⓛ	Ⓛ	Ⓛ	Ⓛ
Ⓜ	Ⓜ	Ⓜ	Ⓜ	Ⓜ	Ⓜ
Ⓝ	Ⓝ	Ⓝ	Ⓝ	Ⓝ	Ⓝ
Ⓞ	Ⓞ	Ⓞ	Ⓞ	Ⓞ	Ⓞ
Ⓟ	Ⓟ	Ⓟ	Ⓟ	Ⓟ	Ⓟ
Ⓠ	Ⓠ	Ⓠ	Ⓠ	Ⓠ	Ⓠ
Ⓡ	Ⓡ	Ⓡ	Ⓡ	Ⓡ	Ⓡ
Ⓢ	Ⓢ	Ⓢ	Ⓢ	Ⓢ	Ⓢ
Ⓣ	Ⓣ	Ⓣ	Ⓣ	Ⓣ	Ⓣ
Ⓤ	Ⓤ	Ⓤ	Ⓤ	Ⓤ	Ⓤ
Ⓥ	Ⓥ	Ⓥ	Ⓥ	Ⓥ	Ⓥ
Ⓦ	Ⓦ	Ⓦ	Ⓦ	Ⓦ	Ⓦ
Ⓧ	Ⓧ	Ⓧ	Ⓧ	Ⓧ	Ⓧ
Ⓨ	Ⓨ	Ⓨ	Ⓨ	Ⓨ	Ⓨ
Ⓩ	Ⓩ	Ⓩ	Ⓩ	Ⓩ	Ⓩ

1. Ⓐ Ⓑ Ⓒ Ⓓ
2. Ⓐ Ⓑ Ⓒ Ⓓ
3. Ⓐ Ⓑ Ⓒ Ⓓ
4. Ⓐ Ⓑ Ⓒ Ⓓ
5. Ⓐ Ⓑ Ⓒ Ⓓ
6. Ⓐ Ⓑ Ⓒ Ⓓ
7. Ⓐ Ⓑ Ⓒ Ⓓ
8. Ⓐ Ⓑ Ⓒ Ⓓ
9. Ⓐ Ⓑ Ⓒ Ⓓ
10. Ⓐ Ⓑ Ⓒ Ⓓ
11. Ⓐ Ⓑ Ⓒ Ⓓ
12. Ⓐ Ⓑ Ⓒ Ⓓ
13. Ⓐ Ⓑ Ⓒ Ⓓ
14. Ⓐ Ⓑ Ⓒ Ⓓ
15. Ⓐ Ⓑ Ⓒ Ⓓ
16. Ⓐ Ⓑ Ⓒ Ⓓ
17. Ⓐ Ⓑ Ⓒ Ⓓ
18. Ⓐ Ⓑ Ⓒ Ⓓ
19. Ⓐ Ⓑ Ⓒ Ⓓ
20. Ⓐ Ⓑ Ⓒ Ⓓ
21. Ⓐ Ⓑ Ⓒ Ⓓ

22. Ⓐ Ⓑ Ⓒ Ⓓ
23. Ⓐ Ⓑ Ⓒ Ⓓ
24. Ⓐ Ⓑ Ⓒ Ⓓ
25. Ⓐ Ⓑ Ⓒ Ⓓ
26. Ⓐ Ⓑ Ⓒ Ⓓ
27. Ⓐ Ⓑ Ⓒ Ⓓ
28. Ⓐ Ⓑ Ⓒ Ⓓ
29. Ⓐ Ⓑ Ⓒ Ⓓ
30. Ⓐ Ⓑ Ⓒ Ⓓ
31. Ⓐ Ⓑ Ⓒ Ⓓ
32. Ⓐ Ⓑ Ⓒ Ⓓ
33. Ⓐ Ⓑ Ⓒ Ⓓ
34. Ⓐ Ⓑ Ⓒ Ⓓ
35. Ⓐ Ⓑ Ⓒ Ⓓ
36. Ⓐ Ⓑ Ⓒ Ⓓ
37. Ⓐ Ⓑ Ⓒ Ⓓ
38. Ⓐ Ⓑ Ⓒ Ⓓ
39. Ⓐ Ⓑ Ⓒ Ⓓ
40. Ⓐ Ⓑ Ⓒ Ⓓ
41. Ⓐ Ⓑ Ⓒ Ⓓ
42. Ⓐ Ⓑ Ⓒ Ⓓ

43. Ⓐ Ⓑ Ⓒ Ⓓ
44. Ⓐ Ⓑ Ⓒ Ⓓ
45. Ⓐ Ⓑ Ⓒ Ⓓ
46. Ⓐ Ⓑ Ⓒ Ⓓ
47. Ⓐ Ⓑ Ⓒ Ⓓ
48. Ⓐ Ⓑ Ⓒ Ⓓ
49. Ⓐ Ⓑ Ⓒ Ⓓ
50. Ⓐ Ⓑ Ⓒ Ⓓ
51. Ⓐ Ⓑ Ⓒ Ⓓ
52. Ⓐ Ⓑ Ⓒ Ⓓ
53. Ⓐ Ⓑ Ⓒ Ⓓ
54. Ⓐ Ⓑ Ⓒ Ⓓ
55. Ⓐ Ⓑ Ⓒ Ⓓ
56. Ⓐ Ⓑ Ⓒ Ⓓ
57. Ⓐ Ⓑ Ⓒ Ⓓ
58. Ⓐ Ⓑ Ⓒ Ⓓ
59. Ⓐ Ⓑ Ⓒ Ⓓ
60. Ⓐ Ⓑ Ⓒ Ⓓ
61. Ⓐ Ⓑ Ⓒ Ⓓ
62. Ⓐ Ⓑ Ⓒ Ⓓ
63. Ⓐ Ⓑ Ⓒ Ⓓ

64. Ⓐ Ⓑ Ⓒ Ⓓ
65. Ⓐ Ⓑ Ⓒ Ⓓ
66. Ⓐ Ⓑ Ⓒ Ⓓ
67. Ⓐ Ⓑ Ⓒ Ⓓ
68. Ⓐ Ⓑ Ⓒ Ⓓ
69. Ⓐ Ⓑ Ⓒ Ⓓ
70. Ⓐ Ⓑ Ⓒ Ⓓ
71. Ⓐ Ⓑ Ⓒ Ⓓ
72. Ⓐ Ⓑ Ⓒ Ⓓ
73. Ⓐ Ⓑ Ⓒ Ⓓ
74. Ⓐ Ⓑ Ⓒ Ⓓ
75. Ⓐ Ⓑ Ⓒ Ⓓ
76. Ⓐ Ⓑ Ⓒ Ⓓ
77. Ⓐ Ⓑ Ⓒ Ⓓ
78. Ⓐ Ⓑ Ⓒ Ⓓ
79. Ⓐ Ⓑ Ⓒ Ⓓ
80. Ⓐ Ⓑ Ⓒ Ⓓ
81. Ⓐ Ⓑ Ⓒ Ⓓ
82. Ⓐ Ⓑ Ⓒ Ⓓ
83. Ⓐ Ⓑ Ⓒ Ⓓ
84. Ⓐ Ⓑ Ⓒ Ⓓ
85. Ⓐ Ⓑ Ⓒ Ⓓ

STUDY GUIDE FOR THE SAT SUBJECT TEST IN FRENCH

Bad news first: there's no one right way to study for a test. If you're looking for a surefire shortcut, there simply isn't one. The good news, however, is that if you're reading this, you're already on the right track—you're putting in the three key resources for successful study habits: time, energy, and focus. The following study guide features a few suggested ways to tackle the French Subject Test, depending on whether the test is just around the corner (**1 Week Cram**) or if you've got more time to practice (**7 Week Stretch**).

Remember that these plans are simply suggestions; everybody learns in their own way and at their own pace. When choosing where to begin, use what you know about your own study habits. If cramming for a test hasn't been effective for you in the past, perhaps it's time to try spreading out your practice over a longer period of time. On the other hand, if you find yourself forgetting key material just before the test, you might want to try an intense refresher in the week leading up to the exam.

If you're not sure how best to prepare, we recommend using Practice Test 1 (pages 17-32) as a diagnostic, which means giving yourself enough time to mirror what will be allotted to you on test day, and then working in a quiet and uninterrupted environment. When you're done, check answers against the answer key on page 34. Make sure to check off which ones you got right and which ones you got wrong so you know where you have to practice. If you're happy with your results, you might just spend a week focusing on the specific section for which you had wrong answers. On the other hand, if you're struggling across the board, you may be best served by building up those content gaps over the course of a few months. Here are our recommendations.

1 Week Cram

The following schedule is an extremely abbreviated way of gaining maximum exposure to the course. It involves reinforcement over a limited amount of time, so you'll be touching on each bit of content four times—once when you skim the chapter to get a general sense of the ideas within, again when you read the summary to remind yourself of what you're expected to have learned, a third time when you test your knowledge against the drill questions, and finally when you mark key terms that you remain unfamiliar or uncomfortable with. If you have extra time on any given day, we recommend reading the portions of each content chapter that you feel least comfortable with.

Day 0, Sunday [2 hours]

Take Practice Test 1, and review the Answers and Explanations, using the Answer Key to keep track of which questions you missed and which you answered correctly. Keep the results of the test in mind as you go through the next week, and slow down your skimming when you hit a section where you struggled.

Day 1, Monday [1 hour]

- Review Chapter 1, "Introduction."

- Familiarize yourself with the exam format and our test-taking strategies in Chapter 2, "General Strategy."

- Skim Chapter 3, "Vocabulary."

Day 2, Tuesday [1.5 hours]

- Review Chapter 4, "Vocabulary Review."

- Complete the Chapter 3 Drills (pages 59-69).

Day 3, Wednesday [2 hours]

- Read Chapter 5, "Grammar Review."

Day 4, Thursday [2.5 hours]

- Complete Chapter 5 Drills (pages 130, 146, 155, 160-163).

Day 5, Friday [3 hours]

- Read Chapter 6, "Reading Comprehension."

- Read Chapter 7, "French Listening."

Day 6, Saturday [3.5 hours]

- Complete Chapter 6 Drills (pages 174-179).

- Take Practice Test 2.

Day 7, Sunday [3 hours]

- Review the Drill Answers and Explanations (starting on page 189).

- Review Practice Test 2 Answers and Explanations.

- Go back and reread any sections where you might still have some difficulty.

This is it, your final chance to review. Look at all the circled Key Terms and look at the questions you got wrong on the Practice Tests. If there's any overlap, that's a clear sign that you need more practice in that section, so spend any remaining time reviewing that content. That said, you've been working hard, so don't burn yourself out by pushing for more than two hours. Rest is an important part of studying, too: It's when the mind processes everything.

7 Week Stretch

This schedule doesn't break things into a day-to-day calendar, but helps to establish what you should aim to accomplish within a given week. For some, that may be a matter of evenly distributing the reading material across the week. For others, it may be to spend one day studying, one day reviewing, and one day testing. We have arranged the material by EARLY, MID, and LATE week.

Week 1

- EARLY: Take Practice Test 1 and read the Answers and Explanations for Practice Test 1.

- MID: Read Chapter 1, "Introduction," and familiarize yourself with our test-taking strategies in Chapter 2, "General Strategy."

- LATE: Read Chapter 3, "Vocabulary."

Week 2

- EARLY: Complete Chapter 3 Drills (pages 59-66).

- MID: Read Chapter 4, "Vocabulary Review."

- LATE: Reread the summaries for Chapters 3-4. Take the Comprehensive Drill (page 67)

Week 3

- EARLY: Read Chapter 5, "Grammar Review."

- MID: Review Grammar charts and Basic Terms.

- LATE: In Chapter 5, complete Drill 1: Pronoun Questions (page 130), and Drill 2: Verb Questions (page 146).

Week 4

- EARLY: Read Chapter 6, "Reading Comprehension."

- MID: In Chapter 5, complete Drill 3: Preposition Questions (page 155) and the Comprehensive Drill (page 160).

- LATE: Review Chapter 3 and Chapter 4.

Week 5

- EARLY: Read Chapter 7, "French Listening."

- MID: Complete Chapter 6 Drills (pages 174-179).

- LATE: Listen to a French podcast or news program.

Week 6

- EARLY: Review Chapter 5 and Chapter 6.

- MID: Re-review vocabulary lists.

- LATE: Take Practice Test 2.

Week 7

- EARLY: Review Drill Answers and Explanations.

- MID: Review Drill Answers and Explanations (starting on page 189)

- LATE: Re-review any topics you feel uncomfortable with and any questions you answered incorrectly on the practice tests and drills.

FINAL NOTES

Don't feel as if you must limit yourself to one of these templates. This is your test and your book; the most effective practice is likely to be that which you feel most comfortable with and able to commit to. That said, here are a few final pointers for adapting the book:

- Spread out the practice tests so that you can track progress and learn from mistakes.

- Don't gloss over reviewing answers, even to problems that you got right, especially if you guessed.

- If possible, don't cram. Your goal isn't to remember material for a single day—unless you're taking the test tomorrow—so the more that you can check back in on how much you remember from a section over the course of your review, the more you'll be able to retain for test day.

Feel free to use other resources! We've given you the best content review and practice tests at our disposal, but if you're still struggling over a difficult concept, and your teacher can't help, another perspective can only help. (Just make sure you fact-check the source!) The College Board's website features an overview of each Subject Test as well as practice questions:

https://collegereadiness.collegeboard.org/sat-subject-tests/subjects/languages/french